THE WHITE PUMPKIN

Denis Hills has been a lecturer in English in Kampala since 1964. In this book he continues the account of his experiences in Uganda, the first part of which, up to 1969, he described in *Man with a Lobelia Flute* (praised by the *Sunday Nation* of Nairobi as 'the best book on Uganda in fifty years'). As one of the dwindling number of British residents in Uganda, Denis Hills has closely observed events there since General Amin seized power. He has well-informed chapters on Amin himself, on the spread of violence, the exodus of Asians, expatriates, education, as well as descriptions of journeys he made among remoter tribal people including the little known Teuso (Ik). The book also contains autobiographical material in which the author recalls the long journey which, as he puts it, has landed him under a mango tree in a Kampala garden. While Denis Hills is critical of Amin's conduct and policies, he is very much in sympathy with the Uganda people. Indeed he hopes that by recording something of their desperate problems, he may have done a small service for them. The book also contains a number of contributions by the author's Ugandan students on the traditional life, customs and beliefs of the people, which are particularly enlightening, and all the illustrations are from the author's own collection.

by the same author

My Travels in Turkey
Man with a Lobelia Flute

THE WHITE PUMPKIN

by Denis Hills

London   George Allen & Unwin Ltd
Ruskin House   Museum Street

First published in 1975
Second impression 1976

© George Allen & Unwin Ltd 1975

ISBN 0 04 910058 0

Printed in Great Britain
in 11 point Plantin type
by Lowe & Brydone Printers Limited
Thetford, Norfolk

For the loved ones
Ingrid, Hansen, Johnny

PREFACE

This book follows on an earlier account I have given of my Uganda experiences up to 1969. Inevitably the emergence of Amin has affected the mood in which I have written the present record; for Uganda has changed, and no one, neither expatriates nor Africans, has shown up very well under the stress of unexpected and sometimes scaring or violent events.

Ugandans, when they cheered Amin's mutineers throughout the early months of 1971, seemed in the moment of euphoria deliberately to have blinded themselves to their own longer term interests; for it was the end of their civil liberties that they were applauding. By subsequently tolerating and then succumbing to a tyranny they have generally come to detest, they have shown lack of resource and public spirit. In permitting a new oligarchy of the wrong people to get their hands on the spoils thrown up by a disrupted society, they have let themselves be cheated.

The British government's hasty decision to recognise Amin within a few days of his usurping power seems to have been an act of miscalculated optimism. For long Britain continued to overlook the inhumanities of Amin's government. Not until the eviction of Indians and seizure of British assets hurt the taxpayer's pocket did British politicians protest; by then it was too late.

True, the *Observer* column on East African affairs has from the start ceaselessly harried Amin. Even this has sometimes been clumsily done. The indiscretions of an *Observer* journalist when visiting Uganda (a list of informants was found on him) may have led to the loss of one life (lawyer Anil Clerk) and imperilled those of others. Another correspondent, David Martin, though filling a necessary role, has tended to overplay it. Not only have his reports been marked by a self-defeating venom against Amin[1]; the element of inaccuracy in his published rolls of the dead and missing has damaged his credibility.

The British expatriate colony took a realistic, decent and self-protective decision when the bulk of it quit, or prepared to quit, Uganda in the wake of the Indian expulsion. Those who have stayed behind (about 1500) deserve some credit for fortitude; but many of us have turned cynical to the point of adopting

---

[1] The bitterness of Martin's feud with Amin is shown by the Uganda government's threat to eliminate him. 'Arrangements have been made by the military officials to arrest David Martin from any corner of the world and put him in Malire Mechanised custody (not in a police custody) for damaging the name of Uganda' (12 December 1972, *Voice of Uganda*).

anti-African attitudes that one had thought long buried. Nor could one help noticing that those Europeans who had looked forward with the keenest relish to David Martin's periodic revelations of the misdeeds of Amin, got very angry with him ('bloody trouble-maker – he's never even set foot inside Uganda!' is what they have said) when Amin suddenly threatened (5 June 1974) that 'if the British government and its agents did not stop their unprovoked attacks', he would deport us all at forty-eight hours' notice.[2]

I started to write this book before Amin took over. Much of the material and many of the observations date back to the time when Uganda, at least for an Englishman, was a happier place to live in. I have resisted the temptation to alter what I then wrote, though in later passages I have found it hard not to show pique and disillusion-ment at the way things have turned out.

Amin has so far survived by skilfully balancing a number of rival forces – in the army, in religion, in the economic sector, and within the tribes. His performance, which amounts to government by elimination, requires a constant and ruthless juggling with the human components in his balancing act.

Meanwhile no love affair could have stood up to the buffetings the Anglo-Ugandan relationship has had to endure over the past three years. A period of separation has been the inevitable conse-quence. Ineradicable damage has already been done to whatever ties of mutual affection and interest underlay the old connection. Free from outside surveillance, from the admonitory wagging white (and sometimes brown) finger, black Ugandans have been finding their own level.

It is a level where the old rules are barely recognisable, and where the African has temporarily lost his way. Uganda has become, with its lawlessness and corruption, another unstable fragment of black Africa.

Vicious rulers demoralise people and Amin's government is destroying souls. Under the soldiers Uganda has identified herself with that special brand of developing politics whose symbols are the gun, the Mercedes Benz driven at top speed, rhetoric, and near-bankruptcy (it is the game rangers themselves who nowadays,

[2] The publication of both the Geneva *Report on Uganda* (May 1974) and of Martin's book *General Amin* at this time, and the publicity given to them by the BBC, were the immediate cause of Amin's anger. Martin's book focuses on the General himself (the 'gentle giant' turned monster) and on the outrages said to have been committed by his Nubian killers. It does not pretend to be a study of the ordinary people in Uganda under Amin's rule.

surrounded by helpless beasts, shoot elephants by the hundred for their contraband ivory). Uganda's new 'friends', with their instant capital projects, their doles of baksheesh, their gifts of deadly weapons, and their small loans of second-rate 'experts', have so far proved a poor substitute for their predecessors.

As I add these words to what I wrote above a few months ago, Amin, following further *Observer* allegations against him (3 November 1974), has again been railing at the British ('The British must kneel before me'). A party of British High Commission officials has been ferried through the night back to London with a few hastily packed belongings and resentment against the journalists who have brought Amin's wrath upon their heads.

One may ask why the BBC and the British press, *The Observer* in particular, make such a fuss about the General, for the world has many other tyrants. In Amin language, it is because 'the British are jealous of me'. The editor of *Punch*, which ran for many months a funny feature on the General (VC, DSO, MC) would say that no journalist can ignore Nero's entertainment value. In a recent BBC interview I heard Colin Legum argue that though he regretted the embarrassment his attacks on Amin might cause British residents in Uganda, *the horrors that had occurred must be told*. Silence would mean collusion. Ugandans wanted to know the truth about what was happening in their country.

But is Colin Legum quite sure of this? Truth that is dangerous may not be agreeable to people who are frightened. '*Mungo* (God),' says many a simple Ugandan, 'will deal with Amin in his own time. The mango will one day fall from the tree. Why shake the branch and disturb snakes?'

Other Ugandans, though, the honourable and the enlightened, of whom there are many, welcome the exposure by the foreign press of Amin's misdeeds. They have, after all, no one else to speak up for them.

For myself, I do not like to be a hostage for a journalist's 'good behaviour'. Yet I believe it is right to watch Amin – a source of instability – and to expose his inhumanity to people who not long ago were in our charge.

And now, four professors and one senior lecturer at Makerere have written an open letter to *The Observer*, copy to General Amin (15 November 1974), complaining about its 'malicious, dishonest, and indiscreet reporting of Uganda affairs'. The reports, say the writers, seem deliberately aimed at breaking relations between

Uganda and those British residents who have taken 'the carefully thought out and very complex decision' to stay and serve her.

I detect some unreality in the professors' implicit picture of a British expatriate community dedicated in Uganda to noble causes. Take away the rewards that abound in a chaotic situation and the homeward-bound planes would be full tomorrow.

The five academics have made a point. In doing so, they have made Amin's point too and earned from him a pat on the back. '*Wie anstrengend es ist, böse zu sein*,' says Brecht, 'How exhausting it is to be evil'. I believe that journalists and writers, even if they do not always get their facts right, will add to Amin's exhaustion and help to erode his tyranny.

Perhaps I shall rejoin some of my old colleagues in another sunny country. I have seen the dogs they left behind mate with strays, their cars driven into ditches, and flowering shrubs in their gardens chopped for firewood. But as friends and teachers they have not been forgotten.

D. C. H.
Kampala

ADDENDUM

While I was under arrest in Uganda (1 April—10 July) I had no knowledge of the concern that was being shown for me by governments and individuals in many countries. I am grateful. I have been told that people prayed for me; I am sure their prayers reached me in my cell.

I have decided not to emasculate this book. To do so would be to deny the dead, the missing, and the fugitive. But a moral dilemma, with political implications, has been dealt with by omitting four words.

It hurts me to retain my earlier criticism of the Makerere letter writers (see opposite page) because they have since shown themselves such splendid colleagues.

D. C. H.
Dorridge, August 1975

CONTENTS

ILLUSTRATIONS

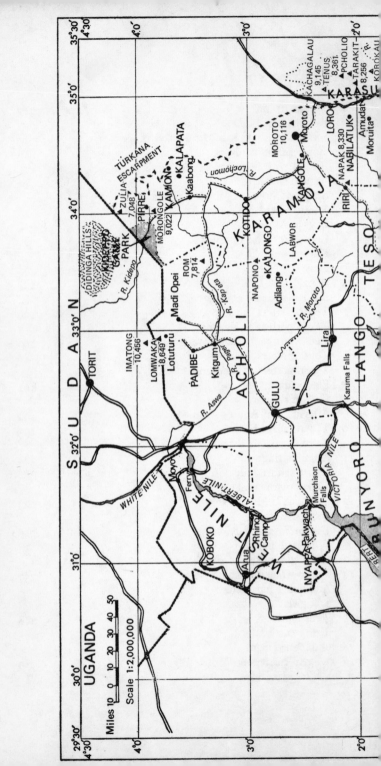

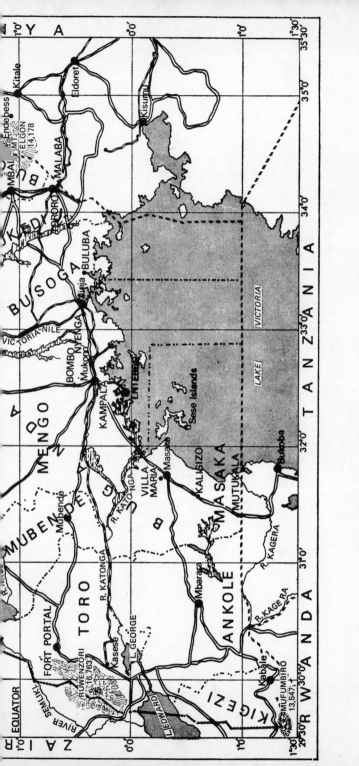

The White Pumpkin

'His gun on his shoulder,
A hat pulled like a basin over his head,
The white pumpkin came over a hill.'

PART I

THE ROAD TO
THE MANGO TREE

CHAPTER 1

Germans

Introduction

The reader may wonder why, in a book about Africa, I am starting off with an account of some of my wanderings in other places. But then, I do not regard my ten years in Uganda as an isolated event: rather, as the latest stage of a single protracted journey whose memories crowd the mind and whose milestones, as I shall indicate, mark intervals in an experience that is even now being shaped by an African landscape.

When, before locking up at night, I search the Kololo skyline for the Great Bear that is shining high over Europe, I feel I am still on a journey that I commenced fifty years ago on a bicycle along Warwickshire lanes. My wartime bivouacking in desert places was an introduction to sleeping under a bush on safari. The same lichen-stained rocks await one on top of Mount Argaeus as on Elgon or Morungole.

A journal would reveal the common threads. In Italy I saw white men in black shirts cheer Mussolini. Here in Uganda I have seen black men in white shirts cheer Amin. In Turkey there was Atatürk worship.

Turkey's economic war filled the shops with home-made junk that no one wanted; Amin's emptied them. Poles used to tell me that the Prussians, over the centuries, had tried to destroy their culture; Uganda Africans say *Wazungu* broke their customs. Europe did not like Jews; Amin has evicted Indians.

Perhaps there are other reasons than mere associated impressions (the approach of journey's end?) for turning back old pages. Sometimes I feel I have been roasting here in the sun long enough. The white coral beaches below Malindi are splendid, but the sea-bathing at Samos was better. Uganda has the banana; but grapes and melons do not grow here.

Nightfall over Mengo is abrupt, dawn brings a flamingo flush and bulbul song. Here there is no soft Northern twilight, no rime on the lawn. One has run away from home – but not for ever.

Ruth

It was a chance meeting with Ruth in an Oxford tea room that, as I see it now, first set me off on the restless journey which has landed me under the mango tree where I am writing these words.

Ruth came from Stuttgart. She was small, she had brown, melancholy eyes, and she was employed as *Kinderpflegerin* (children's governess) by an Oxford don who had acquired temporary fame as originator of Basic English.

The female undergraduettes I had so far met at Oxford had intimidated me.[1] At sherry parties they discussed chamber music and Picasso. They dropped names of literary and theatrical people they knew in London. They were not interested in my skills on the cricket and rugby football fields.

Ruth was different. When I punted her along the Cherwell she praised my body. She responded with true German sentimentality to the old world atmosphere of the Trout Inn at Godstow, where I kissed her in the shadows. For the first time I felt protective rather than on the defensive towards a female. She gave me a thin collection of Rilke's poems which I picked at with a dictionary. There were lines in it which, though they may not have been among Rilke's best (I quote from memory), filled me with romantic melancholy:

> 'Ich finde Dich nicht mehr
> Nein, nicht hier,
> Und nicht in diesem Stein.
> Ich bin allein . . .'

Having discovered Ruth, I was curious to discover Germany. So in summer 1933 I travelled to Berlin and then to Vienna to learn German. This was the start of an obsessive interest in the Germans. For the next three years I spent my vacations

[1] 'Undergraduettes' – a ghastly word, thinks Alan Burgess, who rebukes Evelyn Waugh for using it in his *A Little Learning*.

tramping and travelling in Germany and the adjacent German-speaking lands.

My discovery of Germany, like my friendship with Ruth, was a romantic one. It was bound up with images of old gabled towns, of the great green-black conifer forests of Brandenburg standing on parade like grenadiers, of sunny ploughed fields and vineyards; with its tow-haired, energetic youth, and with the coarse-sounding, powerful language. All this, to me, more than compensated for the ugliness of shaved heads on fleshy necks, of beer bellies and the constant un-wrapping and eating of *belegtes Brot*.

There was sex – romantic sex – too. For it was in Bonn, in an old inn with creaking floorboards, that I had my first sexual experience.

Her name was Magdalene. She wore a hat with a small veil. She was large, clean, and pink. She came from Remagen, and carried a shopping bag. I had, that day, walked the twenty-five or so miles from Cologne with a knapsack on my back. I was in rude health.

She made me undress first, called me her *kleiner Löwe* (little lion), and sprinkled my chest and stomach with Eau-de-Cologne. She wore violet-coloured cotton knickers which, in my haste, I tore. I made love to her eight times, and once again, out of greed, after breakfast.

Magdalene insisted on giving me a proper farewell at the railway station, where she presented me with a handkerchief, a rosy apple, and her photograph. As the train carried me away from her I had a feeling, not of Christian guilt, but of elation.

I have heard some men say that their sexual initiation was an unhappy experience: a sordid act with a drab, an adolescent surrender to a bullying woman, or a bungled surgical operation; it had left a scar. I had been fortunate.

Die Fahne Hoch!

The antics of the Nazis at first awed and startled me. A rally of Berlin University students, with their earnest sabre-slashed faces and their worn but carefully pressed suits, was very different from a friendly-jeering Oxford crowd in casual clothes; the harangues they listened to, and acclaimed with thunderous shouts, were ferocious, and delivered like hammer blows.

In Eggersdorf – a village some twenty miles east of Berlin, where I was the guest of Herr Mark, headmaster of the local school – I watched Storm Troopers exercise in brown shirts and breeches on the football field and listened to them bellow over their beer. Herr Mark took me on a lake steamer to admire the Bismarckturm, and I was photographed on the steps of the palace at Potsdam. A year later, as the atmosphere sharpened, youths jeered at me in a Hamburg cinema because I had a Jewess with me.

Yes, Germany was not only *schön romantisch*, with the mediaeval core of its Düreresque towns still unspoilt, the painted onion spires of its Baroque churches rising over the Bavarian landscape like illustrations to a fairy tale, and the huge farm horses that plodded among Mecklenburg cornfields: a land where girls braided their hair in golden buns and pigtails and where strangers flattered me – '*Sie sehen wie 'n Deutscher aus*, Why, you look just like a German!' Nazi Germany, with its defiant Führer, its hooked-cross banners and marching men, vibrated with political melodrama too.

Encouraged by Hitler, the German minorities who lived outside the frontiers had also begun to assert and make a nuisance of themselves. Wandering in 1934-36 through the Dolomites, Bohemia, the Erzgebirge, and in Lithuania, I observed their behaviour at first hand. The clash of Italian, Austrian, Slav, and German, and the still only partially comprehended phenomenon of anti-Semitism (who in those days could imagine the horrors that were to come?), provided matter to write about that stared me in the face and was, I felt, though my Oxford tutors did not agree, more relevant to 'life' than the weekly essays they required on Kant and the nineteenth-century political theorists. I had started to wander out of naïve curiosity. My curiosity turned into a conscious search for news and journalistic experience.

I attended the Saar plebiscite, the 1935 Nazi Party Rally at Nuremberg, elections in Klaipeda (Memel), illegal Nazi gatherings in the Tirol. These and other events I described for Mr E. W. Record of *The Birmingham Post*. Starting with an impression of Hindenburg's funeral celebrations which I witnessed on my way through the Harz Mountains ('To the tolling of evening bells small parties of peasant mourners carrying oil lanterns came out of the woods to attend the first requiem services for the huge, wooden-faced general who had crushed the Russians at the battle of Tannenberg'), I sent Mr Record over thirty reports in all. He paid me three guineas for every 1,200 words, which covered my travel expenses.

These were ludicrously small, for I travelled rough and often, wrapped in my raincoat, slept in a field or a wood, so that my appearance after two or three weeks on the road would deteriorate. Descending the Brenner Pass, whose cliffs were being blasted for gun emplacements, I was given shelter by Italian road labourers (and met groups of deserters from Mussolini's Abyssinian war call-up escaping by secret paths at night into Austria).

In Danzig I stayed with unemployed workers in their wooden slums. In Königsberg a matronly woman bought me two poppy-seed cakes, and addressed this ditty to me:

'Oh wenn deine Mutter wüsste
Wie es Dir in der Fremde geht –
Strumpf' zerissen, Hemd kaputt,
Und durch die Hosen pfeift der Wind.'[1]

I did not, in my articles for Mr Record, tell the whole truth; for the truth was not entirely respectable. I did not say that while the Saarländer were cheering Hitler's plebiscite victory, I was in the back room of a Saarbrücken inn attending (for the hell of it) the local Communist Party's last meeting – or that I had joined its last defiant street march and been chased through the snow by policemen with truncheons (I got away over a wall).

I did not describe those unpleasant moments in the crowded stadium at Nuremberg when angry Germans tried to raise my arm in the Hitler salute. I did not admit that in Kretinga I had got drunk on *Kornbrand* with Lithuanian peasants who stank

[1] 'Oh if your mother knew
How you are faring in a foreign land –
Torn stockings, ragged shirt,
And the wind whistling through your trousers.'

of garlic and horse manure; or that, stranded without money in a small inn at Bydgoszcz (in the Polish Corridor) I had eaten nothing for a week but rye bread and left-over meat balls.

The only time I tried to write the whole truth, my article was rejected. In it I had described the three days I had spent in a Polish police cell in Gdynia. 'At night my cell filled up with drunks who vomited and quarrelled in the dark . . . A homosexual tried to molest me . . . When a German seaman from Danzig was brought in, the Poles started to beat him. I pulled him into my corner.'

This sort of stuff was not to Mr Record's taste. 'You have no business,' he wrote to me, 'to get into such scrapes, and this newspaper is not interested in them.'

Engländer

It was inevitable that Nazi boastings should arouse my sympathies for the threatened victims. Like calf-love, my affair with the Germans was doomed. I recognised the signs when things that had at first amused me began to make me angry. I had been absorbing experiences. Now I was evaluating them.

Soon after I had come to stay with him, in summer 1933, Herr Mark, who was giving me my first German lessons, had taken me aside and said: 'You must buy a purse. No respectable German carries his money loose in his pocket. And your bicycle', he added (I had brought it with me from England), 'has no bell and no pump. That is against the law.'

I did not, at the time, resent Herr Mark's advice. Later, however, I saw that it fitted into a disastrous pattern of conformity and obedience (*Gehorsamkeit*) on which political authoritarianism, in short the Nazi machine, could thrive.

Again, as an *Engländer*, I was constantly on trial. I would take a book to a lake side, and the local *Sportlehrer* (sports teacher) would immediately challenge me to a swimming race; or sun-tanned youths, flexing their biceps, would ask me to compete in handsprings with them.

When I bicycled with a student group over the north German plain to Rügen, I was expected to pound along at not less than fifteen miles an hour, and never to dawdle or to stop. In youth hostels, among the male hair-nets, the gargling with Odol and the scrubbed trestle-tables, I was rebuked for not having a tooth mug.

I knew, when I went into a beer parlour, that someone was going to pump my hand and say, '*Wir sind blutsverwandt*, we are blood brothers. We must stand together.' This recital, embarrassing at first, was meant to be complimentary and it did not bother me.

Perhaps it ought to have done. For is it not this presumption – or myth? – of blood relationship that makes many Germans and British see in each other an aggravating caricature of themselves (the German, a coarse Englishman, the Englishman, a degenerate German)? The poison of kinship, affinity turned to envy, has helped, I believe, to make us deadly rivals.

What did offend was the copy of *Der Stürmer* that hung over the *Stammtisch* of every inn and came to be displayed in a public reading box in every village square: its cartoons of bottle-nosed Jews mauling blondes, and its mad, evil slogans – '*Raus mit den Dreckjuden* . . . *Mischehe mit Juden ist Volksverrat* . . . *Lenin war Jude* . . . Out with the dirty Jews . . . Marriage with Jews is nation betrayal . . . Lenin was a Jew . . .'

By 1936 I had had enough. I had grown tired of the splendid Badenweiler March, of jackboots thudding over cobblestones, of banners and crowd hysteria and of Nazi art – how many thousands of pictures of Aryan athletes, of farm girls with sickles, and of the Kaiser's glorious naval victory at Skagerrak (Jutland), which in my ignorance I had thought to be a German defeat, must have been painted, sculpted, posted to loved ones and displayed in schools and public places throughout Germany in those days!

Though it never occurred to me that the Nazis would one day burn and exterminate Jews (and none of the Jews whom I met in Germany seemed to have any inkling that this was to be their fate), my experiences had convinced me that Hitler was determined to attack Poland. The jamboree that had exalted ingenuous youths was over. Germany had turned into a war machine.

This conviction had first been planted in me as early as 1933 by Herr Mark. Every evening, during my German lesson, he would open his atlas at the map of the Polish Corridor. He would point to the town of Gnesen (Gniezno, in Polish) and say, '*Da bin Ich geboren*, I was born there.'

He would then take me into his little sandy garden to watch the Warsaw express rumble past. 'That train,' he would say, 'passes through German soil (*deutscher Boden*) which the *Diktat von Versailles* (the dictated Treaty of Versailles) gave to dirty Poles. Under Adolf Hitler we are going to recapture that land with the sword.'

My first short visit to Poland in 1935 had already aroused my interest in the underdog. There, along the Vistula, I had glimpsed things that intrigued me: a Slav culture which, though many Poles wanted to forget them, had old ties with Russia; shabby villages and cab horses; vodka bars, the mazurka, and a language of strange-looking words: *przyjaciel*, friend; *dziewczynka*, girl; *Bóg*, God; *rzecz*, thing.

Back in England, I bought a Polish dictionary and looked round for a job in Poland.

CHAPTER 2

Poles

Gdynia

In January 1937 I sailed from Hay's Wharf in the Polish cargo boat *Lech* for Gdynia. A drunk cabman in a sheepskin coat drove me along icy streets to my new employers, who had advertised themselves in *The Times* as 'The Baltic Institute, an organisation of the Polish Government for the promotion of political, economic and cultural ties with the Baltic and Scandinavian countries.'

The Director, Dr Borowik – his name derives from 'mushroom' – gave me an advance of zlotys, an office whose window I was told never to open (Polish office workers, I was to discover, could not bear fresh air), and set me to sort out a heap of manuscripts.

These were the raw material, which I had to sub-edit, for the next issue of the Institute's journal, whose aim as defined in its statement of editorial policy was not only to assert Poland's voice in Baltic and Scandinavian affairs but to present, in correct and readable English, the Polish case for retaining Upper Silesia and the Polish Corridor (with access to the Baltic through the Free City of Danzig), and to hammer away at Poland's alleged historical 'rights' in Old Prussia (seized centuries earlier by the Teutonic Knights) and in other territories stretching as far as the Elbe and into Czechoslovakia.

Our contributors were mainly Polish academics and sympathetic professors from Sweden, Finland, and the three Baltic States of Latvia, Estonia and Lithuania, with Professor William Rose, a Polish-speaking Canadian from the London School of Slavonic Studies, in support.

The result was a quarterly hotchpotch, in part arid and abstruse, of special pleading for Polish interests, of chauvinism and genuine scholarship, of printers' errors and of altercations over the spelling of place names (should it be Wilno, as the Poles insisted, or Vilnius, the Lithuanian nationalists' version: Tallin or Reval; Teschen or Ćieszyn?).

In the course of just over two years I produced six of these closely printed volumes. I polished up manuscripts on the Ancient Borussi, on the Kashubes (a dying clan of uncouth Pomeranian peasants and fishermen), on bee-keeping among the Mordvinians: on the sixteenth-century grain trade of Livonia, and on the river routes taken across Russia by the Varangians – the 'Red-Headed Ones' (Russ) who gave Russia their name.

Professor Fischer the ethnologist, in his studies of ancient Slav settlements and place names, proved to the world that Polish tribes had once lived far to the west of Poland's current boundaries. Professor Jan Czekanowski of Lwów University propounded comforting racial theories on the basis of skull measurements (a great many Poles, it seemed, were of 'Nordic' origin too!). Professor Halecki demonstrated yet again Poland's indisputable historical claim to the city of Danzig (Gdańsk). And we irritated the Germans, who had opened up a rival institute to ours in Königsberg, by stressing that the astronomer Copernicus, as a citizen of Thorn (Toruń), was by definition a Pole.

Much of the material, though fascinating, seemed irrelevant – those ancient beekeepers of Mordvinia, for instance, who in their gloomy forests traded in beeswax and furs and practised witchcraft, those primeval scavengers of amber washed up on Baltic strands, the function of chain-letters in Estonia. But even the more recondite pieces demonstrated to her neighbours that Poland took a respectful and comradely interest in the minutiae of their cultures.

Above all we were barking back at Hitler's propaganda machine which wanted to diminish Poland, if not push her off the map. Ours was a lost cause, and I do not know what happened to Dr Borowik and my Polish colleagues when in September 1939 the Germans and the Red Army swallowed Poland between them. But it was a cause I enjoyed supporting.

However I learned more in the streets and bars of the realities of Poland's relationship with the Danzigers than I did from Professor Halecki.

Our journal was set, laboriously, in linotype and printed by a dozen Poles who did not know English at a small Polish printers in a Danzig working-class quarter. Nazi louts sometimes tried to beat us up when we left work. We were too tough for them. With German blood on our shirts, I and a couple of Polish colleagues would celebrate our small victories in tumblers of *Goldwasser* – a sweet liqueur with gold leaf floating in it. It was now our turn to boast. 'We will drive,' said the compositor, 'these German swine (*niemiecka świnia*) into the sea.'[1]

There were other ways of getting one's own back. By addressing Danzig tram conductors in Polish I could work them into a frenzy. I would sometimes sit in a restaurant under the picture of Hitler and imitate his voice and gestures. Silly, but it made one feel a little better.

After dark gangs of young men in leather belts and jack-boots would come into the streets of Danzig, looking for something – Jewish shop windows, a synagogue – to damage. I knew that when Heinz got back from his foray, his father would say '*Bravo, mein Junge*', and his mother would have a plate of hot soup ready for him. I had been brought up to detest bullying. Here, in Danzig, and throughout Germany, the bully was being encouraged by loving parents, by girl friends, by school masters, and by public acclaim.

The brand-new port of Gdynia had been built during the twenties and thirties with the help of French capital on the site of what had been a miserable fishing village. Poland was justifiably proud of her 'window on the sea'.

Gdynia was brash, uncultured. It had attracted bankrupts, adventurers, widows, and a new class of Polish seaman who in the absence of a previous national maritime tradition had had to invent a new vocabulary of ships and the sea. There were no Jews, no theatre, and (except for the café orchestras which scraped away at Moniuszko and Lehar) no music. My Polish

---

[1] It is symbolic, I assume, of the Poles' ancient Slav rivalry with Germans that the Polish for 'a German' is '*Niemiec*', from '*nie mówiący*' meaning 'the speechless one', i.e. 'he who does not speak Polish'.

landlady, an attractive virago, quarrelled incessantly with her husband, a worn-out Englishman who exported sweet-cured bacon to England. Visiting seamen rarely bothered to explore farther than the nearest water-front bars, where vodka quickly laid them out. To see something of the 'real' Poland I would have to move to Warsaw. But with the German propaganda machine putting increasing pressure on the Poles, there was clearly not much time left. When early in 1939 I took a job in Warsaw teaching English to classes of elegant Polish house-wives, I felt that I was entering a phase on which the curtain would soon drop.

Warsaw

Now that Chamberlain's government had guaranteed the integrity and independence of Poland, Britain was in favour and learning English the fashion in a society which had long preferred a cultural relationship with France. The Poles knew there would be war. They had a martial tradition, and the prospect excited but did not alarm them. They hoped, and many indeed believed, that their lancers, officered by heroes in four-cornered hats, would push Hitler into the sea, and that British bombers would come roaring out of the sky to help them.

By midsummer a great many of the officer class had been called up. At night, during black-out exercises, the drone of Polish-built monoplanes mingled with the hoof-beats of cab horses. While I entertained the beautiful housewives with readings from Oscar Wilde, and waited for Wanda at the stage-door of the National Theatre, Mars – which glowed unusually big and red during the hot summer nights – was showing omens of the blood that was to flow.

I spent part of the late summer in a Polish farmhouse outside Warsaw. A small train pulled by a tiny nineteenth-century locomotive known as the Samovarek passed it by. Its wooden coaches were much used by poor Jews with old suitcases and newspaper parcels. A travelling fiddler used to entertain them. Neither I nor they knew that they were doomed. The Polish Ukrainian seasonal labourers who were harvesting at the farm slept in a barn under a picture of the slashed Black Madonna of

Częstochowa. I saw them kill a cat by swinging it by its tail against the barn wall. At night they sang doleful religious chants. The Germans, no doubt, later recruited them as slave labour. Many Polish Ukrainians of their type were to become notorious as particularly brutal ghetto and concentration camp guards.

I was on holiday, walking in Galicia, when the Germans invaded Poland. On the third day, in a cobbled village, a Jewish grocer called me excitedly into his shop. I have never forgotten that moment, as I listened to a solemn voice announcing over the Jew's radio that Britain had joined the war. One by one men came into the shop and with intense emotion shook me by the hand. But disillusionment was swift and bitter as Hitler carved his way with merciless speed to Warsaw. Day after day I watched the big cobbled squares of Kuty and Kolomyja fill up with peasants in mocassins waiting in vain for orders. There was no military organisation, no transport, to mobilise them. In hundreds of Galician villages people scanned the cloudless blue skies for the vapour trails of British bombers. They had been deceived.

Yet it was the Red Army, now marshalled along Poland's eastern frontier, that struck the mortal blow. A few hours before they moved in and bundled Polish men off to internment, I walked over a wooden bridge into Romanian Bukovina.

I was in flight, and I had suffered a personal humiliation. My material loss was trivial – some books, a winter overcoat and my Oxford 'smoking', left behind in the ulica hoża in Warsaw. But my shame was deep. I had not kept faith with those men who had shaken me by the hand in the Jew's shop. The Polish policeman who stamped my passport at the bridge seemed to understand my feelings. 'When you return to Poland, Mr Professor,' he said grimly, 'come back in a bomber (*niech pan wróczi bombowcem*).'

CHAPTER 3

War

Bucharest

There followed a frivolous interlude in Bucharest, where to tide myself over I took a teaching post with the British Council. After the short, brutal experience of war in Poland the atmosphere in King Carol's capital struck me as flamboyant and unreal. Here Russia (an uncouth bear with a predatory eye on Bukovina and Bessarabia) not Germany (admired for her efficiency, her economic drive, and her record of opposing the Russian beast) was the hereditary foe. As winter closed in I saw Bucharest fill up with refugees from Poland, with intelligence agents, journalists, and, more significantly, with an infiltration of German 'experts' who were to prepare the ground for Hitler's take-over.

While haggard workmen with rags tied round their feet were building, in bitter cold and snow, an extension to the King's palace, and Romanian officers escorted their ladies to eat sweet Turkish cakes in the cafés, cinemas showed German news-reels of bombers sinking Allied ships.

The British Council, with exemplary tact, carried on as though the war did not exist. My colleagues invited an Anglophile élite to unreal debates ('This house believes that woman's place is in the home'), lectured to them on Bernard Shaw, and produced *Othello* at the National Theatre (when Othello fell dead, his wig came off and skidded slowly into the footlights). Every Sunday I played rugby football with Romanian cavalry officers in the Bucharest league.[1]

A teacher's wife summed up what I think was the majority

[1] Rugby football was introduced into Romania by a rich young banker, Chrissovoleni, who had learned the game at Cambridge. The Romanian national fifteen has always maintained a good standard.

view of my British Council colleagues when she said at a literary party, 'My husband is far too precious to lose his life in some silly battle – let the hearties fight the war.'

War, according to this argument, was for the old sweats shipped over from cantonments in India and Shanghai, for red-faced products of the minor public schools, for Durham coal miners, for bank clerks who wanted to enjoy authority – all of them expendable types of Englishman.

Britain's cause, moreover, was not quite respectable as long as Communist Russia remained in alliance with Hitler. And life in Bucharest was good: caviare and steak, cheap red wine, *cuika* brandy: the wild melodies of Romanian folk music played by pouchy-eyed gypsies to the galloping rhythm of the cymbalon; Marie Tanassi to excite diplomatists with her passionate singing; a semi-official black market to supply us with the *lei*.

Even the Jews – many of them attended our English language courses – did not seem much perturbed by Hitler's lightning victory over Poland. Those who had money dined out, danced, drove cars. The poor orthodox Jews crowded into musty streets, selling cheap wares in village markets, ignorant, fatalistic, seemed unconscious of the storm that was reaching down the Danube to annihilate them.

How totally unrelated to the world shattering events of the day seemed the British Council's cultural mission! How ignoble my own little part in it! I decided to go.

I signed a form at the British Military Attaché's office in which I committed myself to army service, and a little later found myself at Constanza, on the Black Sea, awaiting a passage to Egypt. I was not the only fugitive. A party of British engineers and oil experts whose mission – to put the Romanian oil wells out of action in the event of a German invasion – was no longer acceptable to the increasingly pro-German Romanian government, was also in retreat.

Our ship turned out to be a Haifa-bound hulk manned by Jews whose cloth caps and baggy suits made them look like pedlars. We had to endure some anxious moments before we were allowed to leave. There were rumours of contraband wealth on board. For twenty-four hours Romanian officials searched in vain for jewellery and cash, impeded, in their garish blue uniforms, by fresh paint which the crew with cunning forethought had sprayed around the ship.

As we moved at last into the Black Sea for Istanbul, the local German consul drove up to the quayside. Looking affectedly military in a white motoring helmet and black leather jacket, he waved good-bye.

Soldiering

A few months later, after a brief infantry course at Moascar barracks, I found myself commanding a platoon of regular soldiers in the Western Desert. I had scarcely learned to salute. We lived in holes in the ground. There was no beer.

Wire, minefields, and the naked sky shut us in, with our sunburnt bodies and our dreams of women, over the tedious weeks of waiting.

But when, in late 1940, our first Italian prisoners came streaming in, calling out for aqua, the elation of being a soldier gripped me. I had escaped from the drudgery of earning a living. I had found a role. I had been given the right of leadership over a group of men. The long unknown years of war stretched ahead like the grains of desert sand into a future in which, borne up by the comradeship of soldiers, I imagined I would always sleep under stars and stay young.

I had not forgotten those preparatory street brawls with the enemy in Danzig, or the Polish frontier policeman's words, 'Come back, in a bomber.' Kopanski's Polish Carpathian Brigade, which had been withdrawn from Syria to an encampment near Alexandria, and then sent to reinforce Tobruk, was already making a name for itself. But it was almost two years before I was able to renew my connexion with the men I had left behind in those village squares east of Lwów.

Then, in 1942, Stalin under pressure of Hitler's offensive in the Caucasus felt grudgingly obliged to disgorge thousands of Poles from his internment camps. Oil tankers ferried them across the Caspian. They came in two main drafts. With a detachment of Indian soldiers I was detailed to receive them in staging camps near Baghdad and in Khanaqin (Iraq).

The Poles arrived in open trucks, many suffering from the after-effects of typhus and sick with heat exhaustion. Our medical officer had advised me to welcome them with drums of salty drinking water. They spat it out and cursed me, thinking I was playing a bad joke.

For some months, as a member of a British training and liaison unit, I helped prepare the Poles for battle, and in Italy I was with the same men (I was attached to a brigade of the 5th Kresowa Infantry Division) fighting among the blackened shreds of old corpses – Moroccans, Americans, New Zealanders, Indians, and British – as we advanced on Cassino monastery, a senseless trophy now, battered into a blasphemous pile of rubble under the eye of Monte Cairo.

In later fighting I was mortared and shelled with the Poles in cornfields, in copses and farmhouses, lay down with them in ditches as the *Nebelwerfer* rockets threw fiery brands among us in the night. I saw them force one river after another as we pushed north to Rimini.

I left the Poles on the Senio, south of Bologna. It was Christmas 1944. They had found winter quarters in farms and were sleeping on big peasant beds under strings of onions. They had distilled a sort of vodka from wine, and were eating lumps of sausage with penknives. Only our guns kept up the ritual of war, firing from time to time into a Breughel landscape of farmland and leafless trees where pockets of Germans, stinking of sweat and leather, were lying up in bunkers and farm buildings. The Yalta Agreement, soon after, broke the Polish soldiers' hearts. Men who had dreamed of going back to their farms in the east of Poland woke one day to find they had nothing to go back to.

Russians

By what seemed to my Polish friends an act of apostasy I now found myself unwillingly involved with the machinations of the Soviet Military Mission in Italy. The British had recently captured, near Ravenna, 8,000 former Red Army soldiers whom the Wehrmacht had re-enlisted to fight in its Turkoman Division; and Moscow had sent repatriation officers to make sure that having put these renegades into British uniform, reclassified them as Free Soviet Citizens, fed them like fighting cocks, issued them with NAAFI stores and overpaid them according to the dubious Red Army ranks they had reassumed, we despatched them back to Russia. Under the terms of the Yalta Agreement we were bound to do so. Our Turkomans flocked like sheep on to the ships and trains that carried them off from Taranto to Russia. It seemed that they half-believed in Stalin's promise of an amnesty – or were they too cowed, too foolish, to think for themselves?

The one thousand Turkomans whom I escorted to Odessa had a bitter shock when, well fed, shaved, in clean British battledress and polished boots, they stepped off the gangway in a cold sea mist on to their native soil. Not for them the promised reunion with their loved ones. A few days earlier, as our ship steamed slowly past Greek islands, they had been entertaining us with their marvellous songs and dances. Now in a side street of Odessa I watched them parade under armed escort in front of a picture of Stalin. They were harangued, they cheered obediently, and without more ado were marched off to a nearby concentration camp. Much later I heard from returned German prisoners-of-war that some of our Turkomans had been seen working as convict labour in flooded coal mines of the Donetz basin.

The Turkomans were not alone in their misery. The German prisoners-of-war I saw clearing rubble in the Odessa docks were skeletons in rags. Even the Russians had the sickly look of prolonged privation. One Russian took a handful of *mahorka* (tobacco dust) from his pocket and asked me for a scrap of newspaper to roll cigarettes in. Yet when our British crew had thrown cigarettes to the Russian sentries who stood with fixed bayonets at the foot of the gangway (they would allow no one to land), the sentries without a word had kicked the packets into the water. From their point of view we had succoured and cosseted a shipload of treacherous Moslem trash. We were unforgivably healthy, unscathed, rich – unwelcome.

Not all the displaced Russians in Italy were anxious to revert to the invidious status of 'Free Soviet Citizens', or were as gullible as those bandy-legged Turkomans. A good many of them eluded, with our collusion, the net cast by the Soviet

Military Mission. I doctored the nominal rolls as best I could. Some Russians I registered as Poles. Some I encouraged to run away from their camps, which were not at all closely guarded. Some took shelter with Russikom (an organisation of the Greek Catholic Church in Rome). Others – former soldiers who had disguised themselves as Todt workers or civilian refugees – were denounced by fellow Russians.

Operation East Wind in 1947, in which Ivanov's carefully selected former Red Army and later Wehrmacht soldiers were forcibly repatriated in a sealed train from Rimini, was a small, cruel, and belated token sacrifice to appease the Soviet authorities, who had been trying without success to get their hands on the 8,000 Soviet Ukrainians of the Wehrmacht's Galicia Division that was still under our protection. When the pressure on them slackened, we shipped the Galicia Division to England together with their fifty or so leathery women (whom I listed as 'Red Cross personnel'). It was during these operations that I was gratified to see myself described in the Soviet newspaper *Izvestia* as 'Major Gills, a Fascist officer of the British Armed Forces who has prevented Free Soviet Citizens from returning to their fatherland'.[1]

This was not the end of my connexion with the Russians. For a further two and a half years, until 1950, I was kept busy tracing and interrogating some hundreds of German and Austrian officers and men on their release from captivity in Soviet prisoner-of-war and labour camps.

These men were a valuable catch for British and Allied Intelligence, for the practical Russians had made them work their passage home, and through their employment in factories and building projects they had seen a great deal of what was going on inside the Soviet Union (there was, I believe, no aerial photographic reconnaissance over Russia at that time). I interrogated them on the role of Paulus's phantom 'Freedom Army'; on tank production in Chelyabinsk; on the lay-out of airfields; on road, bridge and power station construction from Kiev to Karaganda.

Later my special field was that of Soviet rocket development.

[1] I have since identified myself as the 'Captain A.' of Bethell's *The Last Secret*. But far more Russians were reprieved than he is aware of.

These and all the other related data that were then being assiduously gathered from many sources were, I understood, collated at JIB headquarters, London.

I have sometimes wondered how much effective use the British made of this encylopaedic mass of information. We learned that when the Americans withdrew from Thuringia, the Russians had dismantled Hitler's V2 rocket plant at Nordhausen and installed it near Moscow. There, with the aid of impressed German specialists, they immediately got on with the job of developing the German V2 rocket prototypes. Did this Russian initiative, I wonder, spur the British into similar activity? Was this episode not significant, perhaps, for Russia's early lead in rocket design? Yet, though the Russians had got Dr Christianssen (inventor of the V1 'Argus-Rohr'), the Americans, as it turned out, had won the trump card in Wernher von Braun.

The information that I recorded day after day in Bruck an der Mur, in Graz, in Vienna and Bad Driburg (Westphalia), was so detailed and repetitive that after a time I could visualise, as though I had seen them with my own eyes, the wretched punishment camps in arid Karaganda: the workers smuggling nails and nuts and bolts from the tank factory at Chelyabinsk; the despicable intrigues of the 'Kasha Communists'[1] whom the Soviet camp authorities used as stool-pigeons; those obdurate Japanese prisoners-of-war whose hunger strike in a camp near Moscow – because they gave their leaders one hundred per cent support – was the only successful action of its kind that I heard of in Russia.

This job, which towards the end I had done with the Control Commission in Germany, ceased in mid-1950 when the stream of prisoners-of-war from Russia dried up – Stalin announcing (what was not true) that there were no more left. I found myself back in London, in a cheap Polish boarding house near Notting Hill Gate.

After an absence of over ten years from normal civilian life, it was time for me to do a little stock-taking and to consider the next move.

[1] *Kasha*, groats. The informer's reward was extra food.

CHAPTER 4

Taking Stock

I was miserable at first. Having enjoyed for so long the comrade-ship of a closed society and the privileges of rank, it was hard for me to become, overnight, a cypher – unknown, utterly undistinguished, and poor – in a great city. Worse, I had absorbed certain habits and attitudes that I would need time to get rid of. 'Civvy street' I had long grown accustomed to thinking of, with awful arrogance, as an alien and rather contemptible world of shopkeepers and unadventurous clerks and of a vague mass of people who performed hateful tasks in factories.[1]

Many hundreds of nights under the stars had made me impatient of paid accommodation. Indeed, having lived for years at a grateful government's expense, I resented not only having to pay money for a roof and a night's sleep, but the constant necessity of producing cash to buy things with.

In the London traffic and on the grey pavements I craved for the open air.

I was opposed on principle to Socialism, which from my undergraduate period I had associated with church-burning in Spain, with Kingsley Martin, with woolly Oxford pacifism and with mawkish thinking about Russia. For me Socialism was now tainted with an act of treachery that had spurned Churchill in the moment of victory and had precipitately surrendered Palestine and India to bloodshed. But I no longer felt the British working man to be a stranger. I had got to know him, toughened by mud and sunshine, as a soldier.

I was embarrassed, not being used to them, by small children. But I had learned compassion for the helpless, a response to

[1] 'The grey mass, *tyomnya massa*', as I once heard an angry Soviet colonel call a group of recalcitrant Ukrainian peasant-soldiers.

my experiences with enemy prisoners-of-war, in hungry Vienna and among the rubble of Munich.

When we had 'liberated' an Italian farm by firing anti-tank shells into it, we found that we had not only killed the enemy, but we had smashed the buildings, slaughtered the big white oxen, and shocked or maimed any of the farmer's people who happened to be sheltering in the cellar. This was war. Cows and civilians should not loiter about a battle area.

It was the military occupation of a beaten country that I had found to be a corrupting experience. The conqueror enforces legalised suffering, and all must be punished alike. The soldier's slab of chocolate offered to a child or to a girl friend, if calculated in self-interest, is a gift with poison in it. It is the captor who is demoralised. The prisoners-of-war he has under his thumb, penned behind wire, are men turned into sheep, castrated. In self-defence against sympathy, he over-reacts; for if he lets them touch his heart, that is the end of discipline.

When three years after the fighting was over I took General Schmalz, formerly of the Hermann Göring Luftwaffe Division, out of his war criminals' cage at Wolfsberg (Carinthia) for a walk, and then on the spur of the moment into a wine shop, and several hours later, in the icy, starlit night, brought him back along a country road singing, I was court martialled. I felt foolish afterwards. But in denting the regulations I had made a small gesture for humanity.

Then there was the incident of the Jewish ship at La Spezia. After fighting ceased in Italy, the Palestinian Jewish Brigade which had been granted only a brief time in the line began on its own initiative to collect Jewish survivors of Hitler's concentration camps with the object of smuggling them to Palestine. An Italian hulk, the *Fide*, crammed with 1,000 of these unhappy people was detained early in 1946 by the British military authorities at La Spezia. GHQ sent me to investigate. I found the detained refugees already on hunger strike. When I went on board they shouted (in Polish) 'Sadist!' Hags tried to claw my face, old men spat at me.

Within a day or two hostile Jewish and American newspaper reporters had descended on La Spezia like vultures. Even

Professor Harold Laski was there. I introduced him, in the tiny candle-lit ship's saloon, to the Jews' leaders. 'Bevin is my friend,' he told them. 'I will speak with him. Trust me.' The Jews were not convinced.

Service regulations do not provide for every situation. I took the humanitarian way out and advised GHQ to let the ship sail. ('The best solution,' grumbled a British staff officer, 'would be to tow the buggers out to sea and sink them.')

So the flag of Zion was hoisted and the Jews sailed away. My decision had been militarily wrong, indeed, a small act of betrayal, for I knew that among the pitiful scarecrows on board there was a hard core of professional Zionists, young men dedicated to liberating Palestine from the British. But I had wanted to show a little human kindness (for which the British would get credit), to dowse, before it flared up, a small glow of hatred.[1]

I had learned that to understand people one should know their language; and that understanding brings sympathy if not downright partisanship (which may not suit official policy). Even so the word 'Wog' still evoked certain responses in me. I recalled the pimps in Cairo, browbeaten women in black with flies sitting on their eyelids, Baghdad contractors who had tried to bribe me with whisky left in my tent (which, of course, I drank).

A lot of Italian women, it seemed to me, had shown more sense and dignity than their men. They had kept homes going, and when the fighting was over managed suddenly to look attractive in a faded cotton dress. I could not forget those silly slogans which the early captured Italians had stencilled on their sun helmets: 'Better to die like a lion than live like a sheep.'

[1] I have since come across a somewhat garbled account of this affair in *The Incomparable Crime* (London 1967) by Manvell and Fraenkel. The Zionists, say the authors, hoped to make anti-British propaganda out of the incident: 'The British must be shamed by world opinion out of their tenure of the Mandate.' As far as I am concerned, the attempt failed. The authors add, by the way, that the Jewish refugees on board the *Fide* were in fact granted Palestine immigration certificates, which were deducted from the legal quota spread over two succeeding months. As for the Kimches' account in *The Secret Roads*, the role they assign to their 'Major Hill' is invented; and their references to me, if part of Israeli folklore, should be rewritten.

(During the Italian campaign I recall seeing a much more telling message painted on a bombed building in Ravenna: *Ecco il lavoro dei Liberatori!* – Behold the work of the Liberators![1])

I admired the Germans as soldiers – had hated them in fact, at first, because they were defeating us. Once we had them on the run I was tempted to fraternise with them. Several times, moved by perverse magnanimity, I had helped wounded enemy to a first-aid post. Yet the Germans had been greedy in victory. Think of all those fur coats and embroidered night-dresses, those hams and foodstuffs, they had looted and sent back to their dear ones from occupied territories. In captivity they had shown themselves lacking in spirit. For the reward of an extra ration German prisoners-of-war would salute a corporal.

The Red Army, as an occupying force, had been a terrifying plague, by turn good-natured and brutal, taking what they wanted at gun point. Sitting on bundles of hay in their little horse-drawn carts, stripping houses of their fittings, they brought with them a chill wind from the hungry steppes of Asia. Their officers and officials I had found to be pathologically suspicious, calculating, avaricious and uncouth. True, they would get drunk with us, loosening their collars as the night wore on, spilling the potato soup on the table, singing, and calling for music. The very next morning, when we met again in conference, they would be as devious and unyielding as ever.

The captured Russian soldiers and refugee families I had handled had struck me as cowed, lacking even the initiative to save their own skins. How foolish it was of them to sit in their tents trusting to fate and to the benevolence of their British guards while office files were earmarking them for sacrifice. Worse, the system under which they had been brought up had corrupted them. They had an ugly tendency to denounce each other.

There were, of course, exceptions. That united band of one hundred Kabardine Mussulmans, for instance, who insisted on being shipped to Syria. Eva Matarashvilli, who taught me the songs of Georgia. Evading in turn the tentacles of the

---

[1] A double-edged reference (Liberator bombers).

Germans, the Russians, the British, and the Italian carabinieri, Eva found safety at last in Buenos Aires.

The Poles had shown not only aggression but a special (in British eyes, a rather flamboyant) sort of bravery in battle. Their national pride (*Honor, Bóg, Ojczyzna* – Honour, God, Fatherland) had been at stake; they were obsessed with avenging the military rout of 1939. Politics, however, confused and eventually destroyed them as a cohesive fighting force, for as the war neared its end they had to reckon with two enemies – the Russians as well as the Germans. How indeed could they have reacted otherwise, with the Red Army in occupation of their homes? When the fighting was over General Anders's men were faced with an agonising choice: to return, in semi-disgrace as 'Fascists', to a Communist-controlled Poland, or to go into exile. Not many chose to go home and of these the final drafts included an embarrassing rabble of turncoat Silesians whom Anders had recruited from surrendered Wehrmacht units.

I felt sad to see the last small party of the genuine Poles depart up the gangway of a Liberty ship that was to take them back to Poland from Naples. The Australian army blankets and the two pairs of boots that dangled from each man's pack seemed a small reward for several years of fortitude and hardship.

Finally, I had tested my nerves in a war and I was glad, though no longer elated, to be alive. The moments of elation had been brief, and they had had to be earned. They were those moments when one realised that the shell that had just pitched in front of one's nose had not exploded: when one turned away from the battle area for a fortnight's rest – when I had jumped naked into the sea at Matruh and Senigallia, or sat in a field after the Cassino battle watching a man with a plough.

And there were those landscapes. The glaring, empty deserts where after the day's heat one shivered under the black escarpments of night. Those Kurdish villages near Kirkuk where the sour smoke curled from dung fires and women like witches watched us from golden stubble fields. Arab boys bringing home their beautiful flocks at dusk in a trail of dust that settled like flour on the old stone walls of Askalon. Blue mountain forests in Umbria. Haycocks on a Styrian *alm* and the blackened eaves of inns stinking of vinegary wine.

It was those images of landscapes that haunted me. I could not rid my mind of them. Nor can I now, though it is the ringed cattle camps of Karamoja, the dikdik and the weaver birds flitting among thorn bush, that come first to mind today when I am on leave in England watching two blackbirds peck at bread crumbs on my brother's lawn. Those images were at the root of my restlessness. A restlessness that no London pavement, no bloated city pigeons, no caw of rooks on a Warwickshire roof, could satisfy.

CHAPTER 5

Germersheim

Escape

To make things worse, I had returned to England several years too late to take advantage of the employers' initial good will towards ex-servicemen. I called on the British Council. No, they would not have me back. 'We are dismissing people,' I was told by a young man with a squeaky voice, 'not recruiting them. And by the way, when you left us to join the services you broke your contract, and you owe us a month's salary.'

So I went to Paddington Labour Exchange, who found me a job as clerk at £5 a week with the Festival of Britain organisation. Declared redundant immediately the Festival opened in 1951, and by now somewhat demoralised, I borrowed my uncle's bicycle and set off down the Old Kent Road.

My reappearance in Bad Driburg as a poor cyclist did not please the Graf von Öynhausen, or his relatives who as impoverished refugees from East Prussia had not long before been glad to drink my NAAFI brandy. Now that the Graf's Kurhaus had been de-requisitioned and paying guests were flocking back to treat their dyspepsia at his mineral springs, he was prospering. Rebuffed, I pedalled off to visit friends in Vienna.

But there was going to be a complication. To enter the Soviet Zone of Austria I would have to be cleared by a Red Army frontier post at the Semmering. In view of my past record I felt certain that my name was on the black list of Soviet Intelligence. I did not want to confront Red Army policemen. To avoid them I left the Vienna road and humped my bicycle into the hills till I came to a grassy plateau overlooking the Semmering Pass, where a few strands of barbed wire and a rough wooden fence marked the frontier. As I sat down to get my breath back, a young man came through the firs towards me, with a suitcase strapped to his back. I was glad to meet a fellow law-breaker. He too, I gathered, had no papers. He had just spent some weeks in gaol, 'cutting logs with a very small saw'.

Once inside the Soviet Zone I bowled quietly downhill to Neuenkirchen and on to Vienna. I had one awkward experience. Just before dark, near Baden, in a Communist inn hung with posters of the 'Bread and Steel' variety, the landlord began to question me rather unpleasantly, and a gendarme came in. I left quickly and dossed down (I always slept out) in a hollow in a field. I would have been in trouble had un-friendly eyes spotted me, for I was on the edge of a Soviet military airfield whose rotating searchlight beams flashed throughout the night around my sleeping place.

Vienna's cobbled streets punished my uncle's pre-War bicycle; my old unit had folded up and my Austrian informants, now adjusted to civilian life, were no longer interested in the past.

But in the Soviet Zone itself the Red Army, though thinner on the ground, was still a sinister nuisance. Among the débris of Wiener Neustadt little yellow men were trying the doors of locked houses. In the town cemetery, where they had buried their dead, the graves of Russian soldiers with their five-pointed red star of flattened tin or roughly carved stone in place of a cross, looked characteristically out of place, aggres-sively pagan. In a separate section of the burial ground I counted the graves of thirty Russian officers with the rank of captain and major whose deaths, according to the inscriptions, had taken place after the war, in 1946 and 1947. Affrays? Drunken driving?

My bicycle excursion and the waking at dawn, in a meadow or clump of pines, to sunlight on strange surroundings and the first chorus of birds, was not simply an impulsive reversal to adolescent habits. On the way back, I found myself a job. I had heard that the Auslandsinstitut of Mainz University in Germersheim (Palatinate) was looking out for a *Lektor* in its English Department. Hiding my bicycle, I called on Professor Jaeger, and I was accepted.

This was, for me, the rebirth of an educative process that

had been interrupted for many years. Naturally I was alarmed at the prospect of facing German university students with my rusty academic background. For three months, therefore, in a Notting Hill Gate café, I crammed German classics – Goethe, Jean-Paul Richter, Gottfried Keller, and Heine whose opening sally in the *Reisebilder* is 'The city of Göttingen, renowned for its sausages and university . . .'.

Drenched with good German prose I went out to confront my first classes.

Students

It is, I think, worth saying a little about Germersheim because it was a significant symbol of Germany's post-War attempt to cultivate among her young people an international outlook in place of the old aggressive contempt and xenophobia.

The Institute, founded on the initiative of the French occupation authorities in 1947, had 700 students. The courses – in English, French and Russian – were designed to qualify them as practical linguists with special knowledge of the countries whose languages they were studying. The Institute's international outlook was based on tolerance – which for years had been a scarce quality among the Germans. I was asked to lecture on British economic history and on current affairs. Since the library (mainly a gift of the Americans) was poor, I had to rely excessively on the *Encyclopaedia Britannica*, which at first, volume by volume, I took to bed with me.

Our students were delightful to teach. They looked, not back into the awful past, for which they did not feel responsible, but to the future; and they eagerly supported the current objective of West Germany's reintegration with Western Europe. But reintegration had its snags. Young Germans regarded the projected rearmament of West Germany with instinctive foreboding, at best as a necessary evil. The possibility of their being used as 'American mercenaries' in a hopeless military rearguard action against Soviet invasion worried them. As for serving in the new West German army, German youth summed up its attitude to the once sacred principle of *Wehrpflicht* in the phrase '*Ohne mich* – You can count me out.'

The Spartan habits, the youthful idealism of our Germersheim students, were splendid. Alas, the West German economic
system was not sympathetic to idealism. The vast mass of the
German people, having lost their possessions and gone hungry
for a while, had become intensely acquisitive and materialistic.
Most of our students were quickly swallowed up in minor
posts in the cut-throat world of Ruhr business and industry.

Garrison Town
The special thing about the small town of Germersheim was its
character as an old German garrison and fortress, rebuilt in
the mid-nineteenth century as a powerful Rhine stronghold
enclosed by massive walls beyond which building was pro-
hibited. Its inns – thirty-eight of them in a town with a resident
population of under 5,000 – used to solace the Kaiser's Bavarian
regiments. They now served a mixed bag of American GIs,
Polish and Bulgarian guard companies and German auxiliaries
from a signals unit. The Pfälzer wine was cheap and gave me
diarrhoea. Drunk warm and spiced as *Glühwein* it left a stupefy-
ing hangover.

I lived in an attic with a smelly iron stove. Though the
Institute's lecturers were poorly paid – we rode bicycles, we
bickered, and we envied colleagues who earned a little extra
money by translating dull German commercial dictionaries
and directories – the townspeople treated us with exaggerated
respect, magnifying our titles.

I used to buy my groceries at Widow Stärk's tiny shop: a
pickled herring (25 pfennigs), a spoonful of mustard in a twist
of paper (10 pfennigs), a pint of butter milk (15 pfennigs), and a
single Rotbart razor blade (8 pfennigs) – total cost one shilling.

'*Wär's das*, Herr Professor?' she would ask as she wrapped my
poor man's supper. 'Is that all you require today, Herr Professor?'

The Rhine swept by between rows of poplar trees – black,
cold, broken by small whirlpools, carrying barges loaded with
oil and coal and slatternly families with dogs and washing lines.
I used to swim in it, hoping I would not be sucked under by the
treacherous current. The streets smelt of midden heaps; gnats
bit at night.

The High Alps

Our students were great hitch-hikers, eager to communicate with their foreign neighbours (though not with the Communist *bloc*), turning up with their rucksacks and rusks of rye bread in Barcelona, Paris, Inverness, but in England disappointed at the narrow range of paid jobs that were open to them (domestic and menial hospital posts for girls, and harvest camps). I followed their example. One summer I cycled to the North Cape. Twice I cycled through the Balkans to Salonica. In winter I made long ski journeys over the high glaciers of the Vorarlberg and the Tirol.

I had learned the elements of ski-ing at an army centre in Bavaria. It was the high lonely slopes of untracked snow not the crowded *pistes* that attracted me, and from a base in the Klein Walsertal (on the Bavarian border with Vorarlberg) that I used to make my favourite glacier tours which in three weeks of hard ski-ing carried me via Lech am Arlberg, Zürs, St Anton, and over the Silvretta glacier to Gargellen, thence over the Swiss frontier to Klosters and Davos, then back by a slightly different route.

On these High Alp ski tours I travelled alone – which is against the rules and not to be recommended – and I had to take the risk of accident, of losing my way in bad weather, and of ski-ing through avalanche areas. But I was in no hurry. I had acquired sufficient skill, and I had sufficient strength, to avoid a disabling fall. There was the nightly comfort of a mountain refuge to look forward to. My reward was the indescribable elation of swooping (when not wearily climbing on skins) through a glittering world of empty glacier slopes.

Frontiers were of no account. Dropping down from Gargellen over the Schlappiner Joch at the end of a long trip, past old avalanche débris and deserted *Almenhütten* on the descent to Klosters, from the Ötztal into Italy, or from the Swiss Vallée du Trient to Argentières in France, unobserved, alone, I felt I had conquered fear, clumsiness, and the ghosts of solitude.

Landscapes

From my long, slow journeys between the Arctic and Mediterranean, and from my unimpeded ski tours through a wintry

Alpine world I learned – what in the pre-War and War-time rivalries of European nations I had tended to forget – that Europe is in truth a small, single and homogeneous territory for ever knitted by language, building and farming styles, by food, and by the Christian tradition whose symbols – a steeple, a dome, an onion-spire pricking a sky-line, a plain wooden cross in a Swedish Lutheran church, an ornate and gilded decoration over a Baroque altar in Carinthia, the plastic crucifix above a street-walker's bed in Naples, the double-barred execution stake of Orthodoxy, a Carpathian ikon – express men's preoccupation with a common vision.

Bumbling along on a bicycle and feeling every jolt of rut and stone one not only feels part of the rolling road itself; the transition from one landscape or way of life to another occurs so gradually – is often quite unrelated to the cartographer's lines – that one scarcely notices the moment of change.

The sad, dripping conifer forests of Sweden were for me an extension of those massed plantations of north Germany. They in turn prepared me, as I travelled north through Haparanda, Rovaniemi (the forests beyond here still scarred by the débris of battle) and Ivalo, for the dwarf birches of the Arctic Circle and those mossy tracts of tundra where herds of reindeer stared gloomily at me as I pedalled past them in the rain.

At the gateway to south-eastern Europe – through Graz and Maribor or over the Loibl Pass – Slovenia still looks like Styria only less prosperous, its painted farmhouses a little more crooked and splashed with the mud and dust of dirt roads.

Montenegro is an aberration, bandits' country, a wasteland of stony mountains with an occasional cottage standing like a cairn among a square of maize stalks. But Tito's Macedonia with its vines and melons ripening in glorious sunshine, the tobacco leaves hanging on stakes to dry, and the sandy summer river beds where water buffaloes look for mud, merges softly into Mediterranean Greece.

Serbia, as I was to discover later when I travelled in Turkey, has already prepared one for Asia. The fierce moustache bristling under a craggy nose, the baggy-seated trousers and thonged footwear, the water buffalo, will occur again and again as one passes the great minarets of Edirne into Turkey and on to the Anatolian plateau. The sweetmeats of honey, sesame seed and spun sugar and the sour *ayran* of the Serbs accompany one on the long journey to Erzurum. The peasant-women of Greece have turned into shawled and shapeless Moslem bundles sitting in ox-carts or preparing food over a fire of dung cakes against a mud wall.

Orient

Where indeed does the Orient begin? In the Taurus foothills where shaggy Bactrian camel trains swing along the Mediterranean coast road under carob trees? In the alleys of Mersin among its swarthy Arab boys and furtive black-draped women? In the bazaars and rug shops of Khoi? There is no demarcation line. Only Red Russia's hideous wire fence that bisects the conjoined hills and plains like a stab wound and separates the free from the unfree.

Persian Azerbaijan is but a poorer, more arid extension of eastern Turkey. At their junction with the two Ararats, Kurdish nomads spill over three frontiers. The stony roads of Azerbaijan wind past mud villages that look like mounds of débris ringed by dust-spattered poplars and a thread of greasy dyke-water.

Perched over two bicycle wheels, viewing the earth as something to be travelled slowly and with laborious effort, one notices – one *has* to notice, for there is nothing else to divert the mind – the details that alone give life and colour to those igneous crusts, details that the mind retains for ever: the bright bee-eater eyeing me from behind a thistle; an Egyptian vulture tearing the bloody flesh of a tortoise; humped cattle, in a cloud of golden chaff, treading out the grain in a stubble field cut by sickle; a samovar shining in a mud-built tea house brightened by a scrap of prayer rug.

The Elbruz range that soars along the northern sky-line changes colour in the sun's arc from ochre to green, from purple to coppery red. Far above the glaring crests, above the Maku gorge and under the snow-streaked cones of Savalan and Sahand, in a cloud-world of their own, herdsmen and their flocks are enjoying cool nights, green grass and sparkling water. Where the ridges that dominate the valleys fall back and the sky empties but for the highest peaks, I have met true Turks: wrinkled, bandy-legged men who live in round felt tents (*yurts*) like mushrooms. Their camels grazed among blue delphiniums, their corralled horses neighed by cold streams. At night the wolf's howl would set off an uproar of men and dogs.

I had first seen the Oriental ritual of sea-bathing, with grave-faced men in baggy underpants and women in skirts squatting in a shallow surf, on a Black Sea strand. Far away at Pahlevi on the Caspian I saw it again – the week-end motorists from Teheran parked in hundreds of little booths along a fine grey beach. Waist-deep, as in a bowl of tepid soup, stand or sit the bathers like flocks of sea-fowl. Melon rinds float beside them.

Westward along the coast from Pahlevi, through the rice fields and giant hornbeam glades, one comes up with a jolt against Europe's most shameful spectacle – the tall watch-towers of Soviet Russia, a double wire fence and parallel to it, following every contour of the long trudge up the pass from Astara, the thin sandy track that reveals footmarks.

How unfriendly it has always seemed to me, this symbol of watchful suspicion, of the prison cage: the gaunt and lonely tower with a wooden box on top, whence high above felled trees and deserted fields unseen eyes stare ceaselessly at the specks and dust of movement on the other side of their world.

Behind the two Ararats the hateful spy-towers run along the Aras, imprisoning Armenia. Not far from Batum, on the Black Sea, Russian wire severs the beach. Far to the west, Bulgarians imitate the master, their watch-towers silhouetted like gallows over maize fields.

My vision of Europe, then, is of a friendly and cohering world that, until one meets the eye of Russia, one can cover in peace, yard by yard: to the north, dissolving in iron fjords and tundra that flickers in the Northern Lights; to the south, rolling down over rough paths and through olive groves to the blue sea furrows that glide past Thassos. To the east, in Asia Minor, becoming desiccated, ochreous, smelling of burnt earth, its minarets turning to signposts pointing through an Arab culture to Africa.

CHAPTER 6

Turks

Writing a Book

Climbers may be attracted to solitary places, but they are not noticeably tongue-tied. I am well aware of the urge to communicate to others the raptures one has felt high up in the thin cold air.[1] Not long after I came to Turkey, to a teaching post in Ankara, I walked up two high mountains – Ararat (16,916 feet), and Demavend (18,603 feet) in Persia, and sent accounts of these experiences to *The Times*. Both articles appeared, to my surprise, on the turnover page.

The Times used to have a soft spot for amateur alpinists. I sent a good many other climbing and travel accounts to its feature editors, and by the time I had had some 10,000 words printed on its turnover page (sometimes, I fear, at the expense of its accredited Ankara correspondent's despatches), it seemed to me that in them I had the makings of a book. All I had to do was to thread the bits together and to introduce a theme.

The theme stared me in the face. It was the huge, eroding Anatolian plateau itself with its bordering ranges falling down to the seas, its marvellous antiquities, and its tough Moslem people who herded livestock in high summer pastures and winnowed grain down in the plains, and in countless lonely outposts guarded with old Mauser rifles Turkey's long frontiers with Soviet Russia and her other neighbours.

I had moved to Kampala by the time (1964) George Allen & Unwin published my book. I learned that some Turks were displeased with it. 'You have portrayed,' the Turkish Press

[1] Robin Fedden (*The Enchanted Mountains*, London 1962) has warned against the romantic approach. 'Description in the language of mysticism and of love', he says, 'had better be left alone.' But was it quite fair of him to say of the moment when he stood at last on top of his beautiful mountain, 'We were merely sitting on a few shattered rocks'?

Attaché in London wrote to me, 'the Turkey of country yokels and of mountains which no one in his senses wants to visit; the Turkey of foreign monuments and of Kurds – who are not Turks at all.'

My book appealed, though, to those indefatigable West Germans who scour the Orient for its *Romantik*; and to some of an older generation of Englishmen in whom, judging by the letters I received from retired military gentlemen disputing points of Anatolian topography, it awakened nostalgic memories of their own youthful excursions in the former Ottoman empire.

I had indeed read extensively in the early travellers' journals. So often had I pored over Fellows, Hamilton and Tozer that I had unwittingly introduced something of their Victorian idiom into my own narrative. No wonder Sir Reader Bullard, Philips Price and W. E. D. Allen, all lovers of the old Turkey, reviewed my book with excessive kindness. Moreover, in the Victorian tradition, I had rediscovered one or two early Georgian churches that had been hidden away and long forgotten in the red gorges of eastern Anatolia.

There was no sex in my Turkey book. For the Rev. H. F. Tozer, Lord Warkworth and the rest of my mentors the subject would have been taboo. Turkey had no Burton to stir things up with notes on pederasty, excision and infibulation. Hamilton was more interested in copying Greek and Roman inscriptions, Warkworth in sitting round a camp fire with camel drivers, than in forbidden female flesh.

For me, Turkey had been an ascetic experience in a Puritanical society and a harsh landscape. Sunbathers had scarcely as yet intruded into Turkey's long Mediterranean beaches. Cafés and tea houses were clubs for old men bunched silently over little glasses of tea. Away from the main towns the overwhelming majority of Turkish women went about in shapeless Moslem wrappings, ducking for cover when I appeared silently round the corner of a Pontic country road. Those coarse skirts and long drawers repelled, as they were intended to, male curiosity and lust. I did not visit the public brothels. In Ankara, I was told, they were under military guard. Craggy-nosed men in cloth caps and long underwear had to queue like post office customers for their turn. The women, some of whom I saw on a shopping expedition, had dyed red hair. They waddled like fattened geese.

I did, however, make a few cautious references to Turkish defecation habits ('Raschid was squatting by the lake and had just cleaned his backside with a finger . . .'), for which W. E. D. Allen chided me in *The Journal of the Royal Geographical Society*. 'It is a pity,' he wrote, 'that Mr Hills is infected with the modern fashion of references to the elimination of the chemical waste of the human body – a process which an older generation did not find of sufficient interest to retail to their readers.' Nor could I resist mentioning the warden whom I caught in an end room of the Istanbul Museum urinating against a piece of sculpture.

Zonguldak

Following the military revolution of 1960 (Prime Minister Menderes was cruelly hanged) I returned from leave to find that a Turkish army officer's wife had appropriated my post as lecturer in English at the Middle East Technical University in Ankara. At short notice I was obliged to move to a school in Zonguldak, a small Black Sea coastal town whose name – in allusion to its early reputation for malarial fever – means 'place of trembling'.

Frogs croaked in an uproar of castanets in the soggy fields of Zonguldak, nightingales piped among the strawberry trees, winter snows piled up against the blackened old timbers of farmsteads. From my cottage window I looked out at vast thickets of rhododendrons and at sea gulls screaming over shoals of silvery fish. Through the winter months, in a demented effort to show the Turks that not all Englishmen were degenerate, I regularly swam, alone with a pair of cormorants, in the cold green sea – an electric shock treatment that made me tingle like a kettle.

By 1963 I had had enough. I did not want to moulder away in a damp cottage on a Black Sea cliff. The flaming sunsets, the thump of breakers, the bony cows wandering through bracken had begun to pall.

I had been eight years in Turkey. I had recorded my experiences in a book. It was time for me and Ingrid to go.

54 The White Pumpkin

In Istanbul, just before I left, I did my last climb – up the dome of the Santa Sofia mosque. David Winfield, who was restoring its mosaics, and I hauled ourselves up to the gilded crescent by an iron chain. The crescent was scratched with Catholic names of Italian workmen.

Turks

Turkey had enriched me. I had been introduced to a fascinating world of antiquities, of Moslem culture and mountain wandering, and to a people of outstanding integrity with a formidable history of military conquest.

Turkish politics were old-fashioned: authoritarian, anti-Socialist and patriotic – the politics of a country that had crystallised its views on foreign relations centuries ago. Russians and Greeks were enemies; Arabs, a former subject race, were inferior. The Germans were true allies who had helped Atatürk thrash the British at Gallipoli and were now offering scores of thousands of Turkish workmen good Deutschmarks in German industry.

We British ranked among Turkey's 'enemies'. We had destroyed the old Ottoman Empire, encouraged the Greeks to invade Smyrna in 1919, and we were still identified with an unpopular régime in Cyprus. 'You are meddlesome people,' an old peasant in a red turban once told me in a tea house near Erzurum, 'you are not to be trusted, and you are for ever changing sides.'

Such stereotyped attitudes, accepted almost to a man by the Turks, made political discussion irrelevant; but they clarified one's own position in society. When travelling in provincial Turkey I was often taken for a German. '*Alman, arkadaş,* A German, a friend!' bus passengers and shoeshine boys would call out with approval when they saw me with my rucksack, '*Hoş geldiniz,* Welcome!' Faces fell when I was unmasked as an Englishman, and they would leave me. But I preferred their ingenuous rebuffs to flattery.

Alpinism as a sport was scarcely known among the Turks, whose educated élite preferred to keep as far away as possible from rural discomfort. The mountain wanderer with his ice-axe and paraphernalia was suspected of looking for gold or precious metals. The only guides I ever found were muleteers or shepherds who would not venture above the snow line, so that beyond the scattered cattle camps of Kurds and Lazes I had to rely entirely on my own resources. Water, however, so scarce on foot safari in East Africa, was never a problem, gushing cold and pure from springs; and there were the plants and flowers – impenetrable thickets of Pontic rhododendrons and yellow azaleas, the dwarf oak hung with galls, flowering capers twisted round a Greek column, saffron crocuses (herdsmen chew the bulbs yet disdain mushrooms), delphiniums.

Europe, I thought, would for ever seem dull to me after Turkey with her stone Hittite warriors and Byzantine walls, her great domed mosques, her bazaars, hand-made rugs, gypsies and peaches.

Driving back to Europe I used to feel that beyond Belgrade, beyond the muddy water-buffalo holes, the apple orchards and the taverns smelling of plum brandy where men got drunk at breakfast, I was re-entering the world of cemented earth and machinery. The German autobahns swooping over anonymous horizons were a nightmare. In Munich, Cologne and Brussels overweight people compulsively munched food. In England there were hairy clowns, the small meat pie, the public library that smelt of sour clothes, grass sprinkled between concrete borders and fields intersected by buzzing lines of cars.

Landscapes

And now that I have recorded those journeys and impressions, let me try to relate them to what was soon to follow.

John Hillaby, who has trudged with camels to Lake Rudolf, footslogged through bog, sewage farm, and Highland glen to John o' Groat's, and again from the Hook of Holland to Nice, says of walking: 'It comes down to the simple fact that if you don't know what you're looking at, you can't be expected to look at it for very long. With his affinities for what makes up the world, the naturalist is able to put a great deal between what he sees and that part of his mind where boredom lurks. As a human being he's neither better nor worse than his fellows, but in the matter of deriving pleasure from the out-of-doors he is definitely more fortunate.'

Clearly my own earlier experiences of walking in Central Europe with its nineteenth-century landscapes had prepared me for the almost mediaeval look of Turkish countryside where black bullocks ploughed beneath crooked walls and wedges of one-eyed sun flowers nodded and stared to the south-east. In their turn the empty spaces of central Anatolia and Persia – whose very 'emptiness' obliges one to look for the gleam of a single wild-flower – prepared me for the East African bush.

There is the prickly armature of spikes that protects the vegetation of the Asian and African territories alike: at the end of the longest foot trail, a water hole, a shepherd in a felt cloak or a black scarified poacher in a cave, someone squatting by a wisp of smoke.

The rhythm of the long walk and the walker's feeling of security are the same wherever you are – a car may break down for want of a bolt, your legs will carry you to journey's end. It is the tiny detail, hidden to the motorist's eye, that gives vibrant life: in a Turkish gorge, a golden oriole in a mulberry tree; in East Africa, the bark of a baboon, the go-away-bird flicking its cockaded head, a man who appears from nowhere carrying nothing but a spear and a snuff-horn. His feet are cracked pads. A drop of spittle shines in the hole in his under-lip. His penis, since he has plucked the pubic hairs, looks curiously impudent and large.

The differences too are absorbing. In the mountains of Uganda I have missed the upland grazing pastures of Anatolia and Persia. The herds stay below, finding safety in numbers and in the proximity of tribal villages, trampling and tearing the eroded tussocks, jostling along dried stream beds, lowing dolefully as the loose and wrinkled skin twitches on their rib cages and flies torment their orifices. The Kurd takes his goat-hair tent and his animals up to summer grazing slopes. When the cold weather sets in he descends to underground hovels whose smoke spirals from vents in the ground. Like the Kurd, the Karamojong cattleman, when he is not roving, settles among dirt and flies.

A Turkish shepherd has powerful long-haired dogs with iron-spiked collars to protect his livestock against wolves and bears. The African has his spear, his game traps; his little yellow dog is a half-starved cur. The Turk, in treeless zones, cooks and warms himself over cattle dung cakes. The African has no use for the precious dung except to smear his hut with it or to anoint a wound.

In the highlands of Turkey and Persia I recall seeing mountain choughs, swifts and eagles. The East African highlands are far richer in birds. On and around them is mountain woodland – stands of bamboo, cedar, hagenias and podocarpus. The Hakkari mountain slopes offer little shade: on the whole of Ararat I have seen but a single poor copse of birches.

But the Turkish mountains are rich in Alpine flowers that shine – primulas, saxifrages, blue gentians – like emeralds. East Africa, though, has familiar species that grow to monsters: giant heather trees bent crooked by wind under the crater lip of Nyiragongo; giant lobelias whose powder-blue inflorescences attract sunbirds; groundsels massive as trees; bushy everlastings, and mosses and lichenous beards that hide the ground orchid in its bed of nettles.

The Pontic Alps are often visited by gentlemen from Kew with flower presses and knapsacks. No gentlemen from Kew bother to photograph the tough and modest flowers of Lomwaka.

The history of Europe is recorded in masonry. In remotest Phrygia the chiselled stones of Ancient Greeks are heaped on a hill like drawn teeth. Where the Greeks settled, their fluted columns still stand or lie.

In East Africa death brings oblivion. No one has built anything permanent in the African bush. There are no castles on crags or marble colonnades. The thatched huts of villagers crumble quickly. Or they are destroyed to purify them of malignant death and evil spirits, burnt down, abandoned. Foot tracks disappear after a single rainy season, under grass thick as hair. Aloes toss their rusty spear heads over unmarked graves. When the tribe moves, no one remembers that the giant fig tree where wood hoopoes cry was once a shrine.

Mombasa – Kampala
As the French ship *La Bourdonnais*, bound for Mombasa and Mauritius, carried me away from Suez towards the Indian

Ocean I felt I was leaving something I could never replace. I thought of those mountains of the Kashgai which I had not yet visited, of sea-bathing at Kuşadasi over embedded marbles, of the Turk bundling off his womenfolk so that a *giaour* could lie down in his parlour.

A stroll through Djibouti disappointed me: heat, an élite of pale Frenchmen, a market buzzing with flies, black men with legs like sticks. It would take time to get Turkey out of my system.

I loitered in Mombasa. Movement was from the opposite direction, for the hotels were crowded with Kenya settlers leaving Africa for ever.

Yet disloyal thoughts were already seeping in. I had left winter behind. Coral sands glittered in glorious sunshine, there were pawpaws and mangoes for breakfast. I was among people who laughed, got drunk and danced. Their women looked one impudently in the eye.

Within an hour of my driving off from Mombasa on the road to Kampala I was surrounded, while I changed a wheel, by half a dozen Giryama women. No respectable Turk could have endured their semi-nudity. Sweat beaded their coffee-coloured breasts. When they laughed they showed mouths crammed with gleaming teeth and crimson tongues that flickered against the gums.

Even the baobab trees, the muddy hulks of elephants, the grotesque helmeted hornbills that I saw seemed to me more ancient than Turkey's historic stones.

In Kampala I suffered at first from a feeling of inadequacy. In Turkey, where Englishmen are few, I had had rarity value. I had managed, moreover, to acquire enough special knowledge of the country to be considered an 'interesting person'.

Here in East Africa I was a nonentity. Not only did I know nothing of the country. I was swamped by hundreds of my countrymen who between them knew everything there was to be known about Kenya and Uganda. What could I possibly add to that store of expert knowledge? As for 'exploration', even Kilimanjaro was climbed by schoolboys.

Yet there was hope. Uganda did indeed abound in pundits

who had studied everything, from the composition of elephant dung to syphilis among Baganda women. But were the Makerere professors, the social anthropologists, the professional hunters and the botanists articulate?

The shelves of Makerere library were proof that they tended to distil their special knowledge into academic papers, journals, symposia, and reports that to a layman were either inaccessible or deadly dull. I at least had a small connexion with journalism. Perhaps I could peep into a few corners and write something after all.

Well aware that hundreds of people had been there before me I described for *The Times* the conventional ascent of Kilimanjaro (it appeared under the heading 'Middle-Aged Fitness Test on Kibo'), and an encounter with Karamojong tribesmen (noting how my guide wiped snot on to the soles of his feet). This was a beginning. By the time Lord Thomson had taken over *The Times* and dropped the turnover-page article for letters on income tax, I had the skeleton of another book.

PART II

JOURNEYS

CHAPTER 7

Lomwaka

By 1969 I had seen a good deal of East Africa and the book I had in mind (*Man With A Lobelia Flute*) was written. But there were still new hills to climb, old places to revisit, and the changing Uganda scene now darkening, alas, under the shadow of politicians and soon to be in the hands of soldiers.

I decided to call on Kalisto and to take him with me to Lomwaka.

Kalisto

Kalisto, now twenty-six, was at last enjoying the first small fruits of his long studies at school and at a teacher training centre. His home was no longer a thatched bachelor hut tucked away among cow droppings and *olim* bush in a corner of Acholi where his father, an old World War II soldier, farmed a few cotton and grain plots. He was the house-proud occupant of a new staff bungalow at Kitgum, where he was teaching mathematics to S1 and S2 classes at the local secondary school.

Kalisto's bungalow, built by a Sikh contractor, had piped water, even though it was only a rusty trickle that discoloured the bath, electricity, and some pieces of furniture of the sort that is supplied to the public service all over Uganda by the Ministry of Works. He had added a Japanese alarm clock, some cushions and pots and pans, a shelf of books. He had a Raleigh bicycle. For the first time in his life he had a little money in his pocket; his salary was £50 a month.

Kalisto – unlike his African colleagues, who all had wives or women to brew their millet beer and share their beds – was still single. When I first visited him in his new post at Kitgum, he was employing two men from his village as servants. He paid their poll tax, and they were happy, squatting for hours in his compound round a fire on which millet porridge or a chicken were cooking. But they could not be bothered to chase away the big brown cockroaches that leapt and scurried over the bungalow. They left greasy finger marks on the white walls and charcoal stains on the waxed cement floor. They breathed beer over his books, and from time to time collapsed drunk on his bed. So Kalisto had sent them home, and he was now fending for himself.

Kalisto was ambitious. The old World War II soldiers back home in Adilang, who spent their days ambling from one hut to another cadging beer, the clansmen with their thin, veined legs, their useless bows and spears, and their boasting, the semi-literate village girls who carried water pots on their heads, who sweated, and picked their noses, and knelt when they came into his compound, were no longer a part of his horizon. Kalisto did not wish to vegetate for ever in the shadows of the teaching profession with a wife who got pregnant every year and a routine of class work that did not tax his abilities. He had set his mind on entering Makerere University and studying for a degree that would open up an entirely new world for him.

People might call him selfish because he did not buy them beer: mad, or impotent, because he did not have a wife. Instead of spending the warm, airless evenings on a stool at the Acholi Pride bar, or on his verandah having his brains hammered to stupefaction by Congolese High Life rhythms from a transistor set, Kalisto would take off his shirt, and with a naked light bulb gleaming on his black shoulders, pore over the history of nineteenth-century Europe.

This was how I found Kalisto when, towards midnight, I drove my Volkswagen into his compound after the 390-mile journey from Kampala. I had brought him more books: histories of the British constitution, of the French Revolution and of Bismarck's Germany, congested with the thousands of examinable facts that thirty-five years earlier I had gladly dismissed from mind when I walked out of my Oxford college and along the Turl for the last time. I no longer remember what Professor Zimmern said in his painstaking analyses of the League of Nations Covenant which I had listened to for a whole term.

1a Mount Ararat, 16,916 feet, from the Erzurum road

1b Little Ararat, 12,840 feet, from Ararat

2a Author with porter in the Kackar range (Turkey)

2b Herdsmen in Moroto
2c Author with herdsboy in the Pontic Alps (Turkey)

I recall G. D. H. Cole's ugly red tie but none of his many words. But I remember the Turl: its noisy Welshmen in ready-made tweed jackets; Jack Lovelock, our sporting hero, who beat Hitler's athletes at the Berlin Olympic Games of 1936. It was into the Turl, and the narrow adjacent passage we called Fornication Lane, that I used to swing down from a college window, or over a wall studded with broken glass and revolving spikes, at midnight. It was a Turl paving stone that had knocked me cold one night, when omitting to secure the rope, I fell twenty feet from the Bursar's window ledge.[1]

Some of Kalisto's colleagues in Kitgum were my old students and they called on me with offerings of beer. I learned that Odong, gangling and yellow-eyed, had run off with a girl of his own Lango tribe, impregnated her, paid the girl's father the fine that custom exacted for elopement, and was now settling down to family life with his college text books and a dozen chickens that walked in and out of his kitchen. He had, incidentally, nothing to be ashamed of in his method of wooing a wife. As Kalisto said, 'You run off with the girl, put a baby in her stomach, then go back to her parents and pay the fine of 250-400 shillings. As long as the parents get their money, everyone's happy.'[2]

Okot was still drinking. He employed a heavy, bare-breasted woman to brew his beer and cook his millet dumplings. His room was a muddle of broken pots and musical instruments, and he was wearing a floppy hat to cover a recent beer wound on his temple. No one objected to Okot drinking at home. But he had begun to fall down under trees, and to giggle and stagger in the class room.

Kalisto's headmaster was an Irish priest of the Verona Fathers' Mission, a man of restless energy who drove a tractor and knew how to box. He had once, it was said, knocked down one of his American staff in front of the boys. The problem of how to prevent the schoolboys – some were grown men – from copulating with the girls tormented him. He tried to keep them apart by housing them in compounds separated by

[1] I climbed back undetected into college but I was identified next day by the lacerations on my face, and rusticated.
[2] See note on 'Elopement in Acholi', p. 257.

several hundred yards of elephant grass, mud, and barbed wire. He was not winning his battle.

Among Kalisto's neighbours was newly arrived Mr Egles, a former RAF bomber pilot who had been shot down into a Romanian peasant's field after a raid on Ploesti. Mr Egles had retained a pink complexion and his flying moustache, now white. Like all expatriate teachers on government contract – and this is a perennial source of irritation – he was better off than the local African teachers. He had a car and a refrigerator; and he and his wife managed to keep their house free of the fine brown dust and the small, persistent flies that plagued everyone else. I asked Mrs Egles how she liked the life. 'A bit different from Putney,' she said, looking through her cotton curtains at a man urinating against a fig tree.

Lotuturu

My object in visiting Kalisto was to climb Lomwaka peak, which stands on the northern horizon, fifty miles away, in a range of hills that seal off the Sudan border. I had brought a Kampala student, Remy Oler, with me. Remy was a Lotuho from the southern Sudan. He had caught my attention with his forthright views and because, in one important point, his prejudices were different from those of the rest of his student group: he was not interested in the local tribal jealousies of a Ugandan. The enemy, for him, were the 'Arabs', who he said were persecuting his people in the Sudan and had forced him as a boy to fly for his life. He was with me now because he wanted to look across the mountains into his Lotuho homeland.

I had already, two years earlier, walked across the plain that leads from a tiny broken ford (where we left my car and recruited porters) to the steep and forested foothill on which Lotuturu Rest House is sited. There were many things I recognised: the marks of iron ploughs dragged on their sides by bullocks scarring the track that runs between grain and cotton plots and under butter-nut trees; scraps of chewed sorghum cane spat out on the path by villagers who moisten and sweeten their mouths with it as they walk under the hot sun. The same old man again offered me a dirty colobus skin for a few shillings. But there was one ominous change. Charred patches showed where Uganda Army patrols had shot up and burnt huts in which Anyanya rebels from across the border were said to have sheltered.[1]

Lotuturu Rest House hardly lives up to its name. It is just a rough cemented shelter with broken shutters. Iridescent sunbirds rustle in a mango tree. Below, the flat and bushy Acholi plain laps stony *inselbergs* that glisten when the sun is on them as though they were drenched in dew.

The stands of pine planted by the forestry station above Lotuturu had grown well since I last saw labourers clearing the ground with the heavy old Nilotic hoes that are bent in the middle and have a heart-shaped blade. The children at the station were cold, dirty, and pot-bellied. Beyond the plantations, frond-ribs of wild bananas gleamed bright red in the swamp where a black stream runs through bamboo and creepers.

At the foot of Lomwaka we rested at a poor, isolated hut that sheltered a dozen ragged people. The lower incisor teeth of all the adults had been so brutally knocked out that when they spoke they sprayed spittle. I was about to sit down on a slab of stone raised like a small table above the mud when I realised, from the monkey tails and jaw-bones attached to it, that it was the owner's ancestral shrine (*abila*). For one shilling I got ten huge cassava roots which my companions immediately ate raw.

I had engaged five men to carry our gear. Early that morning they had grumbled that the loads were too heavy, the *posho* ration too little. They had sulked, and for a time refused to start.

It is my experience with porters that there may be two moments of crisis: the first, soon after setting out, when the men realise that humping spare clothes, bedding, food (and even books) up hill and down dale is harder work than they bargained for; the second, just before journey's end, when they may sit down and demand more money. Once we are well into the hills, I do not expect trouble from my companions. They are too far from home to quit.

[1] 'Anyanya' is a Mahdi word meaning 'snake poison'.

Not that I wish to criticise the dozens of Africans who have helped me over the years up a score of mountains. I could have done nothing without them. I always wonder at their strength, stamina, and resourcefulness, their willingness to trudge miles to look for water, to hack a path through thorn bush and creepers, to endure rain and cold nights, and to risk, quite often, the presence of buffaloes, elephants, even of lions.

Some men carry, of course, better than others. The strongest I have engaged were the Chagga on Kilimanjaro (they are professionals) and the Bahutu in the Virunga mountains. The least satisfactory have been Karamojong – tireless walkers but not used to carrying loads. My best escorts were Teuso, small, active and cheerful, who darted after the honey-guide bird and cut sheaves of soft grass for me to lie on at night.

Indeed, after some years of mountain wandering, I have still not rid myself of the guilt feeling that comes over me when I see my companions – for a, to me, trivial reward – thrusting hour after hour through tall grass that whips the face or plodding uphill with the weight of the head loads glazing their eyes with sweat.

Some of the men who hump my absurd bundles do not even look well. Their eyes are yellow, they are haggard, they have crooked legs. They cough at night over the fire of wet logs. Yet the muscles on their shoulders stand out like oranges as they lift their arms to balance the head load. Their thin legs, with the muscles clamped to the bone like snakes, are iron. The soles of their feet are cracked leather pads, invulnerable to the thorns that draw blood from my hands and to the stones and stumps on which I would bruise and cut my toes if I took off my plimsolls.

At the outset of every journey I have to make a special effort to adjust myself to the dehydration that follows a day's walk through burnt scrub, and to alternate heat and cold. Africans, I try to persuade myself, are inured. Those tiny Tepeth children with spindly legs and bulging stomachs who look like pregnant gnomes and live naked at 7,000 feet on Napak, have adapted themselves early on. Yet I know that my African companion suffers, too, as he sits motionless under a scrap of cloth in a rain storm, or creeps out of the sun into the thin shade of an acacia.

Lomwaka

We spent a wet night under a big fig tree and then started uphill again through drenched grass ten feet high concealing stones and small thorny plants that tore my legs. A gully buttressed with bare rocks and wild date palms runs up the south face of Lomwaka. It is not a good climbing route, so we traversed and camped in a grove just below the summit (8,649 feet). Clouds drowned the stars till dawn.

For two days we explored the summit platforms, startling reedbuck; and we walked several miles into the Sudan along buffalo trails. Rain showers scoured the lichenous rocks, brightened moss cushions where aloes grow, hissed into our camp fire. We had to go carefully, for poachers had set wire noose snares in the undergrowth. There were a great many wildflowers: fire ball lilies and orchids, white *pentas decora*, red-hot pokers, globe thistles (*echinops hispidus*) with a crimson flower-head as big as a tennis ball; and, of course, the giant lobelias and groundsels one expects to find above the line where bearded woodland ceases.

At night we returned to our camp in the grove, near a huge *musanga* tree whose leaves were bunches of pendent fingers so exactly symmetrical, so sharply etched against the blue distance, they reminded me of a Chinese painting.

Immediately to the north the Lolibai mountains which cut off Remy's homeland stuck their tops into black clouds. Remy, as he looked at them, spoke bitterly of the 'Arabs' who had wrecked Christian schools, driven out the white priests who had taught him, murdered villagers in market places. 'It is shameful,' he said, 'that neighbouring black African states do not come to help their brothers in distress.'

Remy thought it would be possible for us to reach his home on foot; he was sure Anyanya rebels would guide a brother and his friends past the 'Arab' military outposts. But our porters would not consider such a venture. They had an uneasy feeling, as we explored the Sudan side of the mountain, that we were being watched. Their fears were certainly groundless. African soldiers, the sort who are accustomed to riding in trucks and who hate rain, would not mount standing patrols in a wild and deserted no-man's-land. Yet, when a branch cracked somewhere like a pistol shot, both Kalisto and Remy started to run.

We returned home by a route that traversed the northern slopes of Lomwaka. It is a relief, at first, to go downhill. But the plunging trails of wet earth and stones that twist and disappear among roots and creepers require firm balance. After a time my knees lose their spring and I begin to slither, using my bamboo stick as a crutch.

We surprised a poacher, an old man in a grey monkey-fur cap, sitting in a cave. His name was Pedro (evidence of early contact with the Verona Fathers' Mission) and he wore a rosary and crucifix across a chest seamed like scratched earth. His hideout was a mess of broken calabashes, monkey skins, bones, ashes and flies.

At the poor hut near the Forestry Station a gap-toothed woman begged me to give her my kettle. There are experts who say that rooting out incisor teeth has been practised by some societies to ensure that if a man gets lock-jaw he can be fed through the gap. Mrs Noni Jabavu, on the other hand, describes how some young Banyoro told her that when the lower front teeth were extracted, a person 'looked like a cow' and therefore beautiful.[1] When I mentioned these theories to Kalisto, he laughed. 'Ask an Acholi why his front teeth were knocked out,' he said, 'and he will simply tell you "It's our custom". Whatever its origin,' he went on, 'young people don't like the practice any more. It makes them lisp when they speak English; and when a man is old and the rest of his teeth grow loose, without incisors he's in trouble.'

An Acholi friend, incidentally, has since given me another explanation of the custom. 'Tooth extraction (*nakko lak*) among the Acholi,' he said, 'seems to have originated in the Sudan, where the Acholi's Lwoo ancestors come from. It was done for beauty. Some teeth are naturally so widely spaced as to show slight gaps in front. The Lwoo are fond of these gaps (*kere*). The smile of such a person is pleasing to them. So the gap was deliberately made by extraction.'

In the plain we met dust again and a scorching heat that had crumpled the coarse, veined leaves of the butter-nut trees.

[1] *Drawn in Colour*, London, 1960.

We walked through plots of ground-nuts and millet where the owners had stuck poles with a yellow potato-flower berry tied to them to avert evil. I threw a stone at a snake that had reared up to seize a chameleon transfixed with terror on a millet stalk.

Back at our start point, I sat on my little Turkish stool (I fancy it lends me authority) and paid off the porters. They went away happily, waving the money (twenty-five shillings each in notes), to their wives. I wondered if the trip had really been worth their while. They had torn their shirts and shorts. They had not speared meat. Yet they had done something. They had been to the top of Lomwaka and would have a tale to tell.

And what had I got out of our expedition? I had endured two wet nights sitting over a fire with the rain spitting in the embers. I had seen some red thistles. My legs would ache for a day or two, and I was thinner. I could look at my map and know that I had stumbled over another tiny portion of Africa. Its image would stay in my mind for ever: a scrub-covered lump of rock, scoured by rain showers, with a crown of green grass that buffaloes had trampled.

Kitgum

It was Sunday afternoon when Kalisto, Remy and I returned to Kitgum. The stores were closed but an Indian beckoned us to come in through his back door.[1] The back of an Indian *duka*, with its swarming domestic life, its tiny passages and cubby-holes, is a puzzle. The labyrinth opens on to a cement space where African houseboys stuff mattresses and wash clothes, children relieve themselves, and raven-haired women ('squatting indecently,' as Kalisto says, 'like frogs') prepare chapattis, rice and curries. The drain that runs round the yard will be cleansed from time to time by rain. When there is no rain, it clots with sludge and rubbish, and smells badly. (Indians, we know, are scrupulous about their ablutions, and they have a ritual fear of contamination; yet the proximity of garbage does not seem to worry them.)

[1] Since I wrote these impressions the up-country *dukawallahs* have disappeared. Local Africans, Nubians, Somalis, and Muslims (many from the north) have taken over their stores.

The box-like rooms are crowded with beds. There is a parlour with tea and dinner sets in a glass-fronted cupboard, crude African paintings bought cheap from a hawker, plastic roses in a bowl. Wedding photographs show a slim, serious couple with sad eyes. Maturity has fattened enormously the woman's hips and cut lines covered with stubble in the bride-groom's face. The source and mainstay of all this teeming domestic life lie in the couple's determination, which is rein-forced by the strongest social pressures, to propagate them-selves; and in the profits, increased by shrewd bookkeeping, from a multitude of small sales. The *dukawallah*, because he lives on his premises, is virtually always 'open'. His evenings are spent playing cards on the pavement outside his shop.

So many obligations consume his profits, though, that the small storekeeper must keep his nose to the grindstone for life. A dozen dependants look up to him as patron, protector, and bread winner. In this he is fulfilling the role ordained by a code that antedates by centuries the Welfare State. Behind him, a fearful spectre, glowers the shadow of that abyss of nameless poverty in the Gujerat from which he has escaped to the relative paradise of East Africa. Somewhere along the road, wrapped in the obscurity of African politics, lies his vision of the future – a suburban home, probably, with a public play park and a school for his children, in the English Midlands.

The *dukawallah*'s African customers say he cheats, which is another way of saying that they would prefer to be cheated by a brother African. They resent, yet so far have been unable to do without him. The services he provides – cheap clothes, bags of sugar, tinned sausages for Europeans, a provisions truck that can be used as a bus – are a godsend to people in country places.

Our obliging shopkeeper sold me six small eggs (two turned out to be bad), some unripe tomatoes, and an old newspaper. The moment I had paid and sat down in his parlour, we became – an endearing gesture – his guests. He opened his refrigerator and set cold drinks before us.

It was late at night when I stopped in a slum near Kampala's Kibuli mosque where Remy shared a room with a Lotuho friend. The dirty shacks were closed and dark. There was a smell of rotting rubbish and urine. From the bar where Jaluo workers drink bottled beer under pictures of Jomo Kenyatta, I could hear the shouts of drunken men. Remy, with the clean mud of Lomwaka on his trousers, disappeared into his world of cockroaches and scuffling rats.

Some months later, after visiting a Lotuho refugee camp in the north, Remy wrote a piece of verse for me. Here are some of the lines with which, in the grief of a small farmer, he tried to symbolise his kinsmen's despair:

> 'Who says I am barren?
> I know I am potent.
> My beautiful wife too is fertile.
> We produce children.
> But when they grow lusty
> God kills them.
> So we are fruitful, yet without fruit.
> There is a blight on us,
> God says we shall die miserably
> With no child to bury us.'

As for Remy's forthright opinions, this is how, in a note on an old Chinese poem, he expressed the traditional African view:

Extract from the poem 'Woman' by Fu Hsüan (died AD 278):
> How sad it is to be a woman!
> Nothing on earth is held so cheap;
> Boys stand leaning at the door
> Like Gods fallen out of Heaven,
> Their hearts brave the Four Oceans,
> The wind and dust of a thousand miles.
> No one is glad when a girl is born:
> By *her* the family sets no store . . .
> No one cries when she leaves her home . . .[1]

'The sentiments expressed by this old Chinese poet would appeal to my people the Lotuho. What he has said is that it is a

[1] Taken from Arthur Waley's translation of *One Hundred and Seventy Chinese Poems*. I have found, while teaching these poems, that they often express old truths which, like the saws of his own elders, appeal to the traditional bias within an African student's mind.

misfortune to bear a daughter who will inevitably, when she grows up, leave her parents for another clan. A typical African family pins its hopes on a son.

'Inheritance among the Lotuho is through the father. For a clan to survive it must produce boys. We have a saying that "A woman is a bird which migrates far and wide". A woman is liable to marry any man regardless of his tribe, race, or even religion; and once married she will be fully integrated into her husband's community. A boy, on the other hand, always remains a member of his clan. He is the one who will perpetuate it. Didn't Isaac Okonkwo, in Achebe's *No Longer At Ease*, name his daughter "A Girl Is Also Good"?

'My people, to put it bluntly, will only praise a daughter if she finds a rich husband and brings in bride wealth. If she fails to do so, she is of no use. And there is a further aspect. Among the tribes of Africa it is good to have plenty of men for self-defence. In the event of a raid, or a clan quarrel over land, men are more useful than women, who can only clack and wave their arms about.

'Yes, it is an unlucky family in which daughters outnumber sons. But ought we to devalue girls? Of course not. Without them we cannot produce the sons we cherish so much. I personally hope to have sons *and* daughters – providing I have more of the former.'

CHAPTER 8

Rom

Moyo

The ferryman taking me across the Upper Nile to Moyo,[1] in the Mahdi district of northern Uganda, dipped an old tin into the grey water that eddied among rotting sedge and lilies and drank slowly, as though the stuff tasted delicious.

Fresh from the city, and with a European's fear of tropical worms and parasites, I felt aversion. I knew, though, that within a few days I would be filling my water-can from some black mud-hole fouled by buffaloes and baboons. The process of surrender to heat and thirst would not take long.

Kalisto had been transferred from Kitgum to the secondary school at Moyo, and he was waiting to guide me through the dark to his bungalow. It was evident that he had learned a good deal about housekeeping. The lavatory worked, the white-washed walls were not smeared by grubby fingers, he had spent money on curtains and a pressure cooker, and – 'like a white woman', as his friends might have said – he prepared for himself real fruit drinks from limes and oranges.

Yet it seemed natural both to Kalisto and to the niece of twelve who washed and cooked for him that she should lie down to sleep on the bare kitchen floor. Each night in her little thin blouse and skirt she curled up on the polished cement as neat and quiet as a cat.

Kalisto told me that he was keeping away from the Top Life Bar. He generally read till midnight, and he had achieved the miracle of saving £500 out of a monthly salary of £50 in less than three years.

Such exemplary conduct, especially his refusal to take a wife even on a temporary basis, had already in Kitgum made Kalisto

[1] In December 1970, just before Amin's take-over.

suspect to his friends; it did not conform to pattern. In Moyo it was again estranging him from his colleagues. But it was all part of a calculated plan; for Kalisto was more than ever determined, through hard study, to force his way into Makerere. It was his dream to go into politics, and one day stir up the government on behalf of his people in Adilang.

I knew Kalisto's homeland conditions. I knew that, scattered among their thatched huts in the heat of an eroding plain, toil-worn, grey with dust, and ragged, Kalisto's kinsmen looked to him as their future emissary to those 'big government men' a glance from whom, they believed, could change their lives. I sympathised with Kalisto's ambitions. Teaching arithmetic for ever in a bush school would destroy him.

Still, even his father, Kalisto admitted, was getting impatient at the absence of grandchildren. The old man had recently visited him. 'He refused to sleep in my spare bed,' said Kalisto, 'he wouldn't even sit on it.'

'Why not?'

'My father feels that my bed is part of my sex life. He associates it with my semen. So it would be improper for him to use it. He wouldn't use the toilet either.'

To Mr Okwonga, the idea of a man defecating inside his own house was disgusting.

Alfred

We were sitting under Kalisto's mango tree when Alfred came up. Alfred used to be a priest. Drink has caused his downfall, and also humanised him. Wherever he goes he carries a cloth airways bag containing a bottle of native spirits (*enguli*) covered, to disguise the smell, with a banana leaf, and, on top, a book. I looked at the book. It was Palgrave's *Golden Treasury*. Alfred's eyes were mud-coloured, his nose slightly swollen.

This amiable man had quickly smelled out an Englishman who might be good for a few bottles of beer. But first, there was something important he wanted to show me.

We followed him unwillingly across a football field at the edge of the township and through some burnt grass till we came to a fine clump of mango and wild fig trees. There, to my surprise, were two graves. I bent down to see what was written on the cement slabs. 'R. W. L. Andrews. W. W. Howard. Air Survey Co. July 1931'.

'The Wazungu,' said Alfred, 'fell from the sky.'

The cement slabs were rotting. The grass around the graves grew wild. But the glorious trees were a natural shrine, and it was a good resting place.

Moyo is a dull, heavy-drinking outpost with a row of shops – some are owned by Somalis, who in northern Uganda have traditionally filled a role played elsewhere by Indian traders – administrative buildings and soldiers' huts, and Kalisto's school. The petrol pump had been empty for months as the owner ('An African,' said Kalisto gloomily) was in debt to his supplier.

We sat with Alfred in the yard of the Top Life Bar. It was midday. Women in drab gowns with thin legs, long fattened hips, and large eyes set in oval faces (they were Somalis) watched me slyly from an outhouse. Two ugly barmaids joined us, with enormous scarred knees. 'They must have been thrown out of a motor car,' remarked Kalisto.

'Very hot girls,' Alfred said to me. 'Buy them a Nile beer, and they're yours for five shillings.'

Some officials wearing fancy shirts came in. 'They will drink five bottles each and stay here till three o'clock,' said Kalisto, nastily. 'They will then drive back to their offices, tell people who have been waiting for them all day to come back in the morning, and go off and drink somewhere else.'

That evening, after the neighbours' babies had been sluiced down in tin basins and put to bed, two of Kalisto's colleagues called on me. The school, they complained, was so overcrowded that pupils had to sleep on the floor and drink their tea out of bottles. Worse, boys were 'screwing' the girls *in broad daylight*. 'They do it on the football field. They call it "cow-cow".'

'Cow-cow,' I said, 'why cow-cow?'

The two teachers laughed. 'Because they do it like cows. It's quick . . . the girls hold on to roots. . . .'

Expulsion of older louts, they said, was the only answer to the problem. 'But then parents would make trouble, and you must know that the governors and authorities have their political interests to consider.'

Alfred, next day, walked us to a village eight miles off,

ostensibly to see a cave where, he said, the local Mahdi used to
hide when Langi and Acholi invaders passed through. The
cave was infested with bats, and I did not feel like poking into
its dark places. The real purpose of Alfred's journey was to
call on an aunt, from whom he appropriated a cock and some
tobacco leaves.

We kept away from the Sudan frontier running a mile or so
to the north. Our stroll took us through cotton fields and tamarind trees where black-headed orioles were piping like flute
players. 'The Verona Fathers,' said Alfred, 'make wine out of
the tamarind fruit.' In the morning Kalisto and I left for Rom.

Jie

The Rom massif stands on the fringe of Karamoja, overlooking
the north Acholi plain. I had already passed the mountain on
my way to Kideppo Game Park. Rom looked large and wild
enough for a long walk, it was well covered with woodland,
and there was said to be game on it.

We motored there over dirt roads. Within an hour of our
halting at a hut near the foot of the mountain, I had found four
Acholi villagers to load our gear on their heads, and we were off.

My friends in Kampala sometimes wonder at the apparent
ease with which I find carriers to escort me on my journeys.
'You arrive out of the blue,' they say, 'park your car under a
tree, and within an hour you have picked up a gang of four
strange men and are off on a week's march. How do you do it?'

It is, of course, the offer of cash that does the trick. Every
village has plenty of able-bodied men with time on their hands.
But they are not likely to have any money in their pockets.
How could they unless they happen to have had a few bags of
cotton or ground-nuts or a poached monkey skin to sell? The
chance to earn twenty-five shillings with a ration of posho,
beans, sugar and tobacco thrown in, is too good to miss. Few
of them bother even to make any special preparations for a
journey. They may bring a panga or an old black cooking pot;
a snuff-horn or a spare lip-plug hidden in their clothes. I have
often found volunteers who came running up ready that very
minute to start on a sixty-mile march.

It was hot and I knew I was going to suffer. Drought and

grass fires had scorched and blackened the earth. It was not long before a cloud of dust resolved itself into a huge herd of Karamojong cattle. We sat under a sausage tree and watched them go slowly by – two thousand or more grey and scrawny beasts with dirty humps and tinkling cowbells, chewing and uprooting coarse grass as they lumbered along, scattering smoking droppings, some of the big bulls trying to mount the cows, with a donkey or two braying among them.

They were escorted by Jie. The Jie were naked. They wore green and blue beads round their necks, and they carried spears and the mashie-shaped sticks with which they whack their gentle beasts. A thirty-mile trek, day after day, means nothing to these herdsmen. Their courage and resourcefulness are astounding. But our Acholi porters looked at them with disgust. For them, the Jie were intruders, driving their voracious cattle into Acholi tribal land, tearing and mauling the grass, stripping and eroding the earth, exhausting water holes. 'Thieves and trespassers,' said our porters.

We camped near a spring that had dwindled to a muddy ooze. The burnt and leafless trees where we sheltered raised their scorched and naked branches against the sky like clusters of stone antlers. Throughout the night rock hyraxes mewed and whistled. In the morning, baboons barked at us like dogs. I do not much care for baboons. They leave their dung at water holes and run off with the poor man's maize cob.

We began to leave the tamarinds, the butter-nut and *opok* (terminalia) trees behind. Soon we were climbing through a belt of the solid-stemmed bamboo that is prized for roof-building; even these splendid trailing clumps had been eaten at the base by fire. I was not enjoying my walk up a charred and sooty mountain; I looked like a coalman, and fire-hardened thorns had lacerated my flesh. When, at last, we came to green and unspoilt slopes, I sat down to rest while Akiron and Loru, the two elder porters, went off to reconnoitre the way.

An hour later I saw a fire suddenly flare up ahead of us and then, to my astonishment, another, followed by scattered points of flame that spread quickly into a sheet of burning scrub. I was dismayed. What had been green, frail, sweet-smelling was being turned to ashes.

The two porters, when they came trotting back, could not understand my anger. Why, I shouted, had they set fire to the mountain? 'To scare the buffalo,' said Akiron. 'To clear the track *for you*,' said Loru. 'It's our custom,' added Akiron.

'It's no use questioning them,' Kalisto told me. 'They have an instinct to burn dry grass, and yesterday you gave them a new box of matches.'

The belt of crackling flames in front of us looked formidable. But dusk was near, I was thirsty, and I said we would go on immediately. I soon found that dodging between patches of leaping fire was an experience which, if I had been alone, I would have thought twice about attempting. We had to judge the wind and skip quickly over corridors of smoking earth. The tortured groves turned incandescent. I saw beautiful wild date palms burst into cascades of fire and sparks. The pink aloes seemed to shudder, then shrivel to lumps of soot. The long grass, reduced instantly to stubble and ash, exposed vicious thorns that tore our legs. Pats of buffalo dung sizzled like boiling porridge. The smoke and smuts made my eyes water. I felt very angry with Akiron and Loru. They had injured the mountain, *my* mountain.

We camped on a clean ridge above the fire and beat the soot off our gear. I had lost part of my eyebrows. I sat on a stone while Kalisto took two small heaps of burning wood and began to cook our beans and posho.

Kaido

In the morning we went up to the main summit (Kaido, 7,814 feet). Two ravens flew off grumbling as we threw down our packs. A klipspringer poked its head from behind a bush. Just below I counted eight buffaloes feeding on a slope.

I like sitting on top of a mountain. From a faraway pimple obscured by clouds, ducking among blue ridges, hiding behind shoulders of the *massif*, it has at last taken shape as a piece of solid moss-covered rock on which I can sit down and unlace my plimsolls. From the moment I set out, the desire to reach it has been an obsession. I have got there at the cost of a little suffering. Now I can relax, study landmarks, adjust my camera (in Kampala, mould has collected on its leather case), make jokes with the porters and offer them my own (more expensive) cigarettes, share my sardines with them.

Until this moment I have, perhaps unjustly, discouraged familiarity in case my companions should take advantage of it and dawdle or turn back.

The swifts swish over our heads. There are beds of wild-flowers kept fresh by cool air and rain showers. The rocks are so clean I sometimes lick the moisture from them. Too soon, alas, worries return: the water can is empty, my knees are going to stiffen, and I wonder whether having reached my car down in the plain I shall be able to get it started again.

Here on Kaido umbrella-shaped acacias etched the skyline, wild date palms and dracaena trees were buttressing the gullies. To the south, the Acholi plain stretched for eighty miles, a vast grey tract of bushy earth studded with *inselbergs* that stuck up like thumbs, like tumours, like carcasses of dinosaurs. Among them the Rock of the Wind marked the site of Kalongo Mission. Somewhere in that haze Kalisto's parents had their homestead. Their dog would be sniffing the compound for bones. I guessed Mr Okwonga would be hunched in the shade of his hut with a calabash of warm beer, his wife pounding millet.

I could see how the fires started by our porters had spread like sores, leaving scabs among the green protea and *opok* groves of the middle slopes. No smoke was coming from them now. But the night wind would seek out lumps of smouldering moss. It would fan them into fresh flame, and the mountain side would go on burning for days.

We had descended to our camp and were loitering about when, suddenly, someone shouted 'Mbogo!' I looked up to find my companions already half-way up a thorn tree. The next moment three buffaloes leapt into sight over a hump. Black, coming downhill like the wind, they seemed to be charging straight at me.

I stood still, holding my mug of tea, gaping. I glimpsed the sweat shining on their great outstretched necks. A flash of thundering muscle, and they had torn past me, a few feet away, and vanished down the slope. It had happened so quickly that I felt neither fear nor exhilaration. To the others it must have seemed that I had just stood there waiting to be mowed down. I knew, though, that I must have reacted instinctively and gauged in an instant the buffaloes' line of approach.

The porters looked shaken. Kalisto had scratched his arms on the thorn tree. I was still holding my mug of tea.

We picked up our pots and pans and continued down through the bamboo. Honey-guide birds were chattering excitedly but our porters were tired and ignored them, saying 'the honey is too high, we would need an axe to get it'. Where the mountain face fell away in bare cliffs, baboons were leaping between branches with a crash that set the trees shaking. In the plain below I glimpsed what looked like a row of grey stones wreathed in dust: the Jie were shifting their cattle.

Kaido peak had disappeared behind its ridges, and doves were calling through the dusk in a hubbub of double notes, so loud, so insistent, they sounded like a chorus of mad cuckoos, when we came to the dirt road at its foot and started the last six-mile lap.

I had forced dehydration and weariness on myself and on my companions, who were lurching under the half-empty loads like exhausted dustmen. Yet I felt very well. I hoped that despite poachers the buffaloes would survive to startle intruders and to graze the tall grass for a long time to come, and that the burnt woodland would soon heal its wound.

Here, in the plain, men were clashing. The Acholi wanted to cultivate cotton plots, sorghum and ground-nuts, to earn a little money for shirts and school fees; the Karamojong, despising the hoe and interested only in grazing and water and the size of their herds, to drive in their cattle and trample the soil.

An enormous young wife, who had kept an eye on my car, brought us a can of washing water when at length we threw down our packs outside her hut. Kalisto and I put up our camp beds on the spot and chatted to her. The nipples on her long breasts were like taps. She had a clean hut, with a tin door, that she planned to convert into a shop. One room was stacked high with cotton.

I went to urinate in the bush, and in the dark I fell into a food storage pit several feet deep that was covered with leaves. I might have broken a leg, but everyone howled with laughter. 'Next time,' I protested, 'prepare your pits for your politicians' (more laughter).

Kalisto and I lay looking into the night. Red flames were flaring on the lower flanks of Rom, a grass fire glowed beyond the hamlet's cotton plots. Above the shadows, the Southern Cross pointed drunkenly the way to Kalisto's old homestead. I looked forward, next day, to boiled chicken and a bowl of millet beer, thick and bubbling, like soup.

Adilang

At Kalisto's homestead in Adilang, I found the old routine unchanged – except that his bachelor hut had been turned into a temporary cotton store and a place for women to spread their sleeping skins. It was the time of drought and cotton picking. Mr Okwonga went early to his fields, and when he had done enough, drank *pombe* in the shade of his hut. His wife prepared our meals of boiled chicken, ground-nut sauce, and chocolate-coloured millet bread, which a daughter brought us on a tray, kneeling as she did so.

Old acquaintances visited me, men with heads scarred in beer fights, ex-soldiers and night watchmen who had come back from the cities to sit in the shade of their butter-nut trees while their sons dug the fields. Their feet were splayed and scarred. Their hands, when I shook them, felt like fire-hardened bark. Some of the women had upper teeth that stuck out so sharply, they looked, in profile, like warthogs; yet no one thought them ugly. The breasts of the older women had shrunk to flaps like dried seed pods, and they were honoured for them; for these flaps, when full and large as pumpkins, had suckled sons.

The children who played all day in the dust between the food bins looked like grey earth balls. The small girl (*lapidi*) in charge of them carried wherever she went a heavy baby on her hip.

A hunting party went out, dressed in rags, with nets and spears. They returned next morning with one small oribi. We called on a local official – a grave man with a bicycle and two wives – and sat formally on chairs outside his hut. When

Kalisto told him about 'cow-cow', he thought deeply for a few moments. 'Well,' he said, 'the school is good for boys.' After further thought, he added, 'But not good for parents.'

The heat knocked one into a stupor. Hot breaths of wind rattled among *olim* leaves and in the stunted cassava plot like a pattering of big rain drops. In the sun's glare two rocky hills on the Labwor border quivered as though they were alive. When the sun fell, the fever left them, and they froze into motionless silhouettes with the acacias etched against their edges like tiny umbrellas.

After supper, when lightning flashed far away, I would sit talking to Kalisto outside his bachelor hut.

'Life in Acholi is hard,' said Kalisto. 'A man digs, eats some food, drinks *pombe*. If there's no food, he just drinks. People are hungry for meat, but the game has been killed off. June and July, when grain bins are empty, are a critical time. Our women are like iron. They accept their chores. Yes, from your point of view they are slaves: old and ugly at thirty. But we know no other life. We accept it.'

'Of course,' he went on, 'we want the government to do more for us. We believe that because many people in this district support the Democratic Party – there is, as you know, a strong Catholic connexion here – Obote has deliberately neglected us.'

Kalisto listed some of the things his people needed: protection against the Karamojong, who raided their homesteads and small kraals, and drove their own enormous herds into Acholi farm land and ruined it; seed for cash crops; more water points – and someone to mend the pumps when they broke down; better trading centres. 'We're not interested in new roads,' he said, 'what use would they be to people who don't own cars? But our trading centres are poor and dirty, and shopkeepers usually fail – they aren't educated and they don't know how to keep accounts. Their wives take things for their own use – paraffin, soap, matches – from the shelves. The owner invites his friends and they drink up the beer. When he's finished his stock he has no money to replace it with. We must train shopkeepers.'

I went with Kalisto to see the dam which British engineers

had built in the days of the Protectorate. It used to be a sheet of clear water with clean edges, a fence round it, and an askari to keep cattle out. Through neglect it is now silting up and almost entirely covered with water lilies and muddy sedge. As a source of good water it is finished; and many of the birds which used it as a sanctuary have been scared away. I saw only a few lily-trotters, a grey heron, some pied kingfishers, and a pair of Egyptian geese.

I filled my water can at a nearby pump (the blackest, greasiest thing in all Africa is surely a wooden pump handle). Here a young man, flirting with a girl, had put his hands on her waist. She, enacting a ritual, was averting her face. The village well is a traditional meeting place of boys and girls, of clandestine lovers, and of courtship. I thought of a Kiga saying: 'An old woman was made love to at a well, and when she returned home she said, "My children, in future you will not fetch water. I will fetch it."'

We visited Kalongo Catholic Mission run by the Verona Fathers thirty miles to the north, under the Rock of the Wind. The church was exactly as I remembered it: neat, polished, and cool, smelling of insecticide. A lay brother had put red oleander blossom in the vases. Again I noticed that the plaster saints had milk-white skins; only the cherubims prancing on clouds above the altar were black.

In contrast to the mission, the small trading centre that has grown up just outside the gates was a place of squalor. Flies covered bread loaves like currants; a drunk lay with his head among chicken droppings.

Apiti Dance

One day, at dusk, to welcome Kalisto and myself, a dozen 'mature' (married) women marched into our compound with the red and blue government colours stuck on a spear. They had come to perform the *apiti* dance, which is traditionally accompanied by songs with words improvised to suit the occasion.[1]

The women wore small cotton skirts and clean white brassières (no other covering) that were too small for their breasts. They had bells on their legs, and their freshly oiled skins shone with

[1] See Lukobo's 'Songs and Dances of the Acholi', p. 272.

an intense, rich blackness that seemed, like polished aubergine, to give off a purplish glow.

The dance leader, who had the tight, muscular body of a hockey player, blew her whistle, the women tensed themselves, then crouching, circling, stamping the hard grey earth with a rhythmic thud, they danced for us. They danced and stamped till their smooth backs ran with sweat, till the grey dust coated their legs and their veins stood out like cords; and they sang songs with words which went like this:

> O husband!
> Get your spear
> Take us home from exile
> To face and fight the foeman
> Of Karamoja.

— a reference to the Jie raiders who two years earlier had murdered a number of Agago villagers and forced many others to flee from their homesteads.

And they sang this praise song:

> We greet the Mzungu (white man)
> He is brave
> He has travelled far
> Through Kitgum and Kakira
> To visit this homestead.

The dance ended when the babies began to howl. The leader thrust her spear into the ground, saluted, and the next moment the dancers had their babies at the breast. Men blew cowhorns, women ululated. Kalisto made a speech. Then soft as shadows the crowd slipped away into the twilight.

'I did what they expected of me,' said Kalisto after his speech. 'No politics. I told them to be proud of their dances and music. What else could I say? It is enough for them that you and I have shown them respect.'

Kalisto has no patience with some Europeans' romantic view of rural life in Africa, with the new fashion of flattering black men, or with its reverse – mawkish pity. He hates the nakedness of a Karamojong. He likes traditional dances and *nanga* and *okemi* music, but he does not write a thesis on them. He knows all the shrubs and trees that have edible berries; he scarcely notices a wildflower.

When we sit on a high place he likes to let his eyes wander over the wide Acholi plain; its magnitude excites him, and the tiny patches of lighter colour that are cultivated land make him feel proud to be an Acholi; the colours of sunset mean little to him. Kalisto wants to help his people, to see that they get modern dispensaries and medicine; yet the sight of a crawling polio cripple does not make him wince; he is used to sick and mutilated bodies. His own younger sister has a limp, his mother a chronically swollen leg.

CHAPTER 9

Pirre-Kaabong

Man With A Lobelia Flute

Meanwhile my book, *Man With A Lobelia Flute*, had appeared in the Uganda Bookshop, Kampala, just too late (January 1970) to catch the Christmas shoppers.

My friends were puzzled by the title. What was a lobelia flute? All right, I had chosen an odd title. But the sort of thing that someone in the editorial department of my publishers had suggested – *Through The Highlands Of Africa* – sounded Victorian and presumptuous.

Today's travel writer dare not, of course, appear to take himself too seriously. Heroics are out. He should give the impression of being vulnerable, even on occasion a sort of clown. A great many others have already preceded him along those forest paths through Angola or up the well-beaten slopes of Kilimanjaro.

A professor of Makerere University to whom I had shown the proof copy of my book had warned me that parts of it were likely to offend Uganda readers. They would, he thought, especially in my chapter on Africans, find evidence of a 'colonial mentality'. He complained of passages that were 'full of cultural upper class arrogance'. If I did not delete them the book was certain to be badly received locally.

My choice of extracts from Dr Cook's *Uganda Memories*, of which the Uganda Society held the copyright, was, thought the professor, 'singularly unfortunate' – 'why remind people of those dreadful and best forgotten days of sleeping sickness?' Finally, what would 'local critics' have to say about my 'frequent references to genitalia'?

Like the professor, an African student friend observed that I had written far more about 'primitive' than educated Africans.

'Where, in your book,' he asked, 'is the modern African without whom your picture is unbalanced?' He was hurt by my photographs of naked men and bare-breasted women. I saw one of our college clerks – a Muganda – give a hiss of disgust when he came to these pictures, and throw the book down.

I deleted only one of the passages that had worried the professor and his copyright committee (in it, Dr Cook remarked that the Bagisu 'used to boil bits of the human frame and use them for flavouring the beer'). Here and there I excised the word 'buttocks' from my text.

My own doubts were that by stressing the violence and *kondoism* that were prevalent in Kampala, and by expressing admiration for tribal societies and 'primitive' people (the 'paternalist' attitude), I might have annoyed someone in authority. Obote's line was to propagate the concept of the Uganda nation: tribes and tribalism, being officially identified with disunity, were out of favour.

So at the very last moment I inserted a preface in which I tried to explain away my obvious interest in simple people and out-of-the-way places. The Teuso with their bare bodies, the Suk with their spears, the Elgon poacher in his skins, the Acholi farmer wielding his bent hoe, had been my hosts and travelling companions. How, I asked, could I ignore them? And why should I? As for the pictures of naked or partly clad people, Morukori and Locham, I said, were more photogenic than a man in a suit holding a folded newspaper.

It was Professor Ali Mazrui who spotted the timidity behind these remarks. My preface, he wrote in his review of my book, struck the jarring note of apology.[1] 'I say jarring because we should by now have got beyond literary embarrassment over questions of nudity in Africa. And yet what was jarring was the presumed necessity to apologise . . . I certainly agree with Hills that Locham is more photogenic than a man in a suit holding a newspaper. I particularly liked the photograph of Locham on top of Zulia. Locham has a *shuka* thrown round his shoulders, but his uncircumcised penis hangs uncovered and unabashed below.'

[1] *East Africa Journal*, Vol. 8, No. 9, Sep. 1971 (Nairobi).

However, I need not have worried. I have not been bundled on to an aeroplane at Entebbe and told to go away. Not many Africans, anyway, have bought my book. Why spend the equivalent of sixteen bottles of Bell beer on a piece of reading matter that will help no one to pass an examination, and has no politics in it?

But I am grateful to Mr Erisa Kironde, former Chairman of the Uganda Electricity Board, for buying *two* copies! In a newspaper article (*The People*, 21 March 1970) in which he argued the case for the Murchison Falls hydro-electric project against the wild life conservationists (the project has for the time being been shelved), he made use of some lines from Okumu pa'Lukobo's 'The Poacher's Lament', which I had published in my book:

> If, boy, you had to choose
> Between an animal to gape at
> And meat in a bowl to eat
> Which in your hunger would you take?

Now that my book was published, I wondered at first whether I was going to lose interest in exploring Uganda. After all, a strong incentive to plodding up and down mountains had been to find the raw material to write about; and having published my record, that incentive had momentarily gone.

But I soon found that slashing the lawn in Kololo or watching *ayahs* trundle white babies in prams along the lake shore at Entebbe was no substitute for that wilderness of bush, with warthogs and dikdik running through it, which lies to the north. I decided to revisit the Turkana escarpment. It is good grassy walking country, where cotton-wool clouds sail over the blunt pyramids of hills converging at the junction of three countries. And the Teuso would be cheerful companions.

Nowadays, when I lay out my kit before going on a journey, it looks like a load of junk ready for the dustbin. The British Army mosquito net which I drew from Kasr-el-Nil barracks, Cairo in 1940 (together with a useless sun helmet) is yellow and darned. My water can has a small hole in it towards the top. My kit bags are blackened with the grease and sweat of many porters' backs. The tins in which I boil porridge and soup are spotted with cockroach droppings. My Volkswagen has been bumping over bad roads for a dozen years.

Nevertheless, I feel it would be wrong to throw away these worn old objects, and that such ingratitude might bring me bad luck. My bamboo stick, which I cut some years ago on a Kigezi mountain, though splitting at the bottom, is just the right weight and length. My old Turkish pullover, though the colour runs in the rain, staining my underwear, has kept me warm at heights of over 18,000 feet. Inside the cocoon of my mosquito net (which I use only in the plains) I enjoy a feeling of privacy which I hope hyenas will respect. Though the engine of my Beetle has a habit of dying, suddenly, on the open road, I can get it going again by putting my mouth to the fuel line and blowing or sucking hard.

To Pirre

Between Kotido and Loyoro I was fiddling with the carburettor when a lion crossed the path some eighty yards ahead. The lion took no notice of us. Still, I was happy when I got the engine going again. Kalisto had not seen a lion before. Lions, for him, were terrifying and dangerous. No one wanted to see a lion.

I learned at Kaabong that the old police Land-Rover track which had been hacked from Kalapata to Pirre was no longer usable. We would have to travel as far as Kideppo Game Park and then turn back to Pirre behind the north face of Mount Morungole. An Army Land-Rover took us along the new route. Kideppo Park had sprouted signposts and camping sites, its dirt tracks were smooth; but over the last eight miles to Pirre, in the no-man's-land at the edge of the park, our truck was badly jolted.

We had scarcely got out of the truck when Atum and Lochere hurried from their stockaded village to welcome us. With them was Atum's daughter – the pretty one who had had affairs with policemen, her small body already starting to wither, her eyes deep-set and wrinkled. The Teuso were as thin and dust-covered as ever. The police post, by contrast, was still manned by large well-fed men. With their shining black boots, their starched shirts, their stout wives in skirts, they looked – among the cow-hides, the tiny chain aprons, and the naked bodies of the Teuso – like urban tourists.

But two or three Teuso schoolboys in shorts were signs of inevitable change; so were the new airstrip, and the recently installed government maize meal relief centre at Kasili.

One doubts if this tribal remnant of some 1,500 Teuso (they are also known as Ik), whose origins the anthropologists have not yet cleared up, will survive. One wonders for how long they will continue to squat round their tiny fires, eating baked tortoise, skinny, chattering, and cheerful, their small heads bunched together like black melons in the starlit nights.

Hunters and gatherers by tradition, a small community without livestock surrounded by cattle-herding and raiding tribes, and now increasingly hemmed in by artificial obstacles – the guarded boundaries of Kenya, the Sudan, and Kideppo Game Park – the Teuso are no longer free to roam at will after game, berries, and the sweet honey that is hidden in black earth or in a hole in a thorn tree. They have had to turn more and more to cultivation.

But drought and baboons spoil their steep little patches of maize and millet. The substitute maize meal ration provided by government charity ('Two mugfuls per man every two weeks,' said Atum, 'and a thirty-mile walk through the bush to get it') is not enough. Meanwhile, their neighbours the cattle-owning Dodoth are ruthlessly pushing their herds into the unravaged Teuso grasslands towards the Turkana escarpment.

Who, one wonders, except for a few foreign anthropologists, is interested anyway in their survival? The anthropologists, of course, need the Teuso a little longer as living evidence for their linguistic and other theories. But once the scholars have completed their questionnaires, proved or disproved their theories, and written their books, what then? The Teuso will inevitably disappear into trousers. They will become poor cultivators, small-town houseboys and porters. Grass will overgrow their stockaded hamlets and the honey-guide bird will call for them in vain.

Yet on the very edge of their territory great herds of game, a small fraction of whose meat would help the Teuso to survive, grow fat within the *galaya* wall of Kideppo Game Park.

Colin Turnbull's old hut, and the yard where his red Land-Rover, looking like a fire engine, used to be parked under a weaver's nest, was now occupied by a Teusó family.[1] Kalisto and I camped for the night outside the stockade. Perhaps 'camped' is too elegant a word; we simply rolled over in our blankets among some pumpkins. In the morning, with Atum and four carriers, we set off towards Kamyon.

Kamyon

Our seven-day march followed a pattern I was familiar with. It was a time of drought. The grass had been seared by the sun, and walking through it was painful, for the sharp seed pods of its trident-headed stalks pricked continuously my soft city legs and penetrated the uppers of my plimsolls. We rested under wild fig trees that towered above the scrub with flaring branches like limbs of giant men petrified in the moment of diving. We sat among their small, fallen fruit while wood hoopoes cackled at us.

My companions, when we halted to rest or eat, would cluster together like schoolboys on a bench. What tiny heads they had – like eggs, or weavers' nests, with a small receding forehead and a bump at the back. Their unwashed skins, patterned with crude scarifications, were the colour of grey mud. Their penises, as they squatted on naked buttocks, dragged in the grit. Only Atum was clothed. He wore shorts that had evidently belonged to someone else, and flat, elephant-hide sandals like boards lashed to his ankles.

One cannot walk in a straight line through bush. The trails zig-zag up hills, wind round thickets and termite mounds, disappear in patches of tall grass, and meander along dry stream beds. One is constantly avoiding something: an over-hanging thorn branch at eye level, stones and holes, leopard and buffalo droppings, perhaps a snake that flees sizzling through grass stalks. So at first, until I have got used again to the trail, my eyes are on my feet and on what is immediately ahead, and for a time I miss things I would like to see: puffs of white blossom on an acacia, an oriole (I hear it piping, but if I stop to look for it my companions will leave me behind and they

[1] See Postscript at the end of this chapter.

will be annoyed at having to wait for me), the brown rump of a hartebeest, wildflowers among the straw-coloured undergrowth.

When we could we camped near a water hole. The water holes were far apart, embedded in sandy gullies among tumbled rocks swept down by torrents during the rains, and they had shrunk to puddles with scum on them. Baboons had smeared the rocks around them with cones of dung. Every pool was infested with small butterflies which fluttered over the mud flakes like scraps of paper ash. Butterflies are associated with fragile beauty and with nectar; yet they feed on dirt and carrion, and settle on the eyes of the dead.

Near Kamyon, on the very edge of the escarpment, we came to a bunch of huts I had been to before. The village now had a sour smell of excrement; and the Teuso had begun to build a new one nearby. They had prepared the posts, the walls of interwoven sticks, and the polished mud floors, and they would soon be thatching with bundles of grass.

A Teuso settlement is a cluster of low beehive huts encircled by a *boma* of thorn scrub with a tiny entrance through which one has to crawl. An unusual feature, said to indicate mutual distrust, is that each small family hut is separated from the others by its own barricade of thorns. In time of famine a man, like a hungry dog its bone, must guard his food and fireplace. I remembered those wasted old men and women I had seen on an earlier visit to Pirre, sitting apart under scattered trees, motionless as lizards, their heads bowed over tiny red embers in which a maize cob or two were privately roasting.

The Teuso had built up the floor of each unfinished hut to a slightly raised platform that would slope down to the fire. On it, in a fug of wood smoke, a family of ten would sleep side by side like the ribs of a fan, with the embers roasting their feet.

We sat on the escarpment edge looking down into the Turkana plain, a vast sunken arena like a drained sea-bed that faded in a far white haze towards Lake Rudolf: thorn freckled, cut by dark spokes of thicket and woodland marking the line of water courses and by the brown snakes of dried sand beds. We were perched on one of the cattle-raiding gateways into

Uganda, much used by Turkana who come with spears and rifles to kill Dodoth herdsmen (often mere boys) and carry away their cattle.

Cattle are currency among the people of the 'Karamojong cluster'. Not only are they a part of tribal myth and folk-lore; they are admired for their own sake. They bestow prestige on the owner and provide him with a diet of milk and blood, above all with the bride wealth without which a man cannot acquire a wife. No wonder the herdsmen of these parts covet, cosset, and steal cattle, guide them patiently to grass and water, sing to them, die for them.

Towards dusk we went down into a ravine and climbed up the far side to camp on the rim. The small plots of maize and sorghum which used to perch on its sides had gone, the women, too, whom I had seen plodding up the cliff wall, their faces lined with exhaustion, carrying pots of water on their heads. The stream was no longer trickling over smooth stones where children played; and we slid down eroded banks of crumbling red dust.

That night the moon rose full, shrinking slowly from a big orange globe banded like a tortoise shell with dark cloud stripes, to a white disc that hovered over Morungole peak. On its slopes grass fires were flaring; they would char the tufted grass before its rebirth in green shoots, scorch the protea blossom into fire-hardened medallions, and leave the *euphorbia candelabrum* stranded on ant hills as bare and black as soot heaps.

While the Teuso cut sheaves of grass to lie on, Atum levelled a place for my camp bed. To lie with the night breeze tickling my feet – this, for me, is the sweetest moment; to feel the thick oatmeal porridge rumble in my stomach, to know that at any moment I can drop off to sleep and that it will not rain. To know that in the morning I shall wake up to bird cries, the beat of a hornbill's wings, and to dew on the grass.

And yet, to be honest, there is another side to these moments. Yes, when I woke up there was indeed dew on the grass, and bird song, but it was the irritating chatter of weaver birds. When I pulled on my socks, I found them full of thorns. The early sun, aiming at the back of my neck, made me slightly dizzy, and the tin in which I was going to brew tea was coated with dried porridge which I was too lazy to scrape off. Atum and the others looked scruffy, their bodies, even their genitals, stained with dust and ash.

As for Kalisto, when I see him skipping with early morning joy, I am jealous of his youth and energy. Alas, I feel in my heart that I am a tyrant driving poor native men, for a few shillings and some Kali cigarettes, to hump my possessions on a useless errand like pack animals, and to cough in the night.

Kalapata

Near Kalapata we entered the Dodoth grazing area, and rested on a mound of rocks whose guardian spirit was a python. It was Atum who saw the python as it lay coiled asleep among some stones I was about to step on. '*Nyoka!*' he whispered, giggling silently.

From the mound, a dozen herds of Dodoth cattle stood like white marble outcrops against a tattered brown landscape. Almost all the trees had been felled for firewood and *manyatta* fences, leaving only scrub, a few green desert dates (*balanites aegyptiaca*), and the *euphorbia candelabrum* lifting grey arms over wasteland. The bald earth, stripped and trampled by voracious cattle, exposed, like a vast cabbage patch, thousands of small aloes. The herds moved slowly, rubbing their wrinkled dewlaps against stems, rattling cowbells made of a tortoise shell, trailing yellow dust; after them, scarcely distinguishable from the blackened tree stumps, came men and boys with spears, sticks, and calabashes of rust-coloured water. It was a familiar dry season scene: the outward peace of it hiding the struggle to survive.

In the morning we passed the white mission church of the Verona Fathers at Kalapata. It was Sunday, and the Italian priest waved to us over the heads of a crowd of Dodoth women gathered at the entrance. Freshly washed and oiled, the women gleamed like kingfishers in their collars of metal hoops and their beaded leather aprons.

We had to dodge through hundreds of cattle making for the noon shade of sand beds where men were scooping holes

3a Iranian shepherd near Khoi (Azerbaijan)

3b Shepherd boys on Mount Savalan (Iran)

3c Kurdish herdsboys near Ararat (Turkey)

3d Boys at Moroto (Karamoja)

4a Companions on Lomwaka, across the Sudan border

4b Kalisto
4c Thistles (Lomwaka)

for a little muddy water. The humped cattle bellowed mourn-fully. Flies clung to their eyes, the loose skin, verminous and caked with dirt, sweated and trembled over their ribs. Their number was enormous; their condition pitiful.

It grew so hot that for a time I could bear to walk only when a small cloud temporarily obscured the sun. The ridges over which we were travelling were tattooed with the dark rings of Dodoth encampments from which flies sailed out to settle on our faces. A boy, seeing me appear suddenly from behind a tree, spilt his calabash of water and ran off howling.

It was dusk when the rock prongs of Kaabong came into sight. I still had an inch or two of water in my old vermouth bottle, which I had filled at breakfast. My kitbags had turned black with the sweat of our carriers. As we came to the tin rest house, a Somali storekeeper went tearing past in a new Japanese lorry. Kalisto had a headache. I was tired and it would take me half an hour to recover.

Kaabong

We found the rest house already occupied by a team of young African veterinary assistants, who moved their ragged blankets and cardboard sleeping mats out of a cubicle to make room for us. They had not long finished primary school, they were strangers to Karamoja, and they were not finding it easy to enforce their regulations.

'The Dodoth,' they told us, 'get quite threatening when we want to destroy a sick cow and burn the carcass – they insist on eating a thigh. They are,' they concluded, 'bad people, and stupid.'

It struck me once more that I have met scarcely a single African with a good word to say for the Karamojong. 'They go naked, they are dirty, they are illiterate, and they steal cattle,' is the usual judgment on them. The reason for the prejudice is clear. The Karamojong are an embarrassing reminder of the 'uncivilised' past. By deliberately preferring to remain 'back-ward' they offend the great majority of Uganda Africans who have identified themselves, if only through their children, with modern ways.

Later that night Kalisto summed up his impressions of our

journey. He had been disturbed by his first glimpse of naked men and of women in skins; by the wretched food plots of the Teuso and by their poverty. He was shocked, he said, to see 'naked men eating raw sorghum from the stalk, like birds, and women collecting rotten fig fruits to make their porridge with'. He thought the government ought to compel the Teuso to move to a more fertile area, where they would be 'made to dig'.

He admired the tall and muscular physique of the Dodoth. But he found nothing 'romantic' in their way of life – he was, indeed, prejudiced against the Karamojong, for it was Jie cattle raiders who from time to time sneaked into the kraals of his father's neighbours near Adilang, killed families, and made off with their cattle. They all, he thought, ought to be made to grow food crops in addition to keeping cattle, to dress, and be brought up to date – the quicker the better.

A Mexican priest at the Verona Fathers' Mission in Kaabong topped up my petrol tank and gave me coffee. Father Flores had served previously in Amudat, where he had feuded gently with the rival Bible Churchmen. Again I felt grateful to the missionaries in remote places of Uganda who have never refused me kindness and hospitality.

Apart from their faith they propagate by word and example certain notions – of social service, hygiene and literacy – that are true gifts to a developing country. They doctor illness and mend machinery. They run schools, they have books and special local knowledge. In their gardens, tidy and full of fine trees, they experiment with flowers and food plants (Nyapea has vines); and in lonely places they have offered me small luxuries: English pudding, a glass of Italian wine. The old white district officers have gone, but in the missionaries much of their best style and spirit remains.

I drove Kalisto to Moroto, where I left him at the rest house. Stew with thick gravy was still being served for lunch, but the mildewed old volumes of Kipling and Gilbert Frankau had vanished. At Soroti I was back among familiar things. In Shamlak's café, among the ketchup bottles, an Indian asked me for sterling currency; an off-duty policeman was quarrelling with a whore, who, he cried, had drunk up his beer. There was a bad smell from a sandy lane where two rows of Indian houses threw their garbage. The bumpy murram road had merged into tarmac, and I now had a smooth run of 230 miles back to Kampala.

POSTSCRIPT

On my two previous visits to Pirre I had met Dr Colin Turnbull who was staying there in his own hut. It was a time of acute famine among the Teuso, and Colin had given me some depressing insights into the consequent suffering and demoralisation of this outwardly cheerful people. Hunger, he said, had destroyed their old social solidarity and made them vicious and cruel to one another. Nothing counted but individual survival. They stole food from the mouths of the old and sick. 'Goodness' meant having a full stomach.

Colin Turnbull has since recorded these experiences of a society apparently at its worst in *The Mountain People* which reviewers have found ghastly, terrifying, gruesome. But this side of Teuso life has not been my concern. I have simply walked in the bush with Atum and a few other Teuso and enjoyed their company.

Modern anthropological studies are generally so specialised, so arid and abstruse, that to the layman they are unreadable. If, like Colin's previous publication on the Ituri pygmies (*The Forest People*), the book is humorous, personal, and sometimes lyrically written, then pundits will accuse the author of romantic journalism; of what Professor Evans-Pritchard has called, in the case of Margaret Mead's *Coming of Age in Samoa*, 'the rustling-of-the-wind-in-the-palm-trees kind of anthropological writing'.

When I recently asked Colin what he thought Evans-Pritchard would have said of *The Mountain People*, he wrote back: 'I think E. P. would have voiced acid disapproval in public and been appreciative privately. It is interesting how some anthropologists understand what I am trying to do and others dismiss the whole thing as a fabrication. I am intrigued myself by the technique of conveying what I believe to be the essential truth underlying the situation and ask myself WHAT would have been achieved by writing a dry (therefore scholarly?)

descriptive account with an analysis in terms of some theoretical model that has no validity for the Ik at all, but which could be made to fit tidily and would upset no theoretical apple carts.'

Atum, incidentally, according to Colin, had been a likeable rogue with an outstanding talent for survival at the expense of others. The real villains were the authorities who by driving this traditional hunting and gathering people into a small enclave squeezed between Kideppo Game Park and two closely guarded State frontiers had deprived them of their traditional sources of food.

Is there not a nasty echo here of the British current love of animals at the expense of people?

END NOTE

Missionaries and the Christian Religion in Karamoja

In terms of environment the Verona Fathers, concentrating their efforts in the northern parts, have had the toughest of the major Christian missionary assignments in Uganda. From Acholi they moved into Karamoja in the 1930s. Their mission at Kangole dates from 1933. Being Italians, Mussolini's colonial aspirations tended for a time to cast a shadow over their presence on British territory. The outbreak of World War II brought them further embarrassment. Later the Verona Fathers opened missions among the Karamojong at Morulem (1949), Kaabong (1955), and Nabilatuk (1960). One of the best known of the Verona Fathers is Father Crazzolara (born 1884, lately retired), a linguistic authority who has written a grammar and vocabulary of the Acholi and Lugbara languages, and a history of the Lwoo.

Protestant missionary activity in Karamoja, represented by the Bible Churchmen's Missionary Society which established itself at Lotome (1933) and Amudat, has been small by comparison. Even so, the two Christian faiths have shown signs of the local rivalry that on a general scale throughout Uganda (duplication of schools, involvement with opposing political factions) has done harm to the Church's reputation.

A Karamojong student, P. R. Odeke, wrote for me the following note on the problems of the Christian religion in Karamoja:

'*Thou shalt have no other gods before me.*'

'Christianity teaches that there is only one God, and that he is the God all men should serve. Well, the Karamojong have Ajuk, the Supreme God. But they believe too in the existence of many subsidiary gods, e.g. the god of cattle, god of rain, god of child-bearing. Christian missionaries considered the Karamojong religion to be pagan and they tried hard to stamp it out. But they were happy that the Karamojong believed in "God". This at least gave them something to work on.

'Christianity says, "*Whosoever shall smite thee on thy right cheek, turn to him the other also.*" This, to a Karamojong, is depriving a man of his basic right to retaliate. More, it makes a woman and a coward of him.

'The Christian bias against "fornication" is the most disagreeable precept of all. The Karamojong agree that adultery between a *married woman* and any man is wrong. But they consider sexual intercourse between an *unmarried* female and a man (married or unmarried) as quite normal and natural. The Karamojong are chronically polygamous. A man has a moral duty to take a second wife if his first wife proves to be barren.

'"*Thou shalt not kill.*" I deny that among the Karamojong to kill someone is an obligatory part of a man's initiation. However, a man who has thus "blooded his spear" will certainly gain prestige and respect, and to this extent a proven "warrior" will impress women and more quickly get promotion to senior status.

'"*Thou shalt not steal.*" Cattle-raiding is endemic among the Karamojong, and it is of course encouraged by the practice of bride wealth, which may be so high that fifty head of cattle are not enough to acquire the girl one wants.

'*Origin of the name "Karamojong"*

'The name "Karamojong" is derived from the phrase "*ekar ngimojong(i)*", meaning "the old men can walk no farther". According to tradition, the Karamojong are said to have migrated from Abyssinia between the sixteenth and seventeenth centuries. When they reached the present Kenya-Ethiopian border a group of them remained there and called themselves Turkana. A second group moved into the Sudan (the Toposa). The main body continued southwards, dropping off another group (the Dodoth) at Apule in the northernmost part of Karamoja. On reaching the territory now occupied by the Jie, the Karamojong are reported to have split up into three fragments – the Jie remained where they were, the Pian, Bokora, and Matheniko moved farther south, and a third body went west and formed the present-day Iteso, Langi and Kumam tribes. It was this last group, who had travelled the farthest, who are said to have used the phrase "the old men can walk no more".'

P. R. ODEKE

CHAPTER 10

Napak

Soroti

Napak (8,330 feet), sixty miles south-west of Moroto, dominates the entry into Karamoja along the road from Soroti. To the motorist it is just another smudge on the skyline that turns into a mountain covered with bush and woodland rising to a jumble of grey stone slabs that lie on the summit like dislodged roof tiles. I had often driven past Napak, hurrying through the gall-strung thorn bush to a meal in Moroto. Now I was going to climb it.

Kalisto was with me. We gave a lift to a Langi forester from Koboko, who had left his job in haste and gone home the morning after Acholi and Langi soldiers of a nearby garrison had been clubbed to death in their quarters by execution squads. The forester felt nervous in his lonely post west of the Nile. Towards the end of July 1971 there had been strong rumours that it might at any moment be the turn of Acholi and Langi professional men and civil servants to be harried and done to death.

The forester was worried but not panicking. I had already been struck by the apparent fatalism with which most of my Acholi and Langi acquaintances accepted the cruel punishment that had befallen so many of their tribesmen. Kalisto accepted that the Acholi had helped put Obote into power and that they had identified themselves with a policy that had oppressed the Baganda. Obote had lost the power struggle. In the context of African tribal politics it was natural that Obote's tribesmen and supporters should be collectively punished with bitter medicine.

'We Acholi,' some of my older students told me in a pessimistic moment, 'are finished. Yes, we made enemies and we must now pay for it.'

An official at the police post at the foot of Napak, whose companion was a soldier asleep under an umbrella, turned us back when he found we had no cholera inoculation certificates. We returned along the dirt road to Soroti, and queued outside the medical reception shed with eleven swarthy Indians who were preparing to emigrate to England. It was easy to find an orderly to inject us, but the Singhalese doctor who had to stamp and sign our certificates could not be traced. So for the second night we put up our camp beds in the garden of Soroti Rest House.

The rest house no longer takes guests. A new motel has been built at the edge of the golf course nearby, one of several put up cheaply by a Danish organisation to a utilitarian design: bar and restaurant surrounding a cement dance floor, rows of whitewashed sleeping cubicles like outhouses, some prickly plants in petrol tins.

I have memories of the old rest house. Visitors used to complain they got food poisoning there. The food was indeed bad, and there was often a rumpus in the night when guests, mostly veterinary or agricultural officers, brought girls back from the town. Worse, the girls, as part of their emoluments, used to have hot baths and occupy the lavatories in the morning, so that denied these facilities one set off to work in a bad temper.

I, too, once ate some rotten fish served for supper at the rest house. I woke in the night gushing at both ends. The night watchman gave me no comfort. 'You are very ill, Bwana,' he said. 'It is the hand of God. Give me a cigarette. (*Wewe gonjwa sana, Bwana. Shauri ya Mungo. Mumpa cigara.*)'

At the bar of the new motel a German smoking a curved pipe told me, 'After the soldiers killed each other in Moroto, I counted thirty-six corpses in the lake near here.' A former African student of mine, now teaching, confirmed this. 'The bodies,' he said, 'were brought down from Moroto in trucks. They were piled on top of each other like sacks of *posho*, with soldiers sitting on them.'

An English film was being shown in the motel lounge. When I heard whistling and laughter I peeped through the door. Across the screen a white woman, quite naked, was swimming in a lagoon. There was more jeering laughter when her nude English lover, covering his private parts with a newspaper, was chased over the sand by a dog. Not far away, in Karamoja, the government had been forcing men at gun point to put on trousers. Here, Europeans were exposing their pale behinds and their pubic hairs on a public screen.

During the night I was awakened by someone tugging at my mosquito net. A black face with a single protruding tooth was looking at me.

'Why are you sleeping outside?' asked the face.

'Because I like it.'

'It is dangerous, and it's going to rain.'

'That's my business, *shauri yangu.*'

'I am an *ayah*. Give me a cigarette.'

I thought the woman was dotty, or drunk. In the morning when I saw her sitting on the grass with her skirt up I realised she was a whore.

Ascent

Our first problem, on getting back to Napak, was to find a start point and porters. So we called on a young African Community Development officer seven miles up the road to Moroto. He was running an Oxfam-founded rehabilitation centre for eighty orphaned Karamojong youths some of whose fathers had been killed in cattle raids.

A dozen of these youths and a few worn-out old men immediately offered to escort us up the mountain. Lobunei, one of the old men, pushed himself forward as leader. He had knock-knees and a bullying manner; he assured us he knew the way to the very top of Napak.

I enjoyed the walk at first. The mountain rose out of the plain directly to the south, roofed at its highest point by stone slabs, and falling away abruptly to the west where, a few miles beyond it, Akisim stands up like an outcast. We turned towards Napak through grass ten feet high and passed a prominent hill split by a flesh-coloured fissure.

'Vagina Hill, that's what we call it,' said the youths laughing and pointing at the fissure, '*Akibon Emiru*, Vagina Hill.'

We went on and on, and sometimes changed direction. The grass got taller, the thorny undergrowth thicker – and there was still no sign of a trail.

Lobunei, I began to realise, was a dud. He had made one of the youths carry part of his load. His knees scraped together as, grumbling incessantly, he forced himself along like a damaged spider. Saliva, seeping through the hole below his lower lip (he had no incisors to stop the flow, and was not using his lip plug), shone in droplets on his straggly beard. At noon on the second day, after an aimless tramp along the foot of the mountain, he sat down and sulked. He had lost the way.

Then heavy rain set in, and we made camp quickly. Within minutes our companions had skilfully improvised rough shelters from thorn acacias. It was simply done. They severed each trunk half-way up, then thatched the fallen mass, which rested at an angle against the stump, with grass and leaves, leaving a sheltered place below into which one could crawl. Lobunei did not help in this work. But as soon as the first shelter – *my* shelter – was ready he crept inside it and began to smoke. We had to drag him out.

It was early August, the time of rains, with thunder booming round the sky and storms that blew up suddenly on streaming rain curtains in the late afternoon or in the evening. In the day-time one quickly dries out after a soaking. But bedding that is still wet at sundown is nasty to lie in. Rain makes the blue dye run out of my pullover on to my shirt. The colour plates of my bird book get stuck together. My trousers feel like wet compresses.

When I am stuck in a downpour under a miserable thin-leafed tree, water drips from my hair, runs under my vest, chills the small of my back. The rucksack in which I have wrapped my camera, matches and cigarettes turns the colour of wet dung. I feel angry with my escort if, after an hour or so, they cannot detect a rift in the clouds.

Before those first rain drops, as big as pebbles, water had seemed one's most precious possession. All day, sweating and dehydrated, I have been husbanding my bottle of boiled drinking water. Now it is the return of the sun's fiery eye that I long for.

I notice that whereas, in the cold and rain, I am most sensitive in my lumbar parts (Turkish peasants sensibly keep a loin-band wrapped about themselves), it is their heads that worry my African companions. Waiting for the rain to stop, cracking their fingers at the advancing rain curtains to make them go away, nursing the small red embers of a spitting fire, they wrap their skimpy *shuka*-cloths or their shirts round their heads, leaving the body bare.

Morning found us close under the western shoulder of Napak still plodding ('Like elephants thrashing about in search of food,' said Kalisto) through wet grass. When at length we found the track Lobunei claimed to have been looking for, it was midday. As the first thunder claps detonated over our heads, we hurried into a copse and rigged up shelters.

It took a little time to collect dry wood and get a fire going. With rain smashing through gaps in the thin tree canopy, our carriers huddled over the tiny finger of flame they were coaxing out of shavings. The rain, washing the dust off their bodies in patches, turned them into piebald ebony carvings crouched with pouting lips over the little heap of smouldering white splinters. When at last the fire took hold, they piled logs over it and began to boil their beans and *posho*, and to sing.

Kalisto woke me in the night. 'A lion,' he said, 'I heard a lion.'

'Don't be silly,' I answered.

'It was a lion,' he repeated, 'I heard it roar.'

'You're dreaming,' I grumbled, and we slept again.

Kalisto and I left early in the morning with two of the youths. We had lost much time, but we were determined to get to the top. A steep and beautiful track overhung with protea flowers in white cones supported by pink fingers led over the shoulder of Napak, opening up a wider view of the plain. We began to meet other men, of the local Bokora tribe: skinny, haggard, in rags, trotting downhill in an odour of sweat and grease with bundles of *kat* leaf.[1]

I had noticed that the track was spattered with discarded leaves where foragers had stopped to chew a little of their treasure. I spoke to some of them.

[1] *Kat* leaf (*catha edulis*) is chewed as a stimulant.

'We sell the leaf,' they told me, 'to Somali traders.'

'Why,' I asked, 'are you all wearing trousers?'

'It is Amin's order. Men were shot by soldiers when they refused to wear them. *Sisi nagopa sana*, now we are afraid.'

Even the women they had with them had discarded their trailing cow-hides for old cotton dresses. I saw one naked youth. But he had twisted a piece of cloth round his hips, ready to pull it down at the approach of a government 'spy'. I met no one with a spear. 'It is forbidden now to carry spears,' the Bokora told me.

'The noble savage is on his way out,' I remarked to Kalisto.

'Thank God for that,' he replied.

Behind the shoulder of Napak we heard a drumming and came to a cascade falling over a cliff into a cold black stream. Above it the track petered out among grassy banks and patches of woodland where the Bokora come to collect the *kat* leaf. The summit was still hidden. Casting about for the direction, we saw a woman. She was sitting as still as a stone, half-concealed by the tall grass, and when she ducked her head I saw she was afraid. We must have looked strange to her: a white man carrying a stick, Kalisto in his bush shirt and khaki trousers looking like a government tax collector, and our two carriers humping bundles like robbers.

The woman was very small: a doll with a tiny wizened face and a large mouth crammed with teeth. Her biceps, when she moved her arms, stood out like small eggs. She was so black that the blackness seemed to have soaked deep into the flesh. On her neck a collar of red beads glowed like geraniums.

She was wrapping a bundle of *kat* leaves in a roll of skin while her husband foraged higher up the mountain.

Rain clouds gathered and we had to halt. Again I stood under a dripping tree. My feet, as I shuffled to keep them warm, crushed the grass into black mud. The rain washed the sweat salt off my face and into my mouth. I began to shiver.

As soon as the sky cleared we made a roaring fire. In the night, as I lay on a swathe of cut grass with my back towards the glowing logs, turning from time to time to let the heat dry out the damp that seeped into my body from the earth, I watched the stars swim one by one from behind the retreating clouds.

Once Kalisto woke us with a scream. 'I was dreaming,' he apologised, 'of the lions of Tsavo.' Poor Kalisto.

We had brought little with us. When we went on in the morning, all we left behind were chewed maize cobs and an empty sardine tin.

Summit

The way to the top – there was no track – led us over grassy ridges broken by copses. We passed an enormous podocarpus with a log-hive slung in its branches sixty feet from the ground. Not until we reached the last knoll 1,500 feet below the summit did we see men. Here was a kraal, muddy and stinking with cattle dung, and a family sheltering in tiny thatched huts. The naked, potbellied children with their stick-like limbs, their runny noses and long penises looked like hungry hobgoblins. Ninety minutes walk from the kraal took us to the top.

I have seen the Karamoja plain from a good many high places. Its landmarks – Moroto mountain, from where I had first looked down on the smouldering tumuli that are strewn between the high ranges, Kadam with its sun-reddened turrets, Kachagalau, and Napak itself standing like a portcullis across the gateway to the north – and my feelings when I see them stretched out below, have become a part of my life in Uganda.

Down in the plains men with flies on their legs are hugging the shade of mutilated trees; it is their women they send to fetch wood and water, the young boys with spidery legs who in the sun's fiery glare must run like salamanders with the goats and cows near the thatched rings of a homestead. I am in a cool high place, where little saucers of rainwater lie in hollowed rocks, and wildflowers stain the black soil with blue dye. Sometimes I think of all the peaks I have climbed in East Africa and I wonder how many hundreds of miles I have walked to get to them.

Here, on top of Napak, I have three good companions: Kalisto, and the two youths who were at first surly, and only yesterday, lost and shivering in the rain, and miserably grubbing for edible roots, had feared 'they were going to die'. Now they are joking about the others who have stayed in camp and are idly eating our food.

As for Kalisto, he is one of Uganda's educated élite and he has no business to be here at all. It is not dignified for an African gentleman to tramp through the bush and sleep like an animal on the ground. It is wrong of him to fraternise with the boors of Karamoja, absurd to spend energy on plodding up a hill that could be put to better use impregnating a woman.

Yes, Kalisto's curious desire to explore his country the hard way sets him apart from his colleagues who, as he puts it, have no other aspirations – why should they have? – than to draw their pay, raise a family, and to keep out of trouble.

Descent

We descended quickly and reached our camp near the foot of the mountain just before dark. We had driven ourselves hard all day and I had been longing for this moment. I wanted a hot meal and a long sleep under a blanket.

The copse was empty! All that remained of our camp were the ashes of the fire.

A man came up the track and told us that our companions had gone down into the plain.

'The lion frightened them,' he said.

I looked at Kalisto. He had, it seemed been right. There really was a lion prowling about. So we picked up our sodden gear and went down into the darkness. It was almost midnight when we found our companions lying in a dirty hut. The hut had been abandoned at the owner's death ('He's probably buried under the floor' said Kalisto nastily), the walls were crumbling and it was verminous. I hated its squalor. But the Bokora were happy to be in a 'real house'. For them a roof, any roof, was better than lying out under the cold starlight.

In the morning we walked to Iriri. I sat on the veranda of a *duka* where a tailor was sewing shorts on an old Singer machine. He smiled when I remarked that the compulsory new dress laws must be good for business. Some children came to stare at me. In their dirty shirts and shorts (one little boy was in long corduroy trousers) they were scarcely recognisable as Karamojong *totos*. Two soldiers with rifles walked past, then a women in a ragged frock and a man in shorts that were black with grease.

If the Karamojong are going to wear rags and clouts, and to use neither soap nor underwear, they are bound, I thought, to become verminous. Perhaps the elders who not long since had complained to the authorities that recent cholera deaths in Moroto were the result of their people being forced into trousers had, in a muddled way, made a valid point. My educated African friends had laughed when I told them of this episode. For them the Karamojong are savages, their elders' complaint against the dress laws based on ridiculous superstition.

One of my northern students (from Nabilatuk) once tried to explain to me a Karamojong's attitude to clothes.

'Europeans,' he wrote, 'have tended to associate the naked or semi-naked state of some African tribes with paganism. Missionaries found nakedness shocking. The Karamojong argue that as man is born naked he is not obliged to cover himself; and they admire the physique and appearance of a naked man. However, men usually carry a length of cloth (*shuka*) with which, tied to a shoulder, they can cover their private parts when necessary, while Karamojong women wear skins that always, in our opinion, cover them adequately.

'The Karamojong,' he added, 'also say that Arab soldiers, who were "heavily dressed", brought back venereal disease from the two European wars. Dress therefore has become suspect as something worn "to hide the disease".'

An Indian magistrate told me of a Karamojong youth who had recently attacked a policeman for making him put on trousers. The trousers, explained the youth in court, were uncomfortable. 'After three days my penis became a snake. It bit me.'

An American professor of Makerere University expressed an outsider's view. 'If I were as well hung as those guys in Karamoja,' he said to me, 'I'd be proud to walk around naked.'

On my first visit to Karamoja, in 1965, I had found it odd to be jostled by stark naked men in a grocer's shop. I soon got over my prudishness. It was I, in my clothes, who felt conspicuous among so much bare flesh. True, the Karamojong smell of rancid fat and leather. But they are not ugly. For they breed from a single stock, and there is no obesity among them.

Amin has emphasised his determination to make the Kara-mojong 'dress like decent people'. Ugandans support him in this. As relics, as part of African wild life, naked Karamojong may provide anthropologists with interesting material and the tourist with curious photographs. But to the educated African they are, in their nakedness, a source of shame and disgrace, and no less unacceptable to modern Uganda than stark naked Scotsmen, drinking cow's blood and carrying clubs, would have been in Dr Johnson's metropolitan England.

PART III

PEOPLE

CHAPTER 11

Coup d'État

A foot safari through the East African bush is for me a physical and emotional rather than an intellectual experience. There are no monuments to photograph. I do not have to worry about dates and inscriptions, art and architecture. What a relief it is, to escape from the tyranny of the Roman amphitheatre, the Byzantine wall, Baedeker.

Not that East Africa's landscapes are mere brutish tracts of coarse grass or forest 'without a past'. Where the tourist looks for elegant animals, the specialist will recognise artefacts, linguistic roots, and ways of life that are his clues to the provenance and wanderings of society. I carry bird and tree books in my rucksack and look forward to a camp fire at night. So it is one's attitude rather than the matter itself that determines the traveller's experience.

I have visited Fort Jesus and the ruins of Gedi. They have been described a thousand times. I cannot identify artefacts. I have other motives for walking: to see what lies beyond that barren escarpment which looks like the end of the world but is the outrider of high open places where the poacher sets his snares and buffaloes beat down the grass and the great lonely trees are unmolested. Also I am curious about people. Their rags and discomfort appal me. But I want to identify myself for a few brief moments with these men and women who build their habitations out of trees, grass and mud; to whom the earth's bare crust is their home, their floor, their food; who tread it barefoot, sleep on it, die in it.

But modern politics, if not history in the shape of masonry, have intruded into the lonely places of East Africa. Under Obote it was the politics of party rallies, of flags and vote-catching. Since the night of 25 January 1971 it has been the politics of the machine gun. The quiet hills of Uganda have looked down on many ant-like figures of soldiers. Villagers have heard the salvoes of executioners in barracks and woods. They have seen the corpses thrown into swamps.

25 January 1971

I was out drinking on the night of Amin's take-over. I had moved from a bar run by an Indian which, with proper respect for the law, he had closed at midnight, to an African place with a juke-box at Bakuli. The customers were mostly taxi-drivers and pimps, with girls in frowsty wigs and mini-skirts that rode up over their prominent buttocks. The juke-box was so loud that no one heard the shooting in the streets – or, if they did, they thought it was just another fire-fight with *kondos*.

Not until I left at 4 a.m. and drove along the Entebbe road looking for another bar did I realise that there was something wrong. The night clubs were closed, there were no drunks under the street lamps, no weaving cars with drunken drivers; and I ran into a smell of cordite and a thick fog of smoke. My engine stalled, somewhere in Katwe, in a dark and rutted place among shanties. I had to knock up two men to give me a push. I heard distant explosions. Army night exercises? I was too concerned with finding another beer to worry about them.

When the kites flew out to their garbage pitches at dawn, the approach roads to the city began to fill as usual with a throng of labourers, clerks, and servants padding silently to work. Sweat was already soaking through their thin white shirts. They looked haggard. The girls had rubbed oil on their legs, which shone like wet sticks. I wondered how many had eaten anything for breakfast – how many had worms, fever, or hangovers thumping behind their ears.

Then I saw the armoured troop carriers chugging up and down with soldiers dangling their legs over the sides, the tarmac and kerbstones crushed by tank tracks, the anxious faces of Indian storekeepers peeping through barred windows, and I knew there had been a military revolution. The early workers who had been trotting townwards realised this too, and went into reverse. They were joined by men in suits, carrying briefcases and airways bags, and by fat women in *busutis* who panted as they hurried away from trouble. I drove to Nakasero preparatory school and took two stranded white children home to Makerere. Some Indians from up-country asked me to shelter them – I dumped them with an Ismaili petrol station owner. There seemed nothing else for me to do except watch the soldiers patrolling the emptied streets in their overloaded, shabby Israeli power wagons.

When a sentry outside the Bank of Uganda pointed his rifle at me, then fired over my head, I went into the Apolo Hotel. Its lounge was crowded with package tourists from Nairobi and with business guests. Everyone had started to drink early. I felt a sudden affection for five silent Japanese bunched at an empty table wondering whether they were present at a panto-mime or a serious political event. I ordered five bottles of cold beer before they could refuse, and we talked about fish-nets and table tennis. When, later, a mob ran cheering through the main street, we knew Obote's government had been ousted. Amin's soldiers had taken control.

On the second night of the *coup*, a little after supper, an immense roar suddenly broke the silence of curfew, rising and swelling into the night air over Mengo as though the entire African population were cheering a goal at a football match. Amin had announced over the radio his decision – a glorious peace offering to the Baganda – to release the political prisoners detained by Obote.

The roaring, the ululations, and the drumming beat in waves across Bat Valley and up the slopes of Kololo hill. I could see my neighbour, a quiet and dignified Muganda inspector of schools, pounding his dustbin lid with a stick among capering elations and servants. 'I'm so happy,' he panted to me, 'I just can't control myself.'

Not a sound, though, came from the large Munyoro family opposite, whose children always made such a cheerful noise after dark. They had doused their lights, and they stayed silent. Buganda's triumph was not theirs.

Hearing the prolonged and savage cry of jubilation that broke like a roaring wind from the throats of the Baganda penned within their darkened compounds, their *shambas*, their shanties, and their gardens, I wondered at the remarkable constancy of loyal emotions they had kept in their hearts during the years of humiliation under Obote. It was a cry that contained, though, a note of ugly tribal gloating. The domination of Bantus by Obote's black Northerners had been temporarily broken. Hysterical tribal feeling centred on the semi-mythical person of the Kabaka, on Buganda separateness and self-esteem, was bursting like pus from an unhealed wound. No political stability, no national cohesion, could be built on such emotion.

Later

Though the military *coup* was officially described as 'bloodless', we learned that two white priests had been killed when soldiers senselessly opened fire on Entebbe airport. Worse, their bodies were thrown into Lake Victoria, an outrageous act and a portent of brutalities to come.

Soon we began to hear of executions of soldiers – 'Obote's men' – in army barracks, and of reprisals, by the Baganda against 'traitors' in villages. That the aftermath of the *coup* would sooner or later demand a blood sacrifice was no surprise. But to describe these victims of political and tribal revenge as *kondos* was an act of cynicism.

I have seen unburied dead on the battlefield. Blackened corpses of Indian soldiers, their boots washed by rain, lying in the cratered dirt at Cassino; New Zealanders, thrown dead from tanks in which, heroically but foolishly, they had managed to reach the upper approaches to Cassino monastery; Polish infantry, freshly shaved, caught by German machine-gunners in a cornfield near Jesi – they found more joy in giving up their lives than I would have done, some, as they died, uttering their own epitaph, '*Niech zyje Polska!* – Long Live Poland!'; piles of German dead sprawled on the Gustav Line at Piedemonte we put them, hurriedly, into a common grave; the dead brought back by stretcher bearers, giving out, like the swollen corpses of our pack mules, a sweet and sickly smell.

In these deaths of fighting men there was logic and a sort of honour; and there were organisations that took care of their remains and of their memory. But the victims of Amin's bloodless revolution were rubbish, embarrassing offal, men to whom

he placation of their ancestral spirits was denied. There they
ay, a small sample of them, the sun-roasted water-soaked
corpses of twenty-six well-built men heaped in grotesque
postures on the lake's edge near Entebbe, three piles of them
ipped out of army trucks, kneeling, praying, prostrate: lumps
of abandoned flesh turning piebald and ivory, the eyes blue,
intestines bursting like sausages through bullet holes.[1]

These men had been soldiers. They had served, rightly or
wrongly, their country. When their commanding officers
quarrelled, they were doomed. But why not bury the dead?
Why cast them, like rotten fish, on the pebbles of a picnic area?

In Kampala the northern faces of Acholi and Langi dis-
ppeared from cafés and bars (and from the police force too).
Men who had sung praises to Obote fell silent and withdrew
to work out their survival. The local Press instantly changed its
line. The students, and there were many, who had been
attracted to the ideology of African Socialism and the African
revolution propounded by Obote, were shocked and confused.
In public places voices that had praised Obote now cheered
min.

It was the day of the Baganda. The beat of their drums
sounded through the banana plantations. In the villages, many
lder people put on bark cloth. For long the Baganda had
ulked at home. Now they drew their money from the banks
nd came to town to spend it. Two hundred tarts, in wigs and
ew dresses, flocked into the central hotel area to enjoy the
indfall of free-spending customers. It was a time of magnifi-
nt ritual mourning for the embalmed body of the Kabaka,
euphoria and extravagance.

Meanwhile, in the north, Langi and Acholi were being hunted
death. The old World War II soldiers in their homesteads
el they have been speared in the back. They are cursing into
eir beer and lamenting the death of sons and brothers. They
e identified with a leader who fell. They and their clansmen
ust suffer, with Obote, the collective punishment that African
dition and the politics of blood-feud and violence demand.

See pictures facing p. 192, I took them on 5 April 1971 at a cove behind
subi School. Penises were missing from at least two bodies. The lorries
t had dumped them had left deep wheel marks.

CHAPTER 12

Aftermath

From the very first moment I was, on principle, against the military take-over. It meant that I – and every other civilian in Uganda – was at the mercy of the soldier with a gun. It meant, in practical terms, that armed men could walk into a class room and arrest the teacher in front of his blackboard. It meant, in view of the accumulation of tribal hatred, and the African tradition of taking cruel revenge on a beaten enemy or a rival, massive bloodshed.

I was disappointed at the enthusiasm with which many, perhaps most, British residents welcomed Amin simply, it seemed, because Obote had irritated them. I found it ominous that the British Information Officer, when he casually asked me how my students had reacted to the take-over, should have shown surprise and unbelief when I said, 'Many students are confused and scared, for you must know that among them Obote's policies had a large following. The Baganda are cheering, of course, but others have gone into a corner and are keeping quiet.'

Eight months after the *coup*, the Features Editor of *The Times* invited me to send him a review of the situation in Uganda. *The Times*, like the rest of the British Press with the exception of *The Observer* (whose Colin Legum seemed to be conducting a personal vendetta against Amin), had been treating Amin gently. Here is the draft of what I wrote (28 Sep. 1971)

'*Early Popularity*

'In Uganda no stable government can be based on her soldiers. Not all General Amin's personal prestige can cover up the internal jealousies, the unpredictability, and the lack of discipline that are associated with his army.

'The military take-over of 25 January 1971 was cheered by the Baganda and by Obote's enemies throughout Uganda. The Baganda would, of course, have welcomed any agent, from divine thunderbolt to the assassin's stroke, that toppled Obote. It happened to be Amin who delivered the blow, and it was Amin who reaped the eulogies.

'Amin's immediate decision to release political detainees (when it was announced, an immense cry of jubilation broke like a thunderclap over Mengo) straightaway consolidated the success of his *coup*; and by arranging for the Kabaka's body to be returned, with pomp and ceremony, to its tribal soil, Amin strengthened his personal image among the Baganda to the point (as he presided over the funeral rites) of temporary adulation.

'During the early period of euphoria[1] Amin's soldiers enjoyed a brief share of their leader's popularity. The Baganda, who up to the very night of the *coup* had treated them as pariahs who in 1966 had fired their Kabaka's palace and "shot down old men on bicycles", now offered them beer and women. When the new heroes carried their weapons into bars and ordered drinks, the customers no longer slipped away. The soldiers even paid, with new bank notes, for what they ordered.

'There were other popular steps taken by the military government, which at first, by blaming Obote for anything that was not right, could do nothing wrong.

'Amin, having partially disarmed and publicly castigated the police for its failure to put down the wave of violent crime that had marked Obote's last months ("You are cowards, you are corrupt, and I will deal drastically with you") – an action

---

[1] Rajat Neogy, editor of *Transition*, wrote in the resuscitated Accra edition (No. 38, June-July 1971), 'We share the joyousness of the people after the events of January 26.' In the next issue (No. 39, October 1971) here was the naïvely enthusiastic letter written by the Professor of Sociology at Makerere, Peter Rigby: '. . . the feeling of excitement as I write this . . . the new sense of hope.' But by 1973, after the expulsion of the Indians, Rajat Neogy was writing in the editorial of No. 42: 'The result of Amin is anarchy and a reign of terror the likes of which Uganda has never experienced in her history . . . Amin has changed one of the most out-going and liberal countries in Africa into a closed society.' *Transition*'s intellectuals, who had barked at Obote and wagged their tails when the soldiers ousted him, now keep quiet or have gone away.

that undermined the reputation and morale of a force that was
in many senses, the army's rival – ordered his soldiers to carry
out a ruthless drive against the armed gangs (*kondos*) who had
been raiding Kampala's shops and restaurants and looting
homes.

'Many private scores were settled, murder committed
under cover of this operation. It was temporarily successful.
In and around Kampala the armed *kondoism* of organised
gangs has for the time being virtually ceased.

'This welcome operation, followed by timely decrees to
restore fringe benefits for civil servants (which pleased the
bureaucracy) and to control prices of such necessities as sugar
and cement (which pleased the common man), further enhanced
as they were intended to, the military government's benevolent
image in the public mind.'

'Bloodshed

'Soon, however, it became known that the "bloodless revolution" was not by any means going to stay bloodless. From
Mbarara to Moyo, in Jinja and Moroto, Acholi and Langi
servicemen were shot, hacked and clubbed to death by fellow
soldiers. There seemed to be a calculated heartlessness in the
way in which corpses were dumped in swamps and rivers like
carrion.

'Not many people sympathised with the dead – or with the
widows and children hastily bundled into trains and buses
and sent back to their villages. They were Acholi and Langi
"Lwoo-speakers": men who in the army and security force
had been largely responsible for putting Obote into dictatorial
power and for oppressing the Baganda. They had lost the
power struggle; "they deserved what they got".

'But the executions were a frightening glimpse into the
realities of military government. Reality was the barrel of a
gun in the hands of men who were instantly ready to use it and
from now on, as in times of curfew and emergency under
Obote, began to harass ordinary Africans.

'Above all, when the soldiers tried to explain away their
self-inflicted casualties as the death toll (no wounded?) resulting
from Tanzanian-inspired guerilla actions in which, they claimed

ellow Chinese led attacks on barracks, they destroyed their own
redibility. Since then the common citizen has had good reason
o suspect especially government statements that deal with
military operations.

'It was, for instance, a psychological blunder – it made the
rmy look silly – to exhibit at Kololo airstrip the doctored body
f a captured "Chinese colonel" who did not look at all like
Chinaman.

'I joined a nondescript crowd of Africans shuffling past the
ody. It had been propped up like a piece of stuffed cardboard.
he face was taut and sallow, the lips swollen, the throat
ound had been stitched up. Here was a propaganda exercise
a sacrilege that might have been thought up by a village
ubaltern. (The dead man turned out to be a half-caste Tan-
anian policeman seized in the border area.)'

'Amin's military government, it is said, has some excellent
inisters. But they work in the shadow of the army. Amin,
ke some village chief on safari, has made them scurry with
im on hand-shaking rallies through the bush, and he has
ometimes publicly rebuked them. They have been enrolled as
military cadets and they are technically, one assumes, liable to
ourt martial. What, one wonders, do they think of the recent
eported machine-gunning of over one hundred Karamojong
ho had formally assembled to protest against Amin's policy
f forcing them into trousers?

'Ugandans say that Obote gave his ministers too much
titude, that they took advantage of this to deceive and
ompromise him. Amin, aware of Obote's error, is loath to
elegate authority. This has committed him to a hectic round
f public duties, rallies and speech-making that often takes him,
y helicopter, from one end of the country to another in a
ngle day. What stamina! and what good peasant humour and
hrewdness gleam among the threats ("If any of you try to
lay politics, I will shoot you like *kondos*"), the promises, the
tterances of befuddled sincerity, with which Dada exhorts
he assembled crowds, the Makerere students, the elders,
he musicians and the traditional dancers. The news bulletins
carcely give news; they are the diary of one man's day.'

'*British Reaction*

'The speed with which traditionally cautious Britain recognised Amin's military government came to most people as a surprise; and in view of other black African states' reluctance to do so, there were some who considered it as almost an act of intervention in African affairs. Britain's action not only conferred respectability on the "rebel" régime; it was seen as a guarantee of its continued stability. The Baganda, whose fortunes the *coup* had restored, interpreted it as a personal gesture of British support and friendship for their own cause. Cynics considered Britain's initiative to be a piece of diplomatic one-upmanship.

'Many Europeans in Uganda felt (at first) gratified by Britain's early sponsorship of Amin. That awful man Obote, who had been abusing Mr Heath at Singapore, was out. An old soldier trained in the traditions of the British Army, who publicly expressed his appreciation of what the British had done for Uganda and rejected Socialism, a man of the right with no time for Obote's Common Man's Charter, had replaced the champion of anti-colonialism.

'What balm it was for a British expatriate to read those words of praise over his breakfast eggs! ("The missionaries were good people. The Queen is my friend.") And justice was being done to the memory of royalty too. Real Cockney guardsmen were flown out to attend the Kabaka's funeral sites. The refined voices of British military officers were heard over Kampala radio in nation-wide broadcasts. What a set-back for those trouble-makers Nyerere and Kaunda who in league with Obote had been manoeuvring to isolate Kenya and to let the Chinese into East Africa!

'Still, a good many Englishmen were surprised that Amin should have been so readily and so amicably received by the British government in London and by the Queen. True, the invitation and visit were seen as a matter of practical politics rather than of moral approbation. It was known that Amin urgently needed arms, and military and police experts to help and advise him. Better that Britain should provide them and so increase her influence over Uganda, than the Russians, the Chinese, or Israel. And yet – Amin had in effect led a mutiny that toppled a lawful government within the Commonwealth and set a precedent for violence in East African politics.

'It was the subsequent inhumanity of the soldiers that, as it became more widely known, has given Europeans and many Africans (they were more prepared for the worst) second thoughts about Amin's military rule. Europeans are upset by butchery. They consider it ungodly to strew corpses by the roadside, to mutilate the dead.

'Meanwhile, Nyerere's refusal to recognise Amin's "rebel" government (the Tanzanian Press calls him "this evil man") and tension on the frontier with Tanzania are a constant reminder of shadows over the future.

'Not much is known about the border situation. People do not accept either the Uganda or the Tanzanian reports as trustworthy. A great many Ugandans do indeed believe that Tanzania is training guerillas for hostile acts against their government. But many believe that Amin is deliberately exaggerating, even provoking, frontier tension, and from various motives: to invent a threat as a pretext for getting arms from abroad; to whip up feelings of national unity; to distract public attention from internal, especially economic, problems.

'The Uganda African does not really believe there will be war with Tanzania. He still trusts Amin to put things right. The very possibility of war fills him with fear and horror. He knows that war in Africa is ruthless, sparing neither woman nor child, an agony of machine-gunning and burning, of flight and hunger and tribal extermination.'

The Future

'The Baganda hold the key to the future and they are biding their time. True there are divisions among them. The older generation want the Kabakaship back; younger people tend to be apathetic or even opposed to its return. Amongst the Baganda, too, there are still old scores to be settled, acts of alleged treachery to be avenged, that date back to the days of party politics and of self-interested manoeuvring under Obote.

'But the Baganda have wealth, education, numbers, and basic tribal solidarity. Will they, one day, outwit the soldiers and assume power? If so, how will they make peace with the

northerners – the Langi and the Acholi, and the men from
West Nile whose present influence they would have to destroy?

'General Idi Amin Dada, for the moment, is a necessary
leader and figure-head. He plays the part of father figure well.
But he would not survive if the politicians reassumed authority.
Like a Hemingway character he has created for himself an
image of personal toughness ("I fear no man, only God").
He may feel one day that he must prove his boast in some violent
adventure.'

Looking Back

Two years later, as I write these lines, I can see that I was not
far wrong in my assessment of Amin. Those who have been
closest to him – ministers, senior officers, advisers, temporary
favourites – have mostly come and gone: fugitive, sacked, or
dead. His soldiers have blood on their hands. With utter disregard for their early promises they have enriched themselves,
as any African knew they would, with loot – houses and property,
cars, shops and businesses, new wives.

No one as yet has called Amin's bluff. He has in turn
successfully bullied and defied the Israeli missions (who
overplayed their hand), the Indians (who were in any case
doomed), and the British, and in their place courted new friends
and gifts among Libyans and Moslems. He has with impunity
threatened Nyerere, calling him in public utterances 'an old
woman', 'a prostitute', and 'a coward'. He has threatened to
bomb Mwanza, to destroy Kigali 'in five minutes', to send his
troops into Israel and Rhodesia.

The Baganda still hold the key to the future. They are sulking
now, intimidated, intent on survival and on exploiting the
commercial opportunities so miraculously offered to them by
Amin's Africanisation of the economy. Amin, a true northerner,
appears at bottom to despise the Baganda ('banana-eaters,
unwarlike, their women soft and loose').

Amin has so far shown extreme skill in crushing conspiracies
and holding on to power. He has, of course, great advantages.
Most Ugandans – the Baganda in particular – would prefer
almost any alternative to the return of Obote. The great blow
he has struck at the Indian community, however harsh in

execution, evokes a cheer in every African heart. It is right that Africans should run their own economy. It is in their own long-term interest that they should be taught to sink or swim.

Amin knows his people very well. The ordinary African expects his leader to deal brutally with rivals and enemies. He has no scruples about looting them. He likes to be harangued. At the same time, in his natural sloth he prefers to be left in peace. The chatter of the machine gun terrifies him. His instinct is to run.

The Africans' old habits of feuding, quarrelling, and of envy tend to hinder every sort of co-operative effort, from running a successful business or a student organisation to affairs of religious leadership. Amin knows that to move people in the direction he requires he has to take them by the scruff of the neck, and to keep the pressure on. The common man, meanwhile, in his thatched hut or under a tin roof, is content to survive. He has learned from experience that when elephants fight it's the grass that gets trampled. And who would want to be a politician? A 'big man' one day; felled like Lucifer the next.[1]

---

[1] The alarming murder (Sep. 1971) of Michael Kaggwa, an outstandingly successful individualist both in business and in public life (he was found incinerated in a back lane inside his white Mercedes Benz), was an early reminder of how success breeds enemies, and how dangerous is life at the top.

CHAPTER 13

Kampala

Other Cities

London, Warsaw, Cairo, Ankara – I have sampled and left them, using them selfishly as staging posts on a journey that, apparently leading nowhere, has landed me under the mango tree where I am writing this sentence in a Kampala garden.

After those acts of desertion it is here I have halted, in a tomato-coloured flat dug into a hill, and it is for ten years now that I have watched the mango tree grow more massive and its leaves change with the seasons from olive to metallic green and then to brown crusts that fall among servants' sludge into the storm drains.

I have always tried to avoid cities. Yet here I am, still rooted in Kampala. Perhaps Kampala is not a real city, only a glorified *boma* two-thirds of whose flimsy houses could be bulldozed, leaving the wild grass growing over the rubble, the latrine pits and the graves, and the vultures and marabou storks to pick the bones.

My aversion to living in cities must go back to my early days in Birmingham: to that impression of grimy trams and rows of monotonous houses petering out in the slums of Small Heath and Deritend; to a memory of ill-looking people who coughed and spat on pavements soiled with dog turds; to my fear of factories and offices where a quarter of a million Birmingham citizens served a life sentence.

Even worse were the loneliness and snobbery of my genteel suburban world where the English of Moseley and Edgbaston hid themselves behind curtains, bolted doors, and high garden walls.

Yet escape was easier then. There was much open ground where boys could play cricket. An hour's bicycle ride away

5a Rom

5b Rom
5c Burnt woodland at Rom

6a Teuso porters in camp

6b Teuso porters in camp

6c Teuso porters at Kaabong

from those slate roofs and brick chimneys one could climb a stile into a field of blackberry hedges; a church steeple would stick out among haycocks and one might hear, far away, the whistle and rumble of a slow train, but not the buzz of cars.

The milkman and the baker, the grocer, the coal merchant and the furniture remover used floats, vans and carts pulled by horses which left droppings in roadways. In the poorer neighbourhoods men with shovels retrieved this precious dung for their gardens (Kurdish women gather it, for their fires, with bare hands).

Later, my first experience of London left a permanent scar. I had been apprenticed through the Oxford University Appointments Board to Shell-Mex. The idea was that I should start from the bottom and one day become a tycoon. One other Oxford graduate – Shaun Wade, a rugby blue and Irish international wing three-quarter – commenced this Odyssey with me.

The dark early morning journeys by tube to a laboratory in Fulham, the job – I had to put on a white smock and test the malleability of lumps of bitumen – the meals in Lyons where I sat among old Jewesses eating poached eggs, and the hideous whores – some wore cloth caps and towed little dogs – who badgered me as I walked back to my digs along the Edgware Road, drove me to despair. I left without drawing a salary, and went to Poland.

During my three years in Poland I avoided Warsaw till the months preceding the War. There was nothing strident, however, or overwhelming about this grey old Slav capital. The horse-drawn droshkies, the bearded Jews in skull caps and kaftans who sat like spectres in tiny ghetto basements, the shawled women pressing their lips to a wayside crucifix, gave Warsaw an old-fashioned look. Rooted in Gogol, too, were the meticulous forms of address, the ritual kissing of a lady's hand, the unworldly chauvinism, and the military officers in their cloaks, their glossy riding boots and their four-cornered hats.

Yet I was often depressed. In Gdynia in the summer I had had the Baltic to swim in. In winter the icy winds blowing off a frozen sea had cleared my head. In Warsaw I lived in frowsty rooms choked with embroidered cushions and old furniture, whose double windows were permanently sealed. Polish food (dumplings and cabbage) was heavy. The whores (*kurwy*) – they had short muscular legs and hard blue eyes – were almost as ugly and brazen as those of the Edgware Road. Street walkers in the city centre specialised in the 'periscope': the customer would mount a woman from behind, in a doorway, while she, grasping her handbag, craning and oscillating her head, looked up and down the pavement to see if a policeman was coming.

Cheap potato vodka was a strong poison that brought both relief and ruined guts to a tense and often melancholy people (they went bald early) living in a poor, friendless and vulnerable country whose past glories still haunted them. The empty vodka bottles in gutters, uncorked by thumping the bottom, and drained and thrown away by early morning workers, were as squalid as the spittle on an English pavement.

Wartime Cairo gave me a guilt feeling. Until I, too, put on uniform I felt cowed by those magnificent soldiers from Australia and New Zealand who lounged, bronzed and muscle-bound, in the streets and bazaars, and took their tarts behind the bushes of the Gezira Club. Later, recalled from the Western Desert for a spell at GHQ, where I censored the other ranks mail and stamped officers' identification cards, the guilt feeling returned. People called us contemptuous names ('Groppi's Grenadiers'). Cairo gave one prickly heat, diarrhoea, and soft white knees. To make my own situation even more unwarlike I was boarded out (with fan allowance) in a guest house among spinster ladies and schoolmasters (Lawrence Durrell, an animated teddy bear with a fairy tale wife – who would have connected his small tubby body with those orgiastic Alexandrian fantasies? – was one of them). A few hundred yards away, at the Gezira Club, a scowling Hammond was belting Freddie Brown through the covers, and nannies trundled sticky white babies in prams.

In the summer of 1945, the war over in Italy, I welcomed posting to Rome, for I felt I had deserved its fleshpots. unrolled my bedroll on the roof of a villa on the Via Appia an cadged my girl friends from a Polish officers' club. There were girls galore, with splendid teeth and black hair that hung to their shoulders.

Rome was quiet then, convalescing in the sunshine. Even the brilliant exhibition of master paintings, when I visited it, I had entirely to myself except for a single private soldier who trailed behind me, his boots clumping, as we passed from one silent hall into another.

For a few drinks a renegade officer from a nearby Russian camp taught me to bawl his native songs: *Blocha* (The Flea); *Volga, Volga, mat rodnaya; Rossiya moya*.

Vienna in the winter of 1945-46 was unspeakable. St Stefan's Kirche was in ruins. The Viennese were hungry. Red Army soldiers in jackboots and dirty forage caps were roaming the streets with broken suitcases looking for loot. No one in the Clusiusgasse, not even the house porters, remembered the Weiss family with whom I had stayed before the War. The Weisses had vanished without trace. They were Jews, happy and harmless, the father a failed commercial traveller, the two children in love with swimming and the opera.

Ankara, the last of the capitals I had stayed in before I came to Kampala, was in a turmoil of rebuilding and expansion, and the Turks would not even recognise it as their chief city – that was *güzel* (lovely) Istanbul, seat of the old sultans. High on its volcanic plug, the old town and fort of Ankara cast a mediaeval silhouette through heat haze as it looked down on the modern apartment blocks, the builders' labourers prostrating themselves at noon in prayer, the rug shops and yoghourt sellers.

It was Turkey with the anachronisms of Islam, a precarious economy, and its military take-over of 1960, that introduced me to the improvisations, the paradoxes and the alarums of a developing society where the élite is nourished by foreign aid and by the labours of a large agricultural population from which it is alienated. Turkey, in short, had prepared me for life in Uganda.

From Ankara, too, as from Kampala, it was easy to escape to empty spaces. The coffee and sugar plantations that surround Kampala merge into forest and thorn bush. The lights of

Ankara shone out among vast steppe lands sprinkled with sheep and prickly plants. Beyond rose the mountains of Armenia.

Kampala[1]

Perhaps Kampala is not so much a city, walled and integrated, as an encampment, a relic of white empire, of missionaries and of Anglo-India, where for a time white administrators pitched their tents and Oriental camp followers their stalls; and where, invested, infiltrated, and finally about to be overrun by the indigenous people, we and our satellites had stayed on as stragglers from our own overcrowded homelands, as last-minute money-grabbers, as spectators unable to tear ourselves away from an exotic experience.

Look at the pattern of this town. Enclaves of residential villas and bungalows set behind hedges in private gardens, for many years the preserve of Europeans and affluent Indians, now largely taken over by African civil servants, and by military men who park their cars and trucks on the flower beds and often have women who carry bundles on their heads; intertwined with them, the old Bombay belt; on the periphery, Africa – her shanties and slums, her small painted cottages, her bars and banana *shambas*. Beyond it all, the papyrus swamp waving blackened pom-poms, the shaggy hills, the emerald forest where turacos flash, and the acacia scrub.

Already, though, tall new cubes constructed by the British, the Italians, the Israelis and the Jugoslavs have sprung up among the tin-roofed shops and invaded the bushy skyline. Green slopes a mile or two beyond the golf course are being dug up into brown patches and rapidly built over. Kololo hill, where expatriates used to tramp to keep their weight down and English ladies walked their dogs, has sprouted a new housing estate that provided but a brief and illusory home for the Indian families who first moved in.

There are incongruities, a sort of rustic privacy even among the slums. No one would guess, from a distance, that those green trees and fronds that run along the railway cutting hide, at Kibuli, a urine-soaked trough of teeming human dens.

[1] For further developments (1973–4) relating to the account given below, see Epilogue.

Where the old Indian belt merges into the poor African suburbs, one side of the Hoima Road at Bakuli used to be occupied by prosperous Indians in well-lit apartments. Indian music sounded through curtained windows. Their big cars and commercial lorries were parked outside, bumper to bumper, guarded by watchmen.

Opposite them were the unpainted hovels of poor Africans, the piles of garbage, the mangy dogs and the children excreting in the drains. Men in ragged shirts came and went out of sheds like chicken coops, quarrelling at night and staggering. The whores stood among the rubbish heaps in the light of an oil lamp, which, shining through a half-open door whose latch was a bent nail, showed the bed, the tin basin, and the frocks draped over a string.

African office workers have now moved into those Indian flats at Bakuli. The curry smells and the coughing watchmen have gone; fluttering strips of cloth have replaced the curtains; holes have appeared in pavements. The hovels opposite and the garbage heaps no longer look so out of place.

The Apolo Hotel (renamed 'Kampala International' since the fall of Milton *Apolo* Obote), when it was raised (1969) seemed to the common man a marvel, an immense up-ended box big enough to house an entire village, filled with artificial air and with liveried servants in enviable jobs.

For a time, under a splendid Austrian manager, its bars and lounges were crowded with tourists and dinner guests. There have been no more tourists for a year or more; and since the hotel became a rendezvous of army and security officers most of its old customers have stayed away. In the lounges a few melancholy Libyans, for ever stroking and straightening their tight-curled hair, look through the windows at an empty garden. In the restaurant Moslem elders in white *kanzus* eat meals at government expense. Only its night club high up on the sixteenth floor, and the girls who resort there, continues to flourish.

After the Apolo Hotel had been built, the Conference Centre and the Nile Hotel, initiated by Obote, soon followed. Hundreds of Jugoslav workmen in singlets and shorts worked day and night to get the buildings ready in time to house the OAU

Conference of June 1971. Obote's opponents resented the cost. Sportsmen were outraged when bulldozers driven by intruders from the Balkans tore up the Kampala Sports Club cricket pitch and football field to make room for the project.[1]

Amin took over from Obote before the buildings were ready. He pressed on with them, hoping that the OAU would meet there and by so doing recognise his legitimacy. It was a blow to Amin's pride when, in the event, the OAU stayed away. It is Amin, though, who has since profited from Obote's prestigious project by using it as a centre for political rallies.

How odd that the golf course, a piece of middle-class England scarcely used by Africans (but popular with Koreans and Japanese), and a nuisance to motorists who have to drive round it, has so far been spared. Cassava patches already threaten its edges. One day we may see soldiers or refugees encamped on the fairway, or men grazing muddy cattle.

Meanwhile the British High Commission has moved from its old colonial style villa to a strong, squat cube designed, in the modern way, to give protection against rioters and stone-throwers. Soon after the new refuge was completed (1968), Indians clamouring to enter Britain discovered that its walls made an ideal blackboard for their slogans. The young men whom I watched shouting abuse and soiling the entrance to the High Commission had anger but little dignity. Parents and friends stood by in cars ready to whisk them out of danger. Many fellow Indians criticised their behaviour.

'They are riff-raff,' an Ismaili told me, 'the sort who get the rest of us a bad name.'

'They are too idle to work,' said another, 'they want to go to England to live on the dole.'

Expatriates

Still, the demonstrators in their jeans and coloured shirts had a point. ('We are British, yet Britain rejects us.') They

[1] Tito has craftily used his Non-Aligned position to win other contracts in Uganda (and elsewhere in Africa). But Uganda is not getting pennies from heaven; she has to pay up promptly – in dollars. The builders, Energoprojekt of Belgrade, run this advertisement in the Uganda Press: 'There is a fact we would like to mention that the Conference Centre and Nile Hotel were completed in 186 days.'

stirred things up, attracted the notice of *The Times*, brought more urgency to the scrutiny of files, incensed the true-blue Englishman who could not understand how a swarthy Hindu 'whose father was a pedlar from Bombay had the nerve to claim to be a Britisher'.

Of the two main non-African communities in Kampala, a good many Indians had quietly left even before Amin's take-over, and like old soldiers most of the European old-timers had faded away, with them the police officers who wore campaign ribbons to remind youngsters that England was once a warlike country, and Mr Flint the Fire Chief – his firemen not only quenched fires, they shot pythons which householders had found in their gardens, and they rescued babies from the bottom of latrine pits.

I knew some of them: big men in wide khaki shorts who chatted up barmaids in Swahili and poured a small fortune into the pockets of the owners of the City and the Kololo International Bar. They had jobs in the Public Works Department, the railway, the post and telegraph service, the electricity board, in sewage and accountancy. They had curious knowledge that was not quite accurate: of clitoridectomy among the Nandi ('it's done to cool off the women so they're more likely to stay faithful'); of the habits of intestinal worms; spear-making; the sex techniques of Ethiopians.

Some, whose jobs were Africanised, had been unhappy to go. Others could not, after Uhuru, adjust themselves to the African way of doing things; believing, though not always for the right reasons, that the African was not yet capable of running his own affairs. A few had slipped through the net of redundancy, taken an African wife, bought a farm in her name or found private employment. Now Amin's policy of expro-priation, directed, for instance, against white tea-planters in Toro, has further diminished their number. The veterans who currently survive either have nowhere else to go or are men clinging to a mistress whom, in spite of her tantrums, they love and cannot do without.

A new sort of Britisher labelled 'expatriate' and employed on short-term contract has largely replaced the older generation. Having no colonial prototype to mould himself on, no war experience, and no imperial ideal to inspire him, he brings with him the current codes of middle-class Britain. He is free-thinking, sceptical, equipped with antibiotics. He knows to the last shilling all the emoluments he is entitled to and how to use import and currency regulations, and the exchange rate, to his advantage. 'Expatriates are mercenaries,' a United Nations officer who had turned sour said to me, 'their one interest is to make money quickly and buy a house in Britain.'

He was unfair. Every expatriate develops some emotional attachment to Africa. The black man's gentle tolerance that overlooks his ignorance and his faults, the sun shining through the window on his breakfast, the heron in his garden, will have changed him in some way for ever. His final experience in present-day Uganda may have been unpleasant – a slap in the face from a soldier, an armed burglar who makes off with his ready-packed suitcases – but he will remember the good things too, and in his rented Hounslow rooms dream of coming back.

Today's expatriate does not want to shoot wild animals. He probably has a young wife who safely delivers her babies on the fifth floor of Mulago Hospital. He keeps a copy of Dr Spock's *Baby And Child Care* in his home. The children flourish, running barefoot over mowed lawns in the tropical sun. Single men often have African girl friends, whom they spoil with presents. They are liable to catch gonorrhoea. No one bothers if white women take African lovers; but there is a problem here. The boy friend will borrow money, and he won't stay faithful. The white homosexual too has his trials. His catamite may be tempted one day to savage him (or get other people to do the job for him) and steal his money.

A bizarre element are – or used to be, till Amin frightened them away – the hitch-hikers. Unkempt, spotty, non-walkers, burdened with immense rucksacks which they could scarcely lift, bold and unembarrassed, they slept rough but haunted the best hotels, where they put their feet up on the chairs. Clean-shaven Englishmen winced when they first appeared on the tropical scene with their jeans and ragged hair and their untidy girls. They, and the teenagers, and European women in mini-skirts who expose their underwear to the pavement hawker, have betrayed that long-guarded image of the white man (aloof, superior, clean).

The young people back on school holidays from Britain – they are far fewer now – seem to be mostly hair and legs. They look impudent. But they are gentle and sensible to talk to.

Africanisation

Africanisation – even before Amin's mass transfer of foreign businesses and shops to black Africans – had not only filled senior administrative posts and the management of the parastatal bodies, initiated under Obote, with favoured native Ugandans. It had produced a rapidly growing class of African office workers, cashiers and shop assistants who handled large sums of money and sophisticated equipment, and did jobs which not long ago people would have said Africans were not suited to perform. Amin has enormously accelerated this process. In addition, by despoiling the Indians, he has created an entirely new element of African business and shop owners (many are women) selling sophisticated commodities in the city centre itself.

Despite initial male resentment and the ingrained belief that 'woman's place is in the kitchen', the African career girl has emerged: elegant, painted, bewigged, often driving her own car, determined to earn a salary even though frequent pregnancy may make her more of a liability than an asset. She is a telephone addict, unscrupulously using it for long private conversations in the vernacular.

In nursery and preparatory schools, trained African mistresses have for some time been helping to look after the little golden-haired boys and girls of white parents. Sports Day at Nakasero School used to be one of the happiest (and best organised) events of the year in Kampala. Black, brown, yellow, and white, the children hopped and sprinted with an uninhibited joy that would have made racially prejudiced people grind their teeth.

In the early stages of this redeployment of African manpower there have been problems. A tradition of incorruptibility and of respect for public funds has not yet taken root. Theft by public servants and by employees, using methods that are often ingenious and impudent, have been so common that the government, the public corporations, banks and businesses lose considerable sums of money. Young bank employees seem to be particularly dishonest.

Here is an earlier and typical letter of complaint (3 December 1971) foreshadowing the spate of protests against cheating and corruption by Africans that have been sent to the *Uganda Argus* (now the *Voice of Uganda*) over the last two or three years:

'It is high time the government stopped the white-collar criminals. The cost of white-collar crime – embezzlement, stock manipulation, bribery, tax frauds, theft from business, consumer fraud, and the like – dwarfs all crimes of violence. The common thief usually steals a person's money and leaves. An embezzler may reach into a family and destroy their equity, bankrupt a whole firm or render valueless the stock of a corporation. When I met a white-collar officer who was busily engaged in selling some office stock, he said "*Owange nzendya ku mulimu gwange* – Hullo, I feed on my job." These white-collar criminals form a large segment of our leadership and as the leadership goes, so goes the nation.'

Dick Ssegirinya

The more restrictions the Government of Uganda places on price levels and on the free flow of trade and currency, the greater the opportunity for astute operators to profit by evading them.

The Indian – once the chief but by no means only offender – was too elusive to be pinned down by controls. He thrived on them, for each new restriction presented him with a profitable loophole. This was an inescapable fact of life that baffled the authorities, exasperated the Indian's business rivals, and angered the moralists.

This does not mean, of course, that the Indians of Uganda, as their enemies say, were parasites and saboteurs. They had, as elsewhere in East Africa, adapted themselves realistically to the opportunities and the ethics of an African situation; and in every field of activity that had to do with hard cash, commerce and documentation, they helped to mould, for the worse, those ethics. Nevertheless Indians were the true founders of modern Uganda. They supplied the economic drive, the capital, the goods and services, introducing these things with patience, hard work, and foresight into what was a rural vacuum.

Predictably, now that the Indians have gone, it is the African traders and shopkeepers replacing them who, in their turn, are being accused of cheating, hoarding and overcharging. In the present chaotic situation of pricing and shortages, it is inevitable that the new men should be called 'black Indians'.

Indians

I have already, in my earlier book, set down some of my impressions of the Indian community. My original verdict, that many of us in Uganda found it hard to feel affection for a people so dedicated to (and so good at) making money, still stands. But on rereading, a little later, those previous impressions, I feel that I should have made more of the kindness, the humanity, that Indians show not only to one another, but in my experience (I cannot speak as an African) to Europeans. Here is a subsequent note that I wrote while the Indians were still here:

'"To be frank with you," Indians have often told me, "we are here to make money." An honest confession. But private actions are fortunately another matter.

'It is not only that there is an ancient cultural (and a physical) affinity between us; and an intellectual parity. Who has kept my old car on the road for nine years? Mr Khan (he tries to hide when I bring it to his garage). Who befriended and entertained my boy in England? Shiraz. Who gives my family sweet cakes and picture calendars? Mr Sood. Who, when I sometimes have to walk home, is most likely to stop and give me a lift? An Indian. And who, in an African bar, will buy me a whisky? A Sikh.

'"Very well," says an African voice in my ear, "but would they do the same for us? Indians underpay us; and they avoid us."

'"They avoid us." Here is the psychological root of the problem. As an African lecturer Dent Ocaya-Lakidi put it in the *Uganda Argus* of 22 November 1971 ("Why Asians have come under Fire"):

'"Asians do not mix with the Africans the way Europeans do.

'"The most difficult part of the Asian problem is their social exclusiveness. Fundamentally it is simply that they won't intermarry with anybody else. This is in stark contrast to the Europeans who appear quite at home with black Africans. A consequence of it is some kind of racial segregation. . . . One Asian went as far as to argue with me, that an Asian-African marriage cannot work. The Asian, he pointed out, does not emphasise sex as the centre of marriage. And the religious factor would also cause problems. . . ."

'Commenting on this article, a letter writer ("Hardcore", *Uganda Argus*, 25 November 1971) exclaimed:

'"You have a point. It really perturbs me to see Asian girls trying to keep their distance from males not of their colour, especially black! Their brothers are terribly mad about black angels! Go to our night clubs!"

'In these terms, the African's case against the Indians in Uganda is not merely an economic one alleging the exploitation of his resources by outsiders. It is a matter of integration. Indians, say the African, are not only chary of committing themselves, for better or for worse, to Uganda by becoming Uganda citizens. They won't on principle intermarry with Africans. To put it bluntly, Indian men may freely enjoy the bodies of black women, but there is no reverse traffic. They put an absolute taboo on their own women having a physical relationship with African men.

'But is the African who argues for physical integration sincere? Scarcely any African male really *wants* to marry an Indian girl. It is the satisfaction of knowing that he *could* do so – that he won't on principle be rebuffed – that his ego desires.[1]

'As for the European relationship with Africans, there is a strong common factor in the Christian code, even if it is only a nominal one (the Bible, church weddings, no nonsense about caste, diet or pollution); and the degree of relationship is a

---

[1] The first officially recorded instance of an Indian girl marrying an African was said to have taken place in Soroti in July 1973. The marriage was acclaimed by the Uganda Press.

matter for the individual to decide, not one of principle. Many younger Europeans seem to feel, indeed, that by whole-heartedly accepting and mixing with the black people, they are in some way making up for the sins of discrimination practised by their fathers.

'It is now the turn of the British people on their home ground to accept and try to understand this gifted brown community uprooted from Africa. There will be many more to come from Kenya. It seems a pity that so many low-class immigrants direct from Pakistan have already staked prior claims to Britain's limited space.'

Tensions

As a by-product of the attempt to settle a multi-racial society in Kampala, parasitic not on land but on each other, there is the overcrowding, the juxtaposition within a small space of peoples of different economic levels, background and values, the tensions and the crime that spring from this.

For years the spread of primary education, the lure of money, the monotony and hardships of village life, have attracted a heavy and uncontrolled migration from the countryside to Uganda's towns. The schoolboy, the labourer, the semi-educated youth seeking a white-collar job, Jaluo wage-earners, Rwanda and Sudanese refugees, servants, thieves and prostitutes have been pouring into Kampala.

The newcomer has to find shelter as best he can. If he is lucky, with relatives, if not in slum corners among rats. For when the Indians were here, the central areas of Kampala – as of other Uganda towns – were already bursting with, for the most part, long-established Indian families (they named and dated the façades of their buildings) who had squeezed themselves into little shops, offices and flats. The replacement of the Indians by Africans has not solved this problem. A new black influx has filled the vacated Indian buildings with its own kinsmen.

As for the residential enclaves, they have always been reserved for officials and the well-to-do, though these areas too, over recent years, have been increasingly overrun by the poor relations of African occupants and by sub-tenants who squeeze into the servants' quarters or sleep and cook in the owner's windowless store shed (a favourite refuge for country boys attending local secondary schools).

It is this uncontrolled flood of people into Kampala, where they face unemployment and hunger, that endangers social stability and is changing Kampala's character from a garden city enjoyed by the privileged into a few pleasant reserves and shopping centres invested by poverty and crime. It is this invasion that by day fills the streets with useless young men, and after dark surrounds the city with a silent and sinister army of the night.

Only five minutes drive from the golden cassias that line the golf course, the drunks of Bakuli and of Mulago village come lurching at you across the road. At Kawempe savage rogues rap your car, and bar girls, shaped like bursting sausages, tilt their bottoms at red-eyed customers.

A few yards from the university compound, in verminous sheds, turbaned women raise broods of fatherless children who act as pimps and watchdogs for their mothers. In the rutted *shambas* between lanes, night cries and the ululations of women mark the trail of the thief.

Since the military take-over, the soldier-bandit has emerged. People disappear. Car theft at gun point and armed burglary have not only increased – there is little police protection for the ordinary citizen. He stays at home after dark. He grumbles. But he dare not protest.

New Attitudes

Concurrent with physical growth and social change, with development projects, urban expansion, the increase of services and of money, are the new attitudes that have taken shape during Uganda's decade of independence.

The emergence of an African élite (the so-called *Wabenzi*, Mercedes-Benz owners), of a large class of officials, of business-men, teachers and journalists, of educated and semi-independent women, and of a mass of secondary school youth: familiarity with decision making, with foreign travel, and with possession of domestic luxuries; all this, as the rat race catches on, has combined to create a new spirit of assertiveness.

Obote encouraged this assertiveness – so long as it was not directed against himself. He urged people to think of and take pride in Uganda as a nation and not a hotch-potch of tribes. In his pronouncements he not only pursued an increasingly strong anti-colonialist line. He made a point of praising the country's youth and the Common Man.

One noted the new assertiveness in education. One noted the boldness, often degenerating into disrespect or hooliganism (strikes, stone-throwing, car-burning), with which schoolboys and students began to challenge alleged anachronisms of organisation, discipline or syllabus that they considered to be the legacy of white educationalists, or humiliating to their sense of 'maturity'.

Obote himself strongly criticised the alleged ivory tower mentality, the academic aloofness and superior airs of Makerere, which he detached from the amorphous University of East Africa and turned into an independent national institution under a new Vice-Chancellor (Kalimuzo) of his own choice.[1] (Kalimuzo replaced the Muganda Lule. Amin subsequently accused Kalimuzo of 'conspiracy'; he has been missing, presumed dead, since the end of 1972.)

The official line – by and large an acceptable one – was that both staff and students should commit themselves ideologically to the African Revolution and to nation building, and that curricula must be readjusted to Uganda's man-power requirements. Makerere students were encouraged to take rooms outside the campus where they would be in touch with the life led by ordinary citizens. Their tribal and regional societies were dissolved.

The English language and its literature were no longer to have everything their own way. The English language was to compete in future with the expanded use of Swahili, and academically with German and French. In literature, Lawrence, Shaw and Eliot would no longer be allowed to overshadow the novels and poetry of native African writers.

[1] At this time Makerere students sharpened their traditional attacks on the university administration for allegedly holding up Africanisation of staff in the interests of white expatriate teachers. Even the Uganda police band and the national football team were castigated by an African lecturer in political science for 'aping the rigidities of a colonial style'.

Obote

On a political level the new spirit of assertiveness had reached a peak at the time of Obote's collision with Heath in Singapore. Uganda politicians and the local press abused the British Government's South African arms sales policy in emotional language that spoilt the Englishman's breakfast. Some expatriates began to recall, with anxiety, the incidents of 16 March 1968 when demonstrators attacked Europeans in Kampala city centre.

Obote spun his dreams. His 'Move to the Left' policy, as he defined it in his Common Man's Charter, purported to be a plan to effect a social revolution based on national unity, on the interests of the ordinary poor citizen, on service and self-sacrific. His Charter was a manifesto of 'African Revolution', with a strong anti-colonialist bias. Many of its ideas it owed to Nyerere's widely admired Arusha Declaration. Students and intellectuals especially were attracted to it. The logic and the apparent humanism of Obote's plan seemed to offer an exciting future in which human dignity based on African values, as well as material progress, count.

But while Obote sat in his office brooding over his blueprints for the future (he made few public appearances after the attempt to assassinate him – he was wounded in the mouth – in December 1969), too many ordinary people were hunting in vain for jobs, searching the shops for milk, barricading their doors against robbers.

Obote had good intentions. He was too slow and not ruthless enough to implement them. His claim that the UPC Party was identical with the nation was blatantly out of accord with the realities. The façade of unity was based, in fact, on suppressing the Baganda. Self-sacrifice was not for those at the top; they wanted larger cars and bigger bank balances. Obote won renown as an international politician and African leader. He failed to keep down the prices of sugar, cement, clothes, meat, and rents.

The common man wanted a bus service not perorations against colonialism. The government tried to stifle criticism, warning people that to grumble – about the nastiness of Uganda milk, for instance, or corruption within the new parastatal National Trading Corporation, which was going bankrupt – was sedition.

Meanwhile too many policemen were harrying motorists for bribes instead of chasing the robbers who maimed private citizens.

Above all, Obote had made implacable enemies of the Baganda.

Ever since that week in 1966 when Obote ordered his soldiers to assault the Kabaka's palace, and the dead had been carted away in lorries, it was clear that he would never again be allowed to sleep in peace. The Baganda, egged on by their virulent women, put their curse on him. Their witchdoctors and their priests prayed that he would die. The howl of triumph that burst from Mengo when Amin ousted him was malignant. Obote had done a great service to Uganda. Surrounded at length by enemies, estranged from his soldiers, loved by few, his downfall was inevitable.

CHAPTER 14

Violence and Crime

The Turks, among whom I had lived for eight years before I moved to Uganda, were a Moslem people with a strong sense of honour (which national pride, and the influence of their pious, white-bearded elders had helped to mould). They generally despised petty theft (deceiving the tax collector and the Customs, and – up to the turn of the century – brigandage, were another matter). I did not have to bolt my cottage door, put away my car at night, keep an eye on the clothes line.

Shopkeepers who discovered they had overcharged me by one halfpenny for a few carrots would run after me to rectify the error. I soon learned that if I offered money to a villager for giving me a bowl of yoghourt or the use of a sleeping rug, I offended him.

So I was ill-prepared for my encounter with the habit of theft, burglary and armed robbery that put a man's property in constant jeopardy in Uganda; and I was disappointed to find that so many ordinary Africans were not embarrassed to accept money as a gift, as a goodwill gesture, or for a service.

Within an hour or two of disembarking at Mombasa I went for a swim and lost my shirt. When, flecked with warm seaweed, I came out of the water at Nyali beach, it had gone.

The beach had seemed to be deserted, and there was no one in sight: only, a few hundred yards away, three boys whom I now surprised behind a coconut palm. They were giggling at something. I looked, and just below me saw a white man and woman copulating on the sand. The man was in military uniform. The two cloth pips on the shoulder tabs revealed him to be a lieutenant of the British Army in Kenya.

'Good for you,' I thought, a little dismayed. In my time with the forward part of the Eighth Army it had been more often than not the sergeants who got the girls. Among officers there had been a strong streak of public school asceticism. We compensated by writing letters to our loved ones, by an occasional furtive call on Mary's House in Cairo (hence, I was told, the name 'brothel creepers' for our soundless crepe-soled desert boots), and by smashing from time to time the mess furniture.

During our long crawl up the leg of Italy it had been considered bad form and bad for discipline for officers – even temporary lieutenants – to hang around farm girls. The Other Ranks, with a clear field, made the most of the platoon cook's surplus rations. Some soldiers I knew perfected a stratagem that involved the co-operation of a comrade whom they dubbed 'the raper's mate'. His job was to distract granny's attention while his companion persuaded her granddaughter into a corner.

I once fancied a hairy farm girl in the hills where we were resting behind Ancona, and with a thumping heart I knocked one night on the door of her bedroom where she slept in a fug of onions and socks.

'Are you there, Teresa?' I whispered.

'Bugger off!' said a voice which I recognised as the staff sergeant's. Had he identified my silly whisper? For a day or two I kept out of his way.

Theft

In Kampala, after I had parked my Volkswagen in the street for a week, the African manager of the hotel where I was staying warned me to lock it in his garage at night.

'But you have a night watchman,' I said.

'The watchman,' replied the manager, 'is only human.'

Later, when I moved to a government flat on Kololo Hill, thieves mounted a number of night operations against my car. I surprised one villain forcing the side window with a bar. Some nights later I was awakened by a bang, and ran out to find my car propped against a tree in a neighbour's garden.

'Never mind,' said Cooper Motors' German mechanic when he saw the dents, 'the more you bash your car, the less likely anyone will want to steal it.'

In Kampala one has learned to live with the risk of being

robbed or burgled as part of the way of life. The old type of burglar, who was usually non-violent, would snatch anything from an alarm clock or a pair of spectacles (the lenses they threw away, the frame they could sell for a few shillings) to one's radio and camera. These days, gangs of armed robbers break boldly into your house, beat and slash you if they feel like it, and clean you out. This may sound an exaggeration. To the victim – many have been my friends – it does not.[1]

As for pickpockets – there are fewer of them now that the number of tourists and of Europeans has diminished – they operate audaciously in shopping centres, bus and taxi parks. I have watched them at work on one of their pitches in the Kampala Road – the victim is bumped from behind and lo! as he turns his head, the money is whipped from his breast pocket and quickly lodged, for temporary safe keeping, with a lottery ticket-seller sitting at her pavement table.

In the case of casual theft, one does not know whom to suspect. The cautious man who *always* bolts his garage door and *never* leaves his bird-watching binoculars in the garden while he slips indoors for tea, and on the one occasion when he omits his customary precautions, is robbed, now realises that someone has been watching him, will continue to watch him, and will try to rob him again.

This is an unsettling thought, for it means he can no longer trust his houseboy or even the children next door. When a European has been burgled three or four times, and his wife has been frightened in the night by a black arm poked through her bedroom window or has had her car seized at gun-point, he turns bitter. Ingrained anti-African prejudices which he thought he had overcome rise to the surface again.

When someone – it must have been a small boy – crawled through the bars across my sitting-room window one night and made off with my shirt and shoes, I was angry. Yet I could not help seeing the thief's point of view. Most Africans are poor, many of them abjectly poor, with breath that smells of hunger. Kampala not only has a parasitic mass of workless youths and men. Thousands of employed but poorly paid

[1] Recently there has been a lull in gang attacks on European property (Nov. 1974).

Africans see, touch, carry, clean, mend, and sell the treasures of other people.

Do we really expect a clerk on 200 shillings a month, the garage hand or the builder's labourer whose midday meal is a roasted maize cob or a handful of ground-nuts in a paper spill, to resist, *always*, the temptation to appropriate a little of the rich man's *mufuta* (fat) simply because we who own things have invented a code of ethics that sanctifies the rule of 'mine is mine'. In this sense pilfering, housebreaking and petty theft may arguably be rationalised as the poor man's revenge.

But during the final months of Obote's rule, and then under Amin, a new species of armed and murderous criminal emerged. While Obote was preoccupied with his political blue-prints for the future, gangs began to rob banks and wages in transit, engage in fire-fights with guards, raid shops and bars. Others broke into private houses, sometimes half a dozen in a row, and stripped them.

Obote's police failed to deal effectively with these gangs, whose sophisticated weapons seemed to be evidence of collusion with soldiers. The night watchman with his whistle and stave simply ran away.

It was the frequency of armed robbery and of car thefts that helped turn people against Obote's government. A president who could not give them police protection was no good, they said.

'What can I do?' a Greek restaurant owner told me. 'Thieves have already reconnoitred my place. I told them they can come and take what they want so long as they don't use violence.'

The thieves left him alone, in fact, till he moved to a bar in Kololo. Since then, under Amin's régime, he has been raided twice, and there have been two murders on the pavement outside.

In earlier days it was the unattended vehicle that was generally taken. Then, during the last months under Obote, armed bandits began to hold up drivers in daylight as well as after dark. Two tough European friends of mine who lost their Mercedes Benz in this way were slashed across the face with pangas, and (they were not ashamed to confess) 'ran like buggery'.

Insecurity

As a fact of life, robbery and theft in Uganda have thrived not only on economic circumstances but on the unwillingness of the ordinary citizen to come to a man's help where there is physical risk. 'I have only one life,' an Indian, who had just watched from his balcony while a neighbour was murdered on the pavement, once told me.

The criminal has thrived on the timidity of the car owner, who when he hears his burglar alarm sounding in the night, turns over in bed and hopes for the best; on the apathy of Europeans (they are insured, they can get their money back). The armed bandit is encouraged above all by the unwillingness of the African to help anyone but a blood relation or a close friend, and on his highly developed instinct to run away from trouble.

Among the lower African classes, the habit of theft can be discouraged by the cruel habit of thief-beating. It can be locally and temporarily halted by brutal sanctions (flogging thieves with bicycle chains in police cells or shooting them on sight). But immediately the pressure is off, the evil breaks out again.

When the security forces themselves practise violent crime, nothing can be done. The victim has no chance; and no redress in law.

Insecurity – the experience of having been violently robbed, manhandled by soldiers, gaoled, which has been the lot of several score Europeans since Amin got angry with the British, has been a prime cause of the exodus of expatriates from Uganda.

The Motor Car

Until 1960, when I bought my first car, a Volkswagen Beetle, from a Hamburg dealer, and a week later, after some driving practice in the quiet streets of Lüneburg (I had acquired a driving licence by post from Dublin), set off with excessive care along the *Autobahn* for Turkey, I had walked, cycled, or used public transport. As a walker I tended to regard the motor car as an enemy. It splashed me, it threw up dust, it made a smell, I had to jump out of its way.

Once I had become a car owner I found I was losing touch

with ordinary people. Ordinary people walked, they queued for buses and crowded with their bundles and suitcases into railway carriages, they rode in carts, chivvied cows along country roads, sat gossiping under wayside trees. For me, a driver, ordinary people had suddenly become a nuisance; they got in the way.

For a time I felt the same temptation as any other driver to flash through landscapes. The great distances and the open roads of Turkey and Persia encouraged speed, as they do in East Africa. The novelty wore off, and now over long distances I generally bumble along. Since I carry rations, a small cooker, and my camp bed, I can stop whenever I want to and I do not have to worry about hotels. In pursuit of mountains, I have for many years past driven to a point somewhere near the range I wish to climb – in rough country it may be several miles away – got out, and started walking. A week or so later, descending a mountain, I have the comfort of knowing that down in the plain my yellow Beetle, with food and fresh clothing in it, will be waiting for me under a tree, or by a farmer's hut, or surrounded by cows.

Car Crime

Here in Uganda the motor car is the symbol *par excellence* of status. It takes priority over a man's house – it is, indeed, a sort of house in its own right, a 'moving house', with glass windows. comfortable seats, ash-trays and electric light, perhaps a radio.

But whatever blessings it has brought, the car in Uganda is a major source of crime, mischief and unhappiness. It causes road deaths. It attracts the thief. It is used by hold-up gangs. Amin's security agents abduct their victims in cars – the boot treatment. The car often confers unmerited status on its owner, and is a source of debt.

No matter that Uganda is one of the world's poorest countries, whose average inhabitant does not even own a bicycle. The number of cars is greatly out of proportion to the country's poverty and debt.

The government car-purchase loan scheme has traditionally enabled officials to take their choice of an expensive Continental car or some cheaper model from Britain or Japan. The

Volkswagen Beetle has long since ceased to confer prestige. It has become the office clerk's or the poor taxi driver's car. Nowadays it is the size of the automobile that counts. But the government car loan has to be paid off. Nagged by debt and garage bills, the owner is tempted to overclaim for mileage expenses or to find other ways of fiddling the money he needs.

Since the Indians were expelled and their cars, vans and lorries either seized, stolen, or sold by auction, a whole new class of African driver, including low-ranking soldiers, wives and girls, has suddenly appeared on the roads. That the owner may live in a house or room with little furniture and naked children playing in a dirty compound, is irrelevant. He has a car. He is *somebody*. Though the price of a second-hand car has trebled since Amin's take-over, there are always buyers.

Observing the conglomeration of expensive cars in Kampala, parked outside hotels, bars, offices and squalid huts, on pavements, at roundabouts and in gardens, one has the impression that if petrol supplies were to dry up, or if repair facilities ceased entirely, there would no longer be an élite. Who can imagine a permanent secretary or an army captain on a bicycle?

The taxi business – it has always been largely piratical despite government attempts to control it – encourages a market for stolen vehicles and parts. Many dealers in motor spares rely directly or indirectly on car thieves. Down the murram lane below Lugard's hill, along the back alleys of Nakivubo, there are sheds crammed with dubiously acquired junk. The Indian dealer sitting in his little office on Visram Street could produce almost anything you wanted.

Uganda's death rate is one of the highest in the world. Who of us here has not had friends or acquaintances killed?

It is all very well to say that children, ignorant villagers, wobbling cyclists, cows or dust clouds are to blame for accidents. The driver's attitude is the key to them – his contempt for the rules of safe driving, the elation at feeling power under his foot. ('Drivers knock you down,' complained a Mr Omeli in a letter to the *Voice of Uganda* on 5 August 1972, 'and run away as if they had knocked down a fox or a rat.') This attitude is the product of a society where, though people mourn loudly at a death bed, there is little respect for life and not much for the law.

Having said this, in the accents, I fear, of auntie, let me confess that despite – perhaps because of – the gay and reckless indifference with which lorries race private cars, and motorists who are drunk steer into ditches or meet in fearful collisions on the open road, I enjoy motoring in Uganda.

There is drama in it: heat and glare; sudden torrential rain storms; the clash of temperament between motorists of different racial backgrounds. Drivers here are not the grim-faced robots of Western Europe, tailing each other in silent fury from one traffic block to another, steering with mathematical precision along triple lanes bordered by barriers and kerbstones. The Uganda motorist is an individualist: a rebel, unpredictable.

And there are those great stretches of lonely, open road running through papyrus swamps, bush and woodland: the red murram tracks that coil through thickets where the colobus monkey peeps out of a tree and borassus palms tower like marble pillars; the green serpentines of Kigezi; night journeys through the black shadows of countryside that smells of rotting leaves and gives out the tinkling music of frogs.

Tips

Here, for what they are worth, are a few tips for survival. Beware of military vehicles, of those green painted garbage trucks with a row of dustmen clinging to the back among the flying rubbish, of contractors' tipper lorries which thunder along on private errands, of stationary vehicles that, without warning, are likely to pull out in front of you.

Allow for cyclists without brakes or lights, drunks, people who rush blindly out of bars, markets and trading centres.

Do not overtake through a cloud of dust. Do not drive over ant-hills – even the smallest are like lumps of concrete. At night, look out for almost invisible villagers meandering along the roadside. Always, always, expect the worst.

No Evidence

The only thief I have ever caught was not the dwarf who climbed through a window and made off with my shirt and shoes, but someone else's thief.

Near Kololo airstrip I saw an Englishman in office collar

and tie pounding along the verge of the road. He was shouting and pointing. The African he was chasing was 200 yards away and rapidly disappearing. Though the road was full of lunch-time traffic, no one stopped.

'Get in,' I said to the man.

'The shit's pinched my briefcase,' he panted.

The thief, as we jumped out of my car, turned into some waste land, dropping the briefcase, which my companion picked up (I never saw him again). Some Africans helped me to run down the thief in a shed. I took him in a state of terror – he was a young Mugisu – to the police station.

'Where is the stolen briefcase?' asked the police officer on duty.

'The owner recovered it.'

'No briefcase,' said the police officer, 'no evidence. Charge dismissed.'

Some days later I had a letter of thanks from the man I had helped. It was signed 'Bryan Lea'. The name meant nothing to me until, a month afterwards, it hit the Press headlines. Mr Lea, a senior official of the British High Commission's Immigration Department, was being accused by the Uganda Government of a kidnapping hoax and of corruption. A great and exaggerated fuss was made of the affair. Obote's government, quite naturally, was immensely pleased to be able to show the world that a white – indeed, a British – diplomat was 'only human' too. Mr Lea was in due course deported.

What, I wondered, when I read the reports of the trial, was in that black briefcase? A middle-aged man in collar and necktie does not sprint, on a hot day, after a ham sandwich.

Thief Beating

The first time I stopped a man from being lynched was in the yard of a petrol station late at night. A crowd was watching four men at work on the victim. When I got him to the police station, a constable rose from his chair and punched the fellow on the back of his neck. After a few more blows, he lay down like a dog.

'What's he done?' the policeman then asked me.

One morning (in January 1971) in the main shopping road

of Kampala I stood over the body of a shop-lifter. A labourer had just split his head open with a stone. The man was alive but the labourer's mates were keen to finish him off. They had all picked up heavy stones and were perched like gargoyles on the wall that fenced their building site from the pavement. When the labourers began to drum on the wall and to jeer at me, I thought I was going to lose control. But I did not intend to give in. Then an African – an educated man with a Makerere beard – joined me. It was twenty minutes before a police car arrived.

'You are a fool to protect *kondos*,' say my African friends, '*kondos* are enemies. *Kondos* must be killed.'

How, though, can we be sure that the man who is being beaten to death is really a thief? Anyone can shout 'Stop thief!' and with the cruel ululations that freeze one's blood start a hue and cry after the wrong rabbit. And is it right to kill a man for stealing a pair of shoes? To beat people to death in the street? Are not the thief-beaters often loafers and *kondos* themselves?

Gunmen

One night, soon after Amin's take-over, I saw two men chasing a third – a big fellow, lacerated and naked except for his striped underpants – round the car park in front of the Grand Hotel. Watching from the balcony was a crowd of waiters and guests.

One of the two men held a pistol. He was jabbering with rage and hysteria. I went up to him and said, in my school-master's voice, 'You're not to kill him here.'

'Go away,' said the gunman. 'We are army officers.'

The naked man, as he dodged for his life among the parked cars, was splashing them with little drops of blood. I tried again.

'If you kill that man here,' I said, 'I'll report you to General Amin. Moreover,' I added, 'I have written down the number of your car.'

It worked. The two officers drove off, no doubt to finish their business elsewhere. The waiters and the guests went back to the lounge. A Norwegian from Nairobi invited me to a brandy. 'You do have fun in Kampala,' he said.

Injustice

The villager who chops up his wife with an axe, or burns his neighbour's hut and the owner with it, will be brought to court. But if the witnesses, for reasons of their own, refuse to give him away, or the defence lawyer, with his educated tongue, confuses them, or the police make a hash of their case, he will be discharged.

The embezzler, the forger, the public servant who takes bribes, when they are brought to a Uganda court, may escape punishment through a technicality of the law (the prosecution's presentation of its case, and police evidence, are often muddled; or a vital file is missing). If they are found guilty, the accused go to gaol, and they survive. It is the petty thief, the youth or the old man, caught with a chicken or a cassava stick under his arm, who pays for his clumsiness with his life. Africans of the lower sort, and villagers, have a habit of lynching him on the spot.

It is an ugly thing to see the killers – corner boys, labourers with lumps of wood, men with heavy stones – hurrying towards their victim. The thief, in his thin torn shirt, his arms pinioned, rolls his eyes in terror and looks in vain for help. Cars pass by. Children run up to watch. A blow fells him, and the battering of flesh begins.

The corpse is left on the ground, the killers vanish. Children stare at it. Women, holding their hands over their mouths, as though they fear the dead man's ghost, stand round like cows. The soles of the dead man's feet shine ivory white against the dark insteps. A boy has stolen his shoes.

An Observation on Crime

The 'man with the Makerere beard' turned out to be Mr Musa T. Mushanga, who as it happened was doing research into crime in Uganda. In an article, 'Observations on Crime in Uganda' (*Mawazo*, Vol. 2, No. 4, Kampala, December 1970), he makes the following observations, which have relevance to some of my own remarks in this chapter:

'There is a generalised lack of faith and trust in law-enforcing agencies. . . . The people know the wrong-doers, they know people who possess firearms illegally, they know who brews and sells illicit waragi, they know the *kondos*; but they are reluctant to communicate this knowledge to the authorities for a number of reasons. One important reason is lack of faith and trust in the law-enforcing agencies. If people begin to regard such agencies as "equally bad" then they will be less interested in giving information regarding wrong-doers. Again, there is great fear of retaliation by the criminals. When criminals find out who reported them to the police, they will attack the reporter. In fact, the tendency is to be as friendly with criminals (especially thieves) as possible if one has to live in a village of thieves and *kondos*. A lot of crimes are committed, and people know about them. . . . Most people live under fear. Fear of robbers who are also murderers; fear of saying what one knows to be the truth; and because of this, people keep quiet and crime spreads. There is also fear of the police, the magistrate and the judge. . . .

'Instead of joining hands with the law-enforcing agencies, people in some parts of Uganda have responded in an unlawful manner by organising the "vigilantes" and the "999" groups to patrol their villages at night to combat robber gangs. This is a response, I conjecture, which is likely to arise spontaneously when society views the law-enforcing agencies as either inefficient, or as inadequate or both. People have a right to be protected by the state and when they define the protection the state gives them as insufficient, then they respond by taking the law into their own hands. Hence the practice of thief-beating that is very prevalent in Uganda. Such measures must be discouraged. Very often they involve innocent individuals.'

'Uganda Argus' Report
Here, from the countless reports of thief-beating that have appeared in the *Uganda Argus*, is one extract (29 October 1970):

'I saw it. They beat him, they kicked him, they jumped on his chest and stepped on his head. He cried like a strangled goat. He cried to be allowed to explain.

'The more he cried the more they dealt him blows. With

difficulty he crept under a parked bus, but one of the "blood-hounds" followed him and pulled him out for a second round of torture.

'Half dead as he was, the thugs – ticket examiners, conductors, and some passengers – continued to beat him. Then some of them decided to strip their victim naked.

'It all started when someone yelled "omubi!" (bad man) and the man was set upon. This is a common experience in Kampala bus park. All it needs is for someone to shout "omubi" and a person is knocked down and beaten.'

Here is another item from the *Uganda Argus* (27 September 1972):

'A judge has said that it is not the law of this country that suspected thieves can be beaten to death.

'Mr Justice Mead was jailing Matiya Sengendo, a muluka chief, to 4½ years for the part he played in beating five suspected thieves.

'Sengendo had jointly been charged with seventeen villagers on a charge of murder. In his judgment yesterday, Mr Justice Mead acquitted eleven of them of murder and found the six guilty of minor offence, that of occasioning actual bodily harm.

'Among the six who were found guilty were Yozefu Bosa and his wife Topista Wasaka Bosa. The husband was sentenced to 2½ years and the wife to fifteen months imprisonment.

'It was the prosecution's case that Sengendo gathered the villagers and ordered them to arm themselves with pangas and sticks. The men were arrested, tied and beaten from 9.30 a.m. until 2 p.m. when they died.

'Relatives of the accused who were acquitted, danced in jubilation after the court had adjourned.'

The Tragedy of Lynching

On the phenomenon of lynching, A. F. Raper (*The Tragedy of Lynching*, New York, 1970) has written:

'Mobs do not come out of the nowhere; they are the logical outcome of dominant assumptions and prevalent thinking.

Lynchings are not the work of men suddenly possessed of a strange madness; they are the logical issues of prejudice and lack of respect for law and personality, plus a sadistic desire to participate in the excitement of mob trials and the brutalities of mob torture and murder.'

On the former American practice of lynching, the author quotes these figures: 3,724 people were lynched in the United States between 1889 and 1930. Over four-fifths of them were negroes. Practically all of the lynchers were native white.

This was racialism and not, as practised in Uganda, a mixture of traditional sanctions and revenge feelings, and a sport.

CHAPTER 15

Women[1]

Liaisons

Let us look at the European relationship with African women as it may be observed in Uganda at certain obvious levels – bearing in mind that in these days the subject can be discussed without embarrassment, that liaisons are far more frequent than they used to be (clean young Englishmen found guilty of going with native women are no longer reprimanded by the High Commissioner's wife), and also that since this is a matter of the private lives of individuals one must be wary of generalisations.

There is, to begin with, the orthodox love affair – it is increasingly common, and sometimes leads to marriage – between the type of young teacher or social welfare worker and an African student or colleague.

The relationship is 'respectable'. It does not (as is more likely in the case of a white man's affair with a semi-literate mistress from a shoe-shop or the City Bar) have to be denied or kept secret. The mercenary factor does not predominate. The couple are not only exploring, in each other, worlds that used to be taboo and are still mysterious. They are striking a small blow for personal freedom against the ingrained codes of white predecessors, of some present colleagues, and of traditional African society itself.

If they marry, they are expected to have children, who are likely to be honey-coloured, beautiful, and intelligent; yet for

[1] The account that follows of the European sex relationship with African women should be taken as especially true of the situation as it was up to the mass departure of Europeans (and Indians) from Uganda that started in autumn 1972. The resultant changes in the social situation and atmosphere have affected that relationship. I have remarked on these changes at the end of this chapter.

7a Teuso on the Turkana
escarpment

7b Teuso porters in camp

7c Teuso porters at waterhole

8a Elgon summit

8b Kadam summit

all that, no matter where they live, will grow up to face special difficulties both of their own and of other people's making.

Then there is the older man – he may be a veteran in his fifties – who has taken up with an African *bibi*. To manage her successfully it is imperative to get her away from her own African society and give her the status of mistress in his own house. Once he has installed her in his home the relationship may be durable, happy and exciting. The man's days of virility may be almost over, while the woman's body, younger, fleshy, and shining with food purchased from the best grocers, grows riper and more sensual. Never mind, a smart car and a generous house-keeping allowance will go a long way to make up for his imperfections as a lover. But he must be patient with the black moods that come over her when, from time to time, she feels she has uprooted herself from her true origins and taken refuge with a stranger.

It is inevitable that in setting up house with an African woman a man may have had to destroy his own former life with a white wife. The latter is sent away, or she leaves him. Thenceforth in some corner of the British Isles she awaits her monthly cheque, which is not only a burden on the wicked husband and frustrating for his new partner, but if it is not forthcoming, produces a solicitor's letter. He lives, then, under the shadow of his native British law: paying twice over for each embrace. An African can escape this predicament. Custom allows him, like Chanticleer, to take co-wives under his wing.

Then there are the many Europeans who maintain discreetly, furtively, or in absolute secrecy an affair with an African girl friend. These liaisons may run smoothly for a long time, but they have a nasty habit of dying suddenly and unexpectedly on the man. He visits his love-nest one day to find the bird has flown. She, however, is likely to have planned for long her flight and its exact moment. Having obtained just what she wanted from her white lover – a nice bank balance, a plot, a small house – she has calculated that it was time for her to leave him: to rejoin her own African people and to raise her own black children among them. The man, if he is a realist, will accept the simple logic of her behaviour. 'Enjoy what you have now.

Do not seek to own it', might have been her motto had she cared to express it.

Bars

Most Europeans, though, who want to take an African woman to bed, do not bother with permanent liaisons. They go to the tarts who attach themselves to bars and night clubs. At this level there is no intrusion. The man has paid – as he pays for a hair-cut – for a single act.

Most Europeans, too, avoid the worst sort of prostitutes – the street walkers in greasy turbans and floppy sandals who hiss to attract your attention, the Congolese whores who quarrel and fight in the back streets of Mengo, the fat girls from low-class bars who are not above suggesting a 'quickie' in the lavatory.

The score or more of chirruping girls who operate from the Hibiscus Bar must have squeezed a small fortune out of the pale loins of white men. This sort of girl is generally young, slender, and healthy looking (though their wigs may smell of glue, and the grease with which they anoint their bodies leaves a smudge on the edge of their clothes). The younger girls, not the older women, speak Primary Seven English. All practise the direct approach. Having touched you for a bottle of beer and assessed to their satisfaction your immediate worth in cash, they put one hand firmly on your thigh and fight off rivals.

Another rendezvous is the lounge bar of the International Hotel. The women sit there quietly, thighs slightly apart showing (before Amin banned the mini-skirt) burnished and often matronly knees the colour of roasted coffee berries. An inexperienced eye might take some of them for housewives waiting for a bus. They specialise in netting the furtive husband and foreign visitors. Who can blame Mr Ohlssen[1] from Uppsala for preferring their embraces to that copy of The Gideon's Bible which an American orgainsation has placed on the bedside table next to his pillow? Who can chide him for his small act of marital betrayal when Felicitas smiles into his face with twenty white teeth each planted perfectly in the crimson gums?

Attempts are made from time to time to remove these

---

[1] Messrs Ohlssen, Tonks, Squipps and Tompkins are fictitious but typical characters and any similarity to real persons is purely coincidental.

courtesans from the three central hotels. They always come back, slipping in through the French windows or in the footsteps of some worthy unsuspecting fellow plodding towards the bar. Their goal is the night club on the sixteenth floor of the International Hotel. Once they have got past its doorman they have not only achieved temporary social status; there are scores of customers to choose from.

There are times when the neighbouring Copper Bar is a dull place with just a few weary looking fellows blinking sluggishly through a haze of stale cigarette smoke; and there are nights when it is bursting with people waving bank notes at the barman. The Copper Bar was at its gayest soon after Amin's takeover, when most of Kampala's night clubs closed early for fear of trouble, and a shoal of tarts migrated from their outlying haunts to the relatively safe and affluent central hotel area. For several months the Copper Bar did a roaring trade. Red and balding Mr Tonks, calling there for a last drink, would find some unpaid beer chits pushed in front of him and the next moment two gay creatures stroking his groin. A priest in what looked like a goalkeeper's jersey ('God made the Church, but the Devil made priests'), a distinguished anthropologist, and a Norwegian diplomat would be penned happily within the scrum of chocolate legs. White wives used to take one look at the prodding, the hugging, and the stroking, and hurry their husbands away.

Jugoslav workers – 400 of them were brought from Belgrade to erect Obote's conference centre and hotel – joined in the fun. At first, after their arrival in Kampala, they had walked about in shy, melancholy groups, citizens of a poor, semi-Communist corner of Europe who had been dropped from the sky into an exotic relic of colonialist exploitation. They looked muscle-bound and surly, weighed down with inferiority feelings, as they clumped up and down on their evening walk past the bright hotel lights. They wore coarse Balkan trousers and shirts, and they had no spending money.

Once they had accumulated a little cash, the bolder ones grew side-burns, invaded the hotel bars and badgered the girls. But they had no English at all. Worse, the girls knew they could raise only a few shillings apiece. Only the toughest sort of tart was prepared to let two or three Serbian carpenters walk her to their dormitory for a grand total of twenty shillings.

The Jugoslavs looked with envy at our cars and bulging wallets. 'Colonialism,' one of them said to me, 'is a fine thing.' 'My friend,' another confessed, 'has caught a very bad syphilis.' When I boasted of having bicycled four times through their country they disbelieved me. But I impressed the Belgrade lawyer attached to their party when I told him how *Izvestia* had once referred to me as 'Major Gills, a Fascist Major.'

'You may certainly be proud of that,' he said. 'Good night, Fascist Major.'

Night Shadows

It is not wise to pick up just any girl, especially the sort who will take you back to slums and shanty areas that teem with pimps and thieves. It will be a shock to wake up in some wretched hut to find your wallet gone, your trousers stolen, or your car stripped of its wheels; embarrassing to be stuck at night in a boggy ground-nut plot from which rutted tracks lead into an alarming maze of shadows.

O pale and vulnerable white man, alone in the black night of Africa with your motor car, your nicely calculated future, and the pound notes in your shirt pocket! If you are set on now, robbed and cut by the silent men who spring out of shadows, there will be no faithful houseboy, no Rwanda watchman, to come to your aid. Fear, a missed heart-beat or two, a painful flurry of self-reproaches – a prayer? Let it be a lesson to you, O night wanderer, not to stir from your peaceful rose garden into the secret and violent places of the poor man's Africa!

I once, in a Mengo street after dark, saw a whore stripping a respectable looking Indian of his jacket and mohair cardigan. A group of men was looking on. As I drove up I saw fear on the man's face. The woman had already snatched his car keys.

'Help me,' he whispered.

I did my white policeman act, and the affair was over in a few seconds. The watching Africans went back into the shadows. Indians, in a street row with Africans, are at a disadvantage. They are timid, they are not respected, and their only hope is to buy themselves out of trouble. Sikhs, hard-fisted and feared, are different. An African, on the other hand, given a chance, will often stand up and fight till blood flows. But surrounded by a mob, he is done for.

Yes, there are the harridans who will summon a fellow with a stick if you dispute the price: the ruthless ones who lock their victim in with the cockroaches until he has paid a ransom; and the sort who conduct their white man to a spring bed without a mattress which leaves him with grazed knees and elbows and a pain across the back.

There is the girl who will take you home, introduce you even like a prize steer to her parents, on condition you undertake to buy her a wig (a kind of bride price?). And there are those fat jolly women in *busuti* gowns who in the smaller bars drink eight bottles of beer on a Saturday night, waggle their buttocks in front of the juke-box, and when they go out to the yard to relieve themselves take you by the hand and expect you to stand by till they have finished.

Girls who have been successful, or in business for a long time, often have their own little cement and breeze-block houses which a former lover has paid for and which local masons have built for her, bit by bit, from her irregular payments. Their houses are not always quite finished. There may have been a quarrel, or her patron may have been posted away, before the ceiling and the paint could be added.

Beware of presenting these women, in a moment of vanity, with your photograph. They keep sheaves of them, and your picture will compromise you, or cause hilarity, when shown to other visitors. That fellow grinning idiotically behind his trade sign – why, it's Mr Squipps! And look at the pathetic little phrase, 'I love you, Topista' which he has written on the back. Who would have thought that such a worthy man . . .

Most girls, though, rent little rooms with a table, chair and transistor set, and a bed screened off by a curtain that is draped with her dresses and underwear. They see to it that their clients can drive up to the door without fouling a huge stone or falling into a half-dug latrine pit. It is the lower sort who live in poor huts among the dust and mud of neglected *shambas*, or in shanties. Their visitors must put up with an overpowering smell of stale urine, cockroaches, the shouts and groans of drunkards, the risk of police raids. Stumbling out of these dens in the morning, with a jigger in your foot, is like emerging from hell.

What, one may ask, is the incidence of venereal disease in these relationships? An Indian businessman once boasted to me that he had been 'wounded' eleven times. Among Makerere students gonorrhoea is so common that they call it 'catching a cold'. 'The halls of residence,' a student told me blithely, 'compete against each other for the highest statistics.'

Attraction

What is it that attracts a white man to African women? In days gone by it would have been easy enough to say what *repelled* (or is alleged to have repelled) him, namely ignorance, fear, prudery, and physical distaste which he expressed (not necessarily with conviction) in allusions to blubber lips, body odour, steatopygia, heathenism, the whole rigmarole of disparagement codified into official attitudes that were intended as a self-protective device for a heavily outnumbered minority group bent on survival.

Graham Greene, brooding (one imagines) over an aperitif with the expression of a melancholy bloodhound, has put this reflection on the conflict between prejudice and attraction into the mind of his police officer Scobie, looking at an African girl.

'He thought: how beautiful she is. It was strange to think that fifteen years ago he would not have noticed her beauty – the small high breasts, the tiny wrists, the thrust of the young buttocks, she would have been indistinguishable from her fellows – a black. In those days he had thought his wife beautiful. A white skin had not then reminded him of an albino. Poor Louise. . . . He watched her go out of the office like fifteen wasted years.'

Yet when it comes to actual physical contact Greene shies away. All he can manage is a brothel scene of farce and squalor.

'. . . the left-hand cell was occupied: in the light of an oil lamp burning on the floor he saw a girl in a dirty shift spread out on the packing cases like a fish on the counter; her bare pink soles dangled over the words "Tate's Sugar" . . . She grinned at Wilson, not bothering to sit up, and said, "Want jig jig, darling? Ten bob."'

Let us not, with hindsight, ridicule those early and still potent fantasies or forget the early 'culture-shock' which underlay them. Sexual attraction must always have been present, asserting a threat to the maintenance of a dominant white caste and its authority that had to be repressed by sanctions.

So what is it that draws so many white men to African women? Is it the large, soft eyes, the cool, glossy skin and its texture – smoothly firm like the sleek hide of a pony? The happy, dazzling smile that has the spontaneity of childhood? The powerful and responsive sex organs? Is it the physical difference, the desire of a deodorised white man from Stoke-on-Trent or Copenhagen to handle and possess something that is easily aroused? A sublimation of his white hunter's instinct to trap and violate the wild thing in its thicket? Is it her good natured tolerance of one's flaws, her ability to sit placidly, her apparent lack of nervous tensions, her old-fashioned deference to the male? Or is it, as one white-haired and giggling Englishman put it to me in a bar, 'The African girl knows how to take the c . . k?'

One is not sure of the answers. It is not simply a matter of enjoying a compliant black body. There may be a vague and perhaps unrecognised desire to expiate one's guilt feeling towards 'blacks'; to erase one's share of the colonial past in an act of love-making; deliberately to find at the body's level the human equality between black and white that society and one's preconditioned prejudices still try to deny.

There is also the loneliness of the white man living among Africans in Africa. The first African baby that he tries to lift from its mother's arms on to his lap flinches from his white face and starts to howl. He has been rebuffed. There are times when listening to the melodious voices, watching the gentle movement of hands, seeing those dark shapes glide over tall grass into the elusive shadows of their private lives, he feels a powerful urge to identify himself with the dark people. And what more intimate than the act of intercourse?

What of the act itself? It is protracted (the woman is used to men of stamina). She expects him, as his first duty, to excite her, to employ his penis as a rubbing-stick. (There are, it is said, polite girls who cry '*Asanti sana* – thank you very much', while this is being done; or '*Wangi sebo* – I am here, sir,' as penetration takes place.) Some Uganda women have deliberately, as children, been taught by an aunt to lengthen the clitoris and the labia minora by pulling them. Baganda men are said to prefer a woman who has thus manipulated herself. The enlarged and greedy parts, adjusted for maximum sensation, fit cosily over the penis like a hat.[1]

She likes you to hold her waist, to caress the small of her back; there may be here a row of tiny keloids which are intended to excite a man when he touches them. Do not disarrange or damage her wig, and do not show aversion to large and protruding buttocks.[2] Provided they are firm, they are her pride, and you should praise them. Intercourse may be accompanied by spurts of *maji*: a token of her body's surrender to the man.

When the battle is over, and if the woman is pleased with you, she will give you a gentle slap before scrupulously washing and drying your genitals with a cloth. The moment she puts on her nightwear you know that it is time to go. Do not irritate her by dawdling; and take care, as you walk out, not to kick or break her jars and cooking pots.

I do not suggest that a majority of Europeans fornicate with African women, or what is obviously not true, that a majority of Uganda women run after European men. The average European is happily married or solidly entrenched among his own kith and kin. He does not seriously scheme to take a black woman to bed. Many more white men (and women too) would no doubt experiment if they had the courage. But in our hearts we are afraid of Africans: afraid of their blackness, of their reputed sexual demands, of their impenetrable background. Was the girl's father a pagan? Did her mother deliver

---

[1] See also notes on pp. 170, 249–51.
[2] A critical moment in the encounter is when the wig comes off. There is a moment of shock. The women's head and face, dominated now by nose and mouth, belong to a more primitive Africa.

her in a corner of some banana *shamba*? Was her umbilical cord severed with a blade of elephant grass? How many hidden worms and viruses have malnutrition and malaria in childhood implanted in her constitution?

As for the ethics of paying for a woman's services, the crumpled bank notes that she tucks into her brassière (where they are safer than in her handbag) will probably be turned into life-giving blood, into *matoke* for her family, into lamp oil, into school fees and clothes, as well as into trashy dresses and bleaching creams. The fornicator, realising this, may take some moral consolation. It should at any rate remind him to be generous towards his partner rather than haggle over the change.

Finally let us admit that in a physical sense the African woman plays her part well, and that in making a gift of her body to Tompkins, she is often (though she may not realise it) giving more than she receives. Who, after enjoying her generous responses, would want to bother with the ravings of Germaine Greer, who sees men as butchers or eunuchs and woman as a clitoris-dominated sex apparatus craving a mechanic to manipulate the right buttons?

The emotional side of one's relationship with her is another matter. It is crippled if it can only be expressed in kitchen Swahili. There are times when she hates us for our tidiness, our haste and abruptness, our food that looks like cooked faeces, and when in our clumsiness we tread on her ancestral shrine. An ill-considered word, a misunderstood gesture, and a mask closes over her face.

POSTSCRIPT

Change

The main changes affecting the picture I have given above include the banning of mini-skirts (offenders – they have included some European women – are charged with being 'idle and disorderly persons'), and of wigs (the soldiers are reported to have told Amin they were 'stinking'), growing pressure on women not to be friendly with Europeans, and of course the mass exodus of Europeans and Indians which has diminished the old night life and left hundreds of foot-loose African women stranded. It is thought that Amin banned the mini-skirt in deference to orthodox Moslem-Arab scruples and under the influence of his new friendship with Colonel Gadaffi and King Feisal. Educated African women have especially resented this act of male interference with their rights.

The army and its sinister associates (vicious young men in smoked glasses and clownish hats) do not approve of African women going out with Europeans. Couples have been insulted or beaten up.

Following the exodus of Europeans and Indians a great many African women have had to transfer their favours to Libyans, Somalis, half-castes, and Africans. This extension of sexual promiscuity has led to a marked (and already publicised) increase of venereal disease in Kampala.

The old professionals have survived. Their familiar faces, a little raddled now, still smile from behind the potted plants at the Speke Hotel.

Anatomy

I have just come across Dr John Baker's learned notes (*Race*, 1974) on the *naturally* enlarged labia minora of the Bushwomen and Hottentots which early attracted the curiosity of white men ('the two labia minora, enormously lengthened, and adhering to look like an unpaired organ'). Dr Baker does not comment on the erotic significance of this peculiarity, nor does he mention the practice – well known among the Baganda and the Banyankole – of artificially elongating the clitoris and labia to give a greater area of engorgement and sexual pleasure. When excited the parts swell and the labia separate.

CHAPTER 16

Neighbours

Tenants

In front of me is a hedge with holes in it. Through the holes I can see a scruffy compound where a girl is braiding her sister's hair into little spikes like candle-wicks, and a woman, using wood chopped from the hedge, is cooking in what used to be the outside toilet. Behind me is a green hill with a television mast on it, at its foot the Sudanese Embassy whose flag is tied to a crooked pole; a man is urinating against the Embassy hedge.

I am sitting in my garden, near the mango tree. I have been slashing the grass, which is an insane occupation because as soon as I have finished one patch I have to start all over again. Left for a fortnight, two-foot long stalks sprout up, on which fire-finches balance.

I think of it as *my* garden, but it is not. I am just one of six tenants, or tenant families, who share it. Yet, since I first took on the job of slashing the grass and cleaning out the storm drains – if I do not, they get blocked with grease and bones from the servants' quarters – I have established a sort of wardenship over the garden.

Moreover, I am, by length of tenancy, the senior resident. Since I first moved into what was then a smart white building where white faces peered through every window, I have seen over a score of tenants come and go. There is only one other white face today. Mr R. is a recluse. Insulated behind trails of cockroach powder, he listens to Bach.

To confirm my standing I have had built in one corner of the garden a thatched hut to read in. With Ingrid I have planted shrubs, trees and flowers, watered and watched them grow, and prevented my neighbours from chopping them for firewood. I am hostile to cats and dogs. I turn away pedlars of wood carvings and banana-fibre mosaics, youths trying to sell bogus charity tickets, strangers who emerge through the hedge.

Some of my fellow tenants have resented my proprietary behaviour. The New Zealand doctor, when I was slashing the grass one afternoon, bawled at me, 'For God's sake stop arseing about!' I used to catch Mrs S., in hair curlers, squinting at me from behind her curtains on the upstairs floor. She saw an angry-looking fellow in torn shorts prowling about with a hoe. She knew I had secreted a pile of stones under a creeper to throw at dogs. Her husband – he was employed by the Public Works Department – said my beautiful thatched pagoda, on which a black-headed heron sometimes perches like a stone weather-cock, was illegal. But neither Mr S. nor his wife had any desire to use the garden. The heat and the glare were too much for them. Not unnaturally they preferred to stay in their cool sitting-room with its Indian brass trays, the brass-studded Mombasa chest, their vacuum cleaner and television set. 'You're too much in the sun,' she shouted at me one day. 'It's spoiling your brain.'

George the police officer from Teso appeared only two or three times in the garden, where he sat under the *nsambya* tree, talking to himself, with a mug of *waragi* which he refilled from an oil can. One night, when he was very drunk, he stood outside our windows and gave tongue to some of the frustrations that were churning within his disordered mind.

'I can see you all,' he cried, 'and I can see your cigarette burning, Mr Jones. I know you don't like me. But I am a police officer. I know you all and I can see you.'

One of the corner flats has its own private garden, protected by an armature of prickly plants. Until recently it was occupied by a series of single European ladies devoted to teaching or to welfare work.[1] They usually kept cats, whose offspring, running wild, twice gave birth to kittens in my wardrobe. Some cats did not last long. Dogs disembowelled them.

---

[1] To stand up to the stresses of Amin's Uganda, a male – a retired colonial officer who lends me *Punch* – has now taken over from the ladies. His orders – regrettable and, one supposes, politically inspired – are to wind up the Uganda branch of his charitable society which a predecessor Miss Enid Levin did so much to promote on behalf of sick and destitute Uganda children.

Cats indeed are out of place in an African garden. They chase away the chameleons and the beautiful blue-headed lizards that bask on trees, and they torture birds. They have scared off the two striped squirrels that used to live in a hole under one of my rose bushes. They break into my room by scratching holes in the window-gauze. A cat once stole my supper.

One lady had a large sex-starved dog which she exercised on a lead, standing by as it peed against my car. Rover once broke free and lolloping through the garden like a bullock, instantly knocked over a playmate of my small boy. Blood and howls, and a charge entered by the boy's German mother at the police station.

Yes, along with porridge oats and afternoon tea we have introduced our suburban brand of neighbour problems to Africa. Here, in the hot sun and the glare, tempers rise more readily to the surface. 'I hate your guts,' shouted the owner of the sex-starved dog at me one day.

How irritating it is, and sometimes sad, to hear one's neighbours' private noises! The love-making, the clatter of Indian brassware thrown against a wall, the abuse ('Swine! Bastard!') and the oaths. There was the African wife of a Dane who would sob uncontrollably for days. There was George's house-girl who, when he had locked her out for some misdemeanour, would howl all night on the verandah. There was 'Cloth Ears': when drunk, he used to fall backwards and gash his neck on a window catch. There are the outbursts of yelling mingled with thumps from the African doctor's house.

Now that almost all the local tenants are Africans, there is the throb of transistor music. Above me I can hear a hammering noise that has brought a crack into the ceiling. It is the Lugbara wife pounding grain on the cement floor.

As for the tumult that comes from the servants' quarters on Sundays and pay days, by nightfall laughter has turned to quarrelling and a little wife-beating.

Changes

The years that I have spent in this government flat dug solidly into a hill have brought changes. The American pine that

Ingrid planted six years ago is now over thirty feet tall. An *nsambya* tree, born of some stray seed, has shot up like an exclamation mark in front of my window, balancing bright yellow flowers which the wind tosses untidily among the spikes of aloes. The mangos, whose fruit, stringy and sour, remains uneatable, have thickened with the years and put on huge crowns of verminous foliage whose blossom turns black with a sweet smell of decay.

The moonflower tree and the red rose bushes left behind by an English lady in the days of the Protectorate have survived, but only just; for they are constantly attacked by white ants which have erected a mound like a great chocolate pudding. The old pawpaws have gone, blown down by gusts of wind, and with them the mouse-birds that used to tear wounds in the fruit and the urchins who crept through the hedge to share it.

I have not heard the wail of the hadada ibis for some months. But crimson-breasted shrikes still skulk, and whistle and rasp in instant duet, among the hibiscus trumpets. Robin chats, when they think they are unobserved, pour out notes of purest melody. A pair of sparrow hawks has lately tried to settle in the eucalyptus tree which was once spotted with weavers' nests, long rotted and dashed to the ground. With ferocious piping anger they drive off kites and crows.

Noisiest and most vulgar of the birds are the plantain eaters, chasing and mounting each other with mad laughter in tree tops. Tiniest are the fire-finches, brightest the iridescent sun-birds that flash and twinkle in the tick-berry bush. Ugliest are the vultures that, attracted by offal, crack sooty wings on the roof.

It is some time since I saw a mongoose sneaking along the storm drain. A great many dogs have come and gone; dogs like foxes, like debased wolf-hounds, like hyenas; pyedogs, dachs-hunds, whippet-like dogs, and large brindled animals. They have unpleasant habits, using my doorstep and my pagoda as a lavatory. When a bitch is on heat they chase her in a pack for days and nights, moaning, slavering, and tearing at each other's legs and ears as they pound past my window under a clouded moon. Regularly they knock over the dustbins (I drag mine into the *dhobi* room before I go to bed) with a crash that sounds like burglars breaking in, and scatter and scavenge the contents. They bark at friends, run away from thieves.

I chased a persistent mob of dogs one night into a nearby garden and laid about them with a stick. As they ran off howling, a light came on in the house to show five men watching me in silence. Next morning the police charged me with trespass and with cruelty to animals. I got no sympathy when I protested that the dogs had recently bitten the captain of the Kampala Sports Club cricket team in the leg, that they fouled my doorstep and kept me awake at night.

'That, sir, is no excuse for breaking into a gentleman's compound at 2 a.m. and beating his animals,' said the police officer.

'And now,' he added, 'let me have your finger-prints.'

Among my fellow tenants who have come and gone have been a dozen expatriates on two-year contracts, and a few African officials. The latter need more space for their children, and are generally off as soon as they can find a detached house of their own. There was the young New Zealand doctor who was immediately burgled. He did not, to my disappointment, show the Anzac spirit that had impressed the Turkish bashi-bazooks and later Kesselring.

'I could hear the buggers taking stuff out of my living room,' he told me.

'Why didn't you call out?'

'And get bashed with a panga?'

George, the police officer, no longer shouts and stamps in the room over my head. A police car used to bring him back drunk at night. Two policemen would carry him upstairs, salute the body and drive off giggling. George was eventually taken to hospital to be dried out. After his release he seemed to be in a state of shock: a sad, silent man, walking slowly, carrying a carton of milk.

Larry and his wife were the perfect American couple. He taught, rode a bicycle so that his wife could use the car for shopping, played tennis, built a sand-pit for his children, grilled steaks on charcoal. They visited the game parks, took

photographs of lions, spoilt their housegirl by overpaying her.
They liked Africans, and left Uganda before things turned sour.

Children

There have been few children to fill the garden with joy and
noise and broken toys. Our African neighbours seeing over the
years so many childless white tenants must think us impotent,
ill, or debauched. (In fact, families with children are more likely
to reside in the larger detached bungalows of Kampala than in
a government flat with only two bedrooms.)

Safely brought into the world on the fifth floor of Mulago
hospital the young of expatriates are put for a time, like portable
dolls, or picnic lunches, in a wicker basket or a carry-cot, then
entrusted to an *ayah*. Their early preparation for life is a warm
bright world of sunshine, bulbul song and shaggy dogs. Lying
out of doors they look up, not at chimney pots, but at green
foliage in which a sunbird rustles. They ride on the *ayah's*
hip.

In normal times the children of expatriates pass through
multi-racial nursery and preparatory schools until they go
away to school in Kenya or Europe. They return from Britain
with long hair and debased accents. Our children help us, in a
tropical world, to keep sane; to remember – under a hot sun –
Christmas.

As a rule our children – until, at any rate, their teens – are
privileged, and yet restricted. They are driven about in cars.
Because of the bilharzia worm which has spread rather than
diminished throughout Uganda, one can never be sure of
pure streams or lake water for them to swim in. There are
no parental farms, as in Kenya, to provide an outdoor childhood. The monotonous warmth, with no seasonal change,
makes some children sluggish. They are fussed over by
servants.

I used to think – till I got used to it – how pale and fragile
our white Uganda children looked as they lined up outside
their school to be driven home by parents. The fierce sunlight
seemed to bleach them to a transparent pallor. Kenya children,
by comparison, look bronzed, muscular, healthier, more self-
assured. Yet white children in Uganda, if given from time to

time a holiday change of climate, have thrived. And what exotic variety there has been to enrich their lives! In the game parks, crocodiles, lions, and elephants. Giraffes that stand like dazzle-painted pylons by the roadside. A flight of pelicans turning their great beaked heads into the wind as they change course like aerial ships of the line. Christmas at a coral lagoon of the Indian Ocean. My two boys have caught dramatic glimpses of drunks, motor accidents, an occasional corpse. They have heard the hue and cry after thieves, gun fire in the night. Safe in their beds they have got used to the immense detonations and lightning flashes of a tropical storm.

Expatriate children have enjoyed, too, and profited from the experience of having African and Indian playmates. Colour consciousness does not seem to be a problem at this early stage of childhood friendships. My younger boy's hero used to be Freddy, one of a large Munyoro family that overflows into the outhouses next door. Johnny never lacked for toys. When he was not 'doing something' he was bored. Freddy owned nothing but his ragged shirt and shorts and his catapults. But Freddy, his muscular black body shining with sweat, was always cheerful; and necessity had made him inventive. He constructed wheels out of wire, model cars from bits of wood and motor tyre, banana fibre footballs. He knew where to find blind snakes, mongooses, chameleons.

My elder boy Hansen, plied with nutritious food from the best grocer, often preferred to take his meals with African or Indian friends, squatting on the floor to eat, with his fingers, dishes of fried ants or grasshoppers, *matoke* plantains, pumpkins and curry.

At a later stage these early childhood friendships tend to break up. The English and the African boy go their separate ways, through different schools, where they are absorbed into societies that emphasise their own diverse values. An African youth, as he grows up, is increasingly drawn within his own family clan and tribal system, in which he matures and is given early responsibility, so that he tends to look inward. It is to the Indian and the half-caste that many European teenagers find themselves attracted as companions – they wear their jeans and their transparent shirts with panache, they have spending money and Japanese motor cycles that scream like electric drills, their hair is a thicket.[1]

There are not many European children left in Uganda now. An exotic and privileged experience is coming to a temporary end. But not far away, across the border in Kenya, white children still play and swim in glorious sunshine, and see elephants and lions.

Servants

The servants' quarters attached to this block of flats are nothing to be proud of. In truth, the single communal water tap and shower, the squatter-type latrine, the two small cubicles per servant family built round a narrow cement yard, were designed to suit houseboys – preferably single – of impeccable habits who were kept up to the mark by white employers whose authority they respected.

That old authority has gone; and by sub-letting their little rooms to kinsmen and hangers-on, the houseboys and maids have turned their quarters into a warren bursting with strangers. Even the windowless storesheds have been broken open to provide a refuge for schoolboys and for idlers with tarts.

The quarters are a happy, tumultuous place, with music, pots cooking over braziers, drink, and girls.

The worst nuisance were some hard men from Teso who for months used George's vacant servants' rooms as an *enguli* bar. It attracted drunks who roared and urinated and fell down in the grass behind my kitchen. Small boys were posted as look-outs, so that when I persuaded the police to make a raid, all they found was an empty bottle or two and a smell.

One night a watchman got me out of bed to help a drunk who was lying outside his door. As no one else offered to do so ('he is not our brother') I slung the body over my shoulder – it was very light – and humped it to one of the cubicles.

[1] I cannot resist quoting here John Aldridge's description of hippies (*In the Country of the Young*, London, 1970). Among male hippies, he writes, the notion that ugliness ('the hairy simian look') is suggestive of 'ferocious sexual vitality . . . has been carried to the point where hair – usually of exactly the right colour and texture – is worn like a pubic growth covering indiscriminately head, face, groin, and armpits, so that the entire person becomes a sex organ.'

'The man died this morning,' my servant told me next day.

'Who was he?'

'No one knows.'

Myself

What of myself? My shaving mirror shows wrinkles and thinning hair, and two scars: one on my scalp made by a Polish vodka bottle; the other, over my left eye, where I was hit with a shoe.

I have not, so far, caught a tropical disease, or knocked any-one down on the road (I have, however, run over a cat, a cock, and a rabbit).

True, I once had a shock when a little girl bolted out of a hedge a few yards in front of me on the Entebbe Road. As I swerved away from her into the ditch I felt a bang on the side of my car. For an awful moment, as I jumped out and saw a little heap of clothes in the road, I thought I had killed her. But no, there she was, half-way across a field, still running. A minute later a gentle old man in a *kanzu* led her back to me by the hand. The little girl was trembling.

'The child is not hurt,' he said. 'Give her a sweet and take her home.'

The old books that I brought with me from Turkey, now stained by mould and cockroaches, surround me like rusty fossils: the new ones, in their bright dust-jackets (*Confessions of an Indian Woman Eater, Clean Young Englishman, The Common Poisonous Plants of East Africa*, and all the rest), like rows of grinning dentures.

I am attached to old things – my car, my school football shirt, the rug which a Turkish *hodja* let me have cheap because one night on a Hakkari mountain Muzaffer and I had shooed a bear away from his sheep.

I read *The Times* and I am pleased when Warwickshire win the county cricket championship. I have given up wearing the two musty-smelling suits I had made in Turkey. I do not feel, after forty years' absence, that I could settle in England again. Here, at least, in a small community, I am *somebody*. In England I am nothing: a pebble, a nondescript person lost in the anonymous, hurrying crowds, buying cheap underwear at Marks & Spencer's and eating a small meat pie for lunch.

England makes me feel old, because it is full of old people, and they talk often of illness and death. The State hospital, the cemetery, are just around the corner.

My two boys seem to have broken with the family tradition of studying hard to pass exams. But they have seen giraffes and lions. They have swum in red creeks among purple mangrove roots, and they have pulled fish out of the Nile.

PART IV

THEMES

CHAPTER 17

Brown Jews

Early in 1968 the Kenya Government's decision to expel certain categories of non-citizen Indians set off a temporary panic among the Indian community in Kenya. Non-citizen Indians in Uganda felt too that their future was threatened. The British Labour Government reacted by passing defence legislation against the threatened rush of Indian immigrants.

Under the influence of these events, which led to a protracted exchange of ill tempered letters between local Indian and British residents in the East African Press, a young Kampala Sikh Jagjit Singh wrote a poem in which he lamented the lot of the 'brown Jew' in East Africa.

There was the ingratitude:

> For the sweat is dry
> That built the railways,
> And black blood must forget
> Swamp sleeping savagery of greenness
> That burst into an Indian bazaar.

And there was humiliation:

> And you will see it always
> In back alleys and government offices
> My subordinate Asian smile of friendship
> That proclaims the Jew also is a citizen
> And the stare of past hostility replying:
> Citizen? . . . Perhaps so,
> But of Asian extraction!

Singh's reference to the sweat of Indian labourers needs comment, for it is widely and fallaciously believed that East

Africa's Indian community is descended – or largely descended – from the coolies who built the railway from Mombasa in 1896-1901. 'The British,' it is said, 'brought them in as the spearhead of imperialism. Their descendants have grown rich at our expense. Now let the British take them away.' Their alleged coolie background has also been held against East African Indians as evidence of low origins. Such people, it is argued, were bound to transmit undesirable characteristics.[1]

The truth is that in the five years of building the Uganda railway, 31,983 workers were brought from India on three-year contracts of indenture. Of this total 25,259 (79 per cent) returned to India, were invalided out of service, or died. Only 6,724 (21 per cent) chose to stay in East Africa. Of these, 2,000 (6 per cent) remained in the employ of the railway.[2]

In short (says Morris) discharged railway coolies added at most 19 per cent to the already existing Indian population of the East African Protectorate (35,000). A further small addition was made by discharged troops (most soldiers serving with the British were Sikhs from the Punjab). Singh regards these maligned coolies in an honourable light, as true pioneers toiling to open up the bush. He is hurt, not only by African ingratitude, but by Britain's reluctance to welcome her brown citizens with open arms.

> And soon we shall be flying
> Unwelcome vultures all over the world,
> Only to unsheathe fresh wrath
> Each time we land.

But gratitude is not an operative factor in politics. As for the gift of economic progress that the Indians brought to East Africa, the trade and the bazaars they introduced into a 'savagery of greenness', the ordinary Uganda African, alas, saw his recently

[1] Sir Frederick Jackson, who became Governor of Uganda in 1911, was one of the first prominent Englishmen to criticise the early type of Indian immigrant. He did so scathingly, referring to them as degenerate camp followers and 'low class parasites', as though he had some personal resentment against these 'lesser breeds' for daring to intrude into the private places of Africa.

[2] H. S. Morris: *The Indians in Uganda*, London, 1968.

departed guests as groups of brown men clustered densely round the honey pots, as alien colonies swarming at the heart of his towns and trading centres.[1] They were not of his race or religion. They did not integrate. They lacked the prestige that military conquerors would have had. The Uganda African enjoyed and was dependent on the goods and services they offered him. But he envied and resented them. They were rich, while he was poor.

Yet it was not the 'common man' who chased the Indians away. It was Amin's own decision and drive, backed up by the officials who carried out his orders and by relentless army pressure, that was responsible for the unbelievably successful and rapid expulsion operation.

[1] A typical, and not unreasonably argued, expression of the African's dislike of the Indian community's domination of trade and of urban housing and premises was given in this editorial in *The People* (now defunct) of 8 November 1971: 'What do we see today? All our major trading centres are occupied by non-Africans and to make it worse a good number of them non-citizens. If we have to achieve economic independence, the economy of this country must be in the hands of the indigenous people. We have been exploited enough. Our people have been pushed around for a long time and this must stop. The African must run the trade business, he must come to town, trade there and live there. It hurts us to see our people cycling or driving like mad every evening, running away from our towns back to the villages as if they were foreigners here. We see castles in Kampala and in some other towns all owned by non-African landlords. Where do they get the money to put up such buildings? The answer is simple: from this country. We know of nobody who came to this country with sacks of money. All the bank overdrafts these people use to accumulate profits are savings of our people. We therefore urge the government to come out with a drastic policy that will change the order of the day once and for all. Because the economy must be in the hands of the citizens of this country. Because the African must have a right to enter the business trade. Because the African must have the right not only to trade but to live in our towns.'

A letter writer in the *Uganda Argus* (George Kyamulesire, 19 August 1972) expressed his grievances more crudely. 'During colonial days, Europeans were rulers, Asians were middle class, and Africans were labourers. This has been practised by Asians until now, whereby their shop attendants could boil water for coffee, clean the shop windows, and collect mail from the post office! On top of all these duties were insults. Yet they paid their employees a salary ranging from sh. 70/- to sh. 150/- a month. I have always been in disgust with these stupid Asians. As history tells us, they came as labourers, therefore Britain should thank Uganda to have kept their people for so long. Yet they already have overflowing accounts in London, the money they have got through African sweat. We have had Wazungu friends, but never in history an African has ever had an Asian friend. To Asians I say bye-bye . . .'.

Expulsion

The Indians themselves were too realistic to deny that they were in Uganda to make money. To a degree not easily comprehensible to an Englishman – still less to the salaried overseas Englishman who has turned his back on the rat race in Europe – the Indian looked on money making as vital to his very survival as a distinct human being. Behind him in India and Pakistan glowered that nightmare of overcrowding and poverty which it was his dominant aim to escape. Before him, sooner or later, lay the probability of a future in some other foreign land. He was migrant: temporarily buttressed by money, but without permanent roots.

Over recent years the Indians of Uganda had become increasingly aware that time was running out for them. Though their instinct was to procrastinate, they felt after Obote's warning of 1968 an added incentive to make money quickly and to transfer it abroad. Even those who had gambled on Uganda citizenship hedged their bets by seeing to it that some members of their families retained their British passports. Meanwhile they trusted to the forces of law and order and to the presence of the British to ensure their continued security among the black people.

General Amin's military take-over of January 1971 did not excite undue alarm among Uganda's Indians. Indeed they welcomed the first new measures that checked, for a time, the robbery by armed gangs of their shops and premises.

It was not until Amin, towards the end of 1971, summoned a meeting of the eighteen Indian communities and publicly rebuked them for lack of public spirit, then ordered an immediate physical count of every Indian man, woman and child, that Indian suspicions were really aroused. Now, alerted and angered by Amin's insults, the business community decided that the time had finally come for them to sell off their stocks and get their capital out of the country. 'Now we shall really soak the Africans,' several prominent Indian traders told me.

Few people imagined, though, that Amin's expulsion order of August 1972 would be so drastic, the terms so brutal and short. Amin rightly calculated that any extension of the deadline for their departure would only enable the Indians to drain Uganda of further desperately needed currency. Having announced his decision he shrewdly maintained the pressure by threats. 'You are cheats, rogues, saboteurs,' he told the Indians. 'Any British Asian who delays his departure will be sitting on fire.'

Amin's tactics were successful. Not only did he frighten the Indians away – both British and non-British Indians, for both alike felt equally in danger. He seems to have paralysed British diplomatic initiative. The British Government let him have his own way. Africans everywhere, even Amin's critics, could not help but admire the ex-sergeant-major who had so forcibly imposed his will on their former colonial masters. True, the expulsion order had been severe and peremptory. But what, after all, was wrong with letting the black man be master in his own house?

Consequences

Some Indians had of course reason to welcome Amin's drastic decision. He had forced Britain's hand. The British Government was now obliged for humanitarian reasons to waive the quota restrictions and to accept all her brown citizens.

But not everyone looked forward to being dumped in cold, unwelcoming Britain. Many energetic individuals with professional skills preferred to try their luck in the British Dominions (especially Canada) or in America. To young Indians displacement opened up exciting prospects. To older people it was a terrible blow. Theirs had been a cocooned community life centred on mosques and temples, on clubs, schools and the homes of neighbours and kinsmen. In a warm climate, among familiar mango trees, they had been able to eat their customary food, to wear their customary dress, to sit on their own verandahs. They had been relatively affluent and privileged. All this they would have to abandon for the wintry streets of industrial England.

Apart from their stranglehold over a large sector of the Uganda economy, it was the very intensity and exclusiveness of their community life, the gregariousness, that contributed to the unpopularity of the Indians. A stranger might have thought the towns belonged to them, not to Africans. They lived over their shops and offices, crowded the verandahs, the pavements, the public gardens and the big day schools. There were too many of them, they were too conspicuous, and they pursued a social and cultural life in which non-Indians did not share.

The *sari* denoted the separate identity, moral codes and unapproachableness of their women. The car parades were an unwise demonstration of wealth. The swarming school playgrounds were an ominous pointer to the future off-loading of thousands of young Indians on to the Uganda economy. If only there had been fewer Indians!

Their abrupt departure has a tragic side. A way of life, a distinct, valuable and fascinating culture which one had come to accept as part and parcel of the urban Uganda scene, has been destroyed for ever. Africans will not quickly be able to replace their skills.

But in the context of Uganda's development it is vital that Africans should have been given this chance to do so. An élite – politicians, military officers, managers, civil servants, and intellectuals – have already got their hands on the nation's money. It is right that a middle-class of African artisans and traders should now emerge to create more wealth and to enjoy their share of it. The turn of the town labourer and of the peasant with a hoe has yet to come.

Now that the Indians have gone, Europeans at any rate realise how much they miss them (so, too, do a good many Africans, who have begun to call the new class of traders and shopkeepers now banging the cash registers 'black Patels'). For the Indians were not only grocers, stocking English biscuits and pickles. They were dentists, doctors and nurses with an acceptable standard of efficiency: hairdressers, tailors and dressmakers, mechanics, teachers and sportsmen. Their presence in tropical Africa added greatly to the European's comfort and boosted his morale.

The Indians were a non-violent people. After work, their old men liked to play cards under mango trees. They did not bother much about drains, but they had flower beds in their gardens. They did not divorce their wives. As an extension of the Orient into tropical Africa they exerted a civilising influence.

Paul Theroux, in one of his articles for *Transition* (No. 33, October/November 1967, Kampala), asserted 'In East Africa nearly everyone hates the Asians. . . . The British have hated the Asians longest.' But the European felt that he and the brown man had much in common. They shared the same mental processes. Their departure from Uganda leaves him feeling lonelier and more exposed.

CHAPTER 18

Naipaul's Africa

V. S. Naipaul: IN A FREE STATE, *London,* 1971

Bobby, a homosexual expatriate, and Linda, a 'man-eating' colonial wife, are driving through an East African country at a time of disturbance. The king ('a London playboy . . . a very foolish man') has fled and is being hunted by soldiers. Through their chatter, much of it, one might think, scarcely worth recording were it not so authentic, we see the expatriate's Africa, and Naipaul's.

Bobby, in a fancy native shirt, woos African men with a murmured, 'I love Africa. I wish I was your colour.' To school-boys he offers a few shillings: 'Look, my colour, your colour. I give you shilling buy schoolbooks. . . . When I born again I want your colour. You no frighten. You want five shillings?'

Bobby's advances are not, in the encounters revealed to us, successful. A Zulu corner-boy spits in his face in a hotel. He scares and bewilders the up-country barman. When Bobby, the day's adventures and terror over, is most in need of caresses, his own houseboy jeers at him.

Linda, on the other hand, cannot bear the thought of touching African flesh. 'Africans smell,' she says. 'Let's open the window. You can smell the filth they've been eating.'

Linda (she uses a vaginal deodorant with 'an appalling name') has an obsession with smells. 'This smell of Africa,' she says. 'I got it this time, when we came back from leave. It lasts about half an hour or so, no more. It is a smell of rotting vegetation and Africans. One is very much like the other.'

Yet 'it was this smell, in a warm, shuttered room, that Bobby liked'.

For Linda the élite are bogus black gentlemen with European hair-partings, ruling over brutes whom they ignore. 'You go out with Sammy Kisenyi, making educated conversation, and you see a naked savage with a penis a foot long. You pretend you've seen nothing. You see two naked boys painted white running about the public highway, and you don't talk about it.'

'Fat savages,' she calls the soldiers at a road block. 'Fat black savages. I can't bear it when they grin like that.'

It is the offended voice of Naipaul himself that we are listening to; his voice that says of the hotel servant 'his smell swirled about the room', that finds Africans physically distasteful, loutish ('the squealing and the chatter in the kitchen'), and ignorant ('you can train them so far and so far only'). It is Naipaul, looking at the barboy, who notes on top of his head 'particles of fluff trapped between the springs'.

Naipaul's African townships are, as we would expect, squalid and tumbledown. 'Walls mud splashed. . . . Crooked telegraph poles, sagging wires, the broken edges of the asphalt road, scuffed grass sidewalks, dust, scattered rubbish.' How could they have been otherwise? The town dwellers, even the élite, have not long since been 'flushed from the forest', from 'horrible little huts'.

Only the king's people are conceded to be a little more attractive than the others. Some prisoners, sitting by the road under guard, were the 'slender, small-boned, very black people of the king's tribe, a clothed people, builders of roads'.

One wonders why Naipaul has this pitiless antipathy to Africans. Did he, when a guest of the English Department, at Makerere, find their presence too physical, their fumbling for words to express sophisticated thoughts crude and infantile, their minds not subtle enough for his own fastidious sensibilities? Does Naipaul *fear* Africans? Has his Trinidad background among rough and extrovert West Indian negroes left a scar that throbs when he meets real black people? Or is he more honest than lesser writers, who in these days of being nice to black men dare not hurt their feelings?

Brilliantly malicious and sensitive, Naipaul, when he described in his earlier *An Area Of Darkness* the fearful poverty and injustices of Indian society, stressed his 'horror of the unclean' – of Indian excretory habits, for instance, and of polluted food.

Yet he showed compassion, even a faint feeling of identity with the awful Indian scene.

True, at the end of his year in India he wrote, 'India remained for me an area of darkness into which I knew I could not penetrate. . . . I had learned my separateness from India, and was content to be a colonial, without a past, without ancestors.'

But on returning to the loneliness of London, he understood on further reflection, 'It was only now, as my experience of India defined itself more properly against my own homelessness, that I saw how close in the past year I had been to the total Indian negation, how much it had become the basis of thought and feeling.'

Naipaul's *In A Free State* reveals, however, no sympathy at all for the black figures that slop through his uncouth landscapes. Even his old-timer, the white colonel, crippled, bad-tempered and contemptuous, is a grotesque caricature of some Boer farmer or embittered Kenya settler. 'They say,' observed the colonel, 'there's good and bad everywhere. There's no good and bad here. They're just Africans.'

The day's car journey that Naipaul describes, with Bobby and Linda chattering in their special 'Makerere' idiom, is made in an atmosphere of mounting tension – the yak-yak-yak-yak of a government helicopter flying low, the menacing rifles at road blocks – that explodes into brutality. Soldiers seize Bobby and beat him up in a roadside shed.

'The boots probed his ribs, his belly, probed and kicked. . . . He didn't open his eyes, fearing that he might not be able to see. Then he felt the boot hard on his right wrist, and he could have cried then, at the clear pure pain, the knowledge of the fracture, so deliberate, the knowledge that what had been whole all his life had been broken.'

One reviewer sees in the day's spiralling humiliations an allegory of the 'Colonial Retreat'.[1] Whatever symbolism Naipaul intended, violence had rightly to be a part of it. For violence is basic to African society and its environment. It thrives on the black man's docile acceptance of brutality and sudden death. It lurks in the beer pot, behind the steering wheel, at funeral and initiation ceremones and in the bridal night. It leaves the

<hr />

[1] *The Times Literary Supplement,* 8 October 1971.

a to c Aftermath of Amin's coup; partly bleached corpses at the edge of Lake Victoria

10a Teuso village huts

10b Kurdish goat-hair tents (on saddle between the two Ararats)

poor man bleeding in the gutter. No one stops to help him; the man is poor, he is unknown, and the ordinary citizen has learned that the police station is a place better to avoid.

At a time (1966) when many of us in Uganda regarded the persecution of the Baganda and their king as a temporary – perhaps necessary – lapse from the customary processes of civilised government, Naipaul, with remarkable prescience, seems to have glimpsed the permanency of terror.[1]

Shortly after reading Naipaul, I came across Nadine Gordimer's description of another climactic assault on a white man in a Central African republic.[2] The white man, clean, fit, wearing glasses, is dragged out of his car and battered to death – his body, staved in under the dirtied bush jacket, left in the dust.

Nadine Gordimer's Englishman is killed by many small black men using stones and farm tools. Flabby well-meaning Bobby does not stand a chance against the soldier's nailed boots. In both incidents it is made clear that a superior person is being bashed by mindless apes. Both victims love Africa. The violence that lies so close to the surface of Africa has suddenly reared up and struck the god from across the seas with his large brain and fragile body, his western magic and insufferable arrogance. The black man, violating in his rage the taboos that normally protect the aloof and gifted albino, has assaulted him.

These are the dreaded moments of unpalatable truth; for we white people, clustered in small colonies and outposts among the huge populations of Africa, are vulnerable; and we know it. Why, otherwise, the watchman, the guard dogs, the fences and the barred windows behind which we retire in our brightly lit enclaves at night? Why in July 1960 did 20,000 Belgians flee instantly in panic from the Congo after an army mutiny at Thysville during which some wives of Belgian officers had been

---

[1] Elsewhere (*The Mimic Men*, 1967) Naipaul has written: 'The order to which the colonial politician succeeds is not his order. It is something he is compelled to destroy; destruction comes with his emergence and is a condition of his power. . . . The pace of colonial events is quick, the turnover of leaders rapid. . . . The career of the colonial politician is short and ends brutally.' Under Amin, his body may be found in the Nile.

[2] *A Guest of Honour*, London, 1971.

raped?[1] Why the rapid exodus of so many expatriates from Uganda towards the end of 1972 after soldiers had threatened some Europeans with guns?

And yet, apart from Mau Mau and the Congo episode, and his irritating exposure to robbery, it seems that the white man in Africa has so far been let off lightly. Is this a tribute to African good manners, to fear of retribution, or to the European's caution (do not get drunk in the slums, never challenge an armed thief), and to the technical resources that in times of trouble enable him to make his getaway?

In Uganda, to be fair, it is a fact that a great many Africans genuinely like British people. They deplore the abuse, the blows, the nights in gaol, the arbitrary deportations, that many of us have had to suffer under the military government. It is the undisciplined soldier, the *kondo*, who have broken the rules.

The Stanleyville Operation

Dr Conor Cruise O'Brien, the Irishman who can be nasty about Europeans in Africa, has this hostile comment to make on the Belgian paratroop operation to rescue white hostages in Stanleyville (1964):[2]

'Are white people in Africa to be regarded as covered by a sort of Caucasian providence insurance policy, with a guarantee that if the natives get rough, the metropolitan forces will once again come to their rescue? . . . The only real security for white people in Africa lies in convincing the Africans among whom they live that their presence is genuinely useful to Africa, and that they are not out to trick, rob or murder Africans.'

The flaw in Dr O'Brien's assertion is, of course, that an African government which is in trouble and wants a scapegoat is liable to pick on the 'imperialists' – in effect, on its own resident white community irrespective of occupation, merit or morals.

As for the dozens of Europeans in Uganda who to my own

[1] Ian Scott, first British Ambassador in Léopoldville (now Kinshasha), said that by morning on the day following the mutiny, for a quarter of a mile round the ferry departure point at Léopoldville there was a solid block of abandoned cars. See his *Tumbled House*, London, 1969.

[2] 'Mercy and Mercenaries,' *Writers and Politics*, New York, 1965.

knowledge, over the last two years, have been robbed at gun-point or cut and beaten in their homes with pangas, they know better than Dr O'Brien. The *kondo* and the soldier do not want to know whether you are useful or useless, charitable or uncharitable, to Africans. They want loot; with the added bonus, probably, of enjoying the moment of white humiliation.

Dr O'Brien does concede that 'In most parts of Africa – everywhere except where there were numerous white settlers – British rule, unlike Belgian rule, has not left a legacy of hatred; on the contrary, there is a real fund of good will towards Britain in English-speaking Africa.' But he cannot resist a last thrust at the Stanleyville operation. 'It might be well for Europeans and Americans,' he says, 'having rescued some hundreds of whites from blacks, now to set about rescuing several millions of blacks from whites.'

Mr K. (*22 December 1972*)

To conclude with the realities of Uganda, with an incident that was not even reported in the local Press.

Mr K., an Anglo-Greek businessman, lay on his back outside the baker's shop at Kololo on the spot where a few minutes earlier he had parked his Peugeot car, which the bandits had driven off. Someone had put a towel over his face, leaving uncovered only the faded orange shirt, crumpled trousers and dusty shoes, and the olive-coloured arms sprayed with black hairs. His wife, a plain middle-aged woman wearing glasses, stood by him. She was a trained nurse. When the bullet entered her husband's left breast she knew he was dead, and that there was nothing she could do but to wait for the police and the ambulance, to control her grief and protect her husband's body against indignity.

She behaved very well. Some Greek friends of her husband joined her. When I looked up I saw a row of Indians peering down from a roof top (strange, I thought, the building had looked deserted yet Indians must be hiding inside like cock-roaches). 'To kill a European is not good for the image of Africa,' an African said to me. 'The soldiers did it,' added a woman. A hundred yards away, at the grocer's, I could see people going about their usual business of buying milk.

CHAPTER 19

Expatriates

'Will there ever be a time or a place in which I am no longer homesick for Africa?'

Trevor Huddleston, Bishop of Stepney
Letter to *The Times*, 24 October 1970

'No Englishman could live in Africa for long and remain a gentleman.'

J. Morris
Spectator, 25 September 1971

'Anyone who knew the "natives" never bothered to expect gratitude, and the natives certainly never expected gratitude from the white man who had been supplied with an interesting life and a certain amount of power, and with a pension at the end for enjoying it.'

Gerald Hanley
Warriors and Strangers, 1971

Paul Theroux: GIRLS AT PLAY, *London, 1969*

Girls at Play is an American's sick joke:[1] a satire of malevolent ferocity focused on white, unmarried schoolmistresses at a bush school for African girls somewhere in Kenya's White Highlands. These wretched women – bitchy, cranky, unloved, afraid of the shadows and the night noises outside their barred windows, clinging together for protection over horrid meals spoilt by bickering – are exiles: 'unmarried among bananas'.

Miss Poole, the headmistress, keeps pets. 'Even after a bath, she smelt strongly of her cats.' Her dogs, sitting at her feet, used to gnaw their bottoms for fleas while she drank tea. Yet human dirt – that is, Africans' dirt – nauseated her. The thought that, in a Nairobi hotel, an African might have slept in her very bed the night before, turned her stomach.

Heather Monkhouse, newly posted to the school after her

[1] Theroux was for three years a lecturer in Mass Media at Makerere University.

expulsion – the result of a sex scandal – from Nairobi, is an already raddled woman of thirty-six 'who had had on the average one and a half affairs every year since she was twenty-five'. Her lingering memory is of an elderly, methodical man in Croydon, 'who had made love to her in a way a man might eat a soft-boiled egg . . . all the while he stared at what he was doing . . . then the dunking of the spoon'.

Heather had come to Africa five years before 'to get away from it all' – the crowded London subways, the ugly working-class faces, the swollen women with shopping bags. Yet she fears and hates Africa and Africans. 'Africans were all around her, but she never saw them.' 'Who wants to live in Africa, what white people?' she says to B.J., the gushing American Peace Corps girl, 'only cranks, fools, failures. . . . We're the best they'll ever get, the best.'

B.J., plump and pretty, had flown to Africa from New York with a plane-load of Peace Corps Volunteers ('serious little buggers with sun-glasses and handbooks and rucksacks, greeting each other in too-loud Swahili'). She looked forward to fraternising with Africans, or as the Peace Corps put it, 'getting to know the Host Country Nationals'. She wanted to have an African boy friend, to eat native food, to tramp in a sun-helmet with porters through elephant grass.

But her Hollywood vision of Africa (savage, romantic, mysterious) remains an illusion. She finds Africa a dull place, not at all mysterious, only disorganised. 'Africa was the endless staring of Wangi' (the timid clerk whom she dates from time to time). 'The game parks were no different from Southern Cal., there were no throbbing jungle drums.'

The old-timer, the Kenya settler, is represented by unspeak-able, foul-mouthed Fitch, owner of *The Horse and Hunter*, 'a drunkard living unwashed in the East African bush, perspiring heavily, cursing in forces' slang' ('the bugger shits through his teeth after two beers' is one of his picturesque phrases); 'mean with money, evil-smelling, spitting tobacco into his moustache, punching up Auntie' (Auntie, his wife, is a very black Nilotic woman with her lower front teeth knocked out), 'cursing Africa and hating England'. But though Fitch despises Africans they are his customers and he cannot afford to offend them. To ingratiate himself, he has repainted his hotel signboard; it is the horse that is now white, the hunter black.

There are some glimpses of village life – decrepit shacks, goats, dog-turds, and 'people in stinking rags who dug with small pointed sticks, and with shards of glass circumcised little girls spread on mats'.

We meet the schoolgirls only on the hockey field. They are heavy-buttocked, they wear green bloomers, and yelp.

Heather's arrival at this awful school precipitates disaster. She provokes a feud among the staff and undermines discipline. One week-end after an orgy of drink, quarrelling and violence, B.J. is raped by Wangi and then drowns herself in a bog, Miss Poole is deported, and Heather, dreaming of 'a nice dirty old time' with a man at Mombasa, is murdered in her bed by an albino half-wit. Miss Virjee, the bow-legged Indian games mistress, who was never invited to tea ('she licked her fingers'), runs off to Nairobi. Miss Male packs her curios. The school closes.

What is Theroux up to? What has he tried to demonstrate with his doomed expatriates, exhibited in macabre farce? He evidently means us to take his caricatures seriously, for in his Author's Note to *Girls at Play* he specifically states: 'It would be misleading for me to suggest that the teachers in this book are different from others in Africa. Most expatriates there consider their work a kind of ritual penance for getting so much fresh air and tropical sunshine, tolerated because it requires little thought and does not intrude very much on their passions.'

More detailed clues to Theroux's aims are to be found in the article 'Tarzan is an Expatriate' which he wrote earlier for *Transition* (No. 32, August/September 1967, Kampala), an article which outraged some expatriates, amused others, and provoked a sheaf of petulant letters to the editor.

In this article Theroux diagnoses five main reasons why expatriates come to East Africa:

'An active curiosity in things strange; a vague premonition that Africa rewards her visitors; a disgust with the anonymity of the industrial setting; a wish to be special; and an unconscious desire to stop thinking and let the body take over. All of these reasons are selfish to a degree. Mixed with them may be the

desire to do a little good, to help in some way; but this is
desire together with the knowledge that the good deeds will
be performed in a pleasant climate. This, in the end, is not so
much a reason for coming as it is an excuse. The wish to be
special (and rewarded) is dominant; the need for assertion –
the passive assertion, the assertion of colour – by a man's mere
physical presence eventually dominates the life of the expatriate.
Tarzan must stand out; he is non-violent but his muscles show.'

'The realisation,' he concludes, 'that he is white in a black
country, and respected for it, is the turning point in the
expatriate's career. He can either forget it, or capitalise on it.
Most choose the latter.' The result is a feeling of racial superiority.

So in terms of Theroux's categories, B.J. had curiosity,
and she wanted to do a little good. Miss Poole, the Kenya-born
settler's daughter who had spent seven miserable years in a
boarding house in England, was driven back to Africa by
nostalgia for the happy days of childhood. Heather, the London
shop assistant, had wanted some swimming, the sun, a man.
In Africa Miss Poole, Heather, and dim Miss Male were somebody. They had status. They were white. Decanted back home
from an aeroplane they would disappear into the crowd:
nonentities with yellowed skins, looking for cheap lodgings.

Among the readers annoyed by Theroux's article was a
Mr Alex Smith of Kampala. Trying very hard to be honest with
himself he had this to say in a letter in the next issue (No. 33)
of *Transition*.

'Let us face the unadorned facts; we come here, attracted by
the conditions that are offered to us, salaries, allowances and
all, to do a job that the Government of this country wants us to
do. We are not altruistic, few of us pretend to be, and we are
under no illusion that we are here for any other purpose than to
be used, treated well while we are being used, and when our
usefulness is at an end sent on our way with a word of thanks
and a useful gratuity. Perhaps while we are working, a little
human sympathy for those whom we are employed to help may
induce us to work a little harder. We may feel that we would

like to see the children we notice in the villages enjoy a better life than their parents as a result of our efforts. . . . The reality is that we are paid to do a job and it is our duty to see that we give value for money, not to waste our time examining our consciences.'

So for Mr Smith we are little better than mercenaries. Enright's mendicant professors. At best, honest shoemakers cobbling adequately for a wage. But Mr Smith's no-nonsense attitude begs a lot of questions. What about the rakes, the zealots, the romantics, those who respond so passionately to Africa that they fall in love with a knobbly mountain, a tribal culture, with black protest and black skin?

Where, in his scheme of things, do the Irish nuns of Buluba, who touch the rotting skin of lepers, fit in?[1] Or the missionaries who have grown old in the course of turning *shenzi* schoolboys into black gentlemen (not a type with much survival value once unsympathetic politicians turn the heat on them.)?

Statistics
To see this matter from the angle of statistical investigation let us look at the findings of Ríta Cruise O'Brien, a sociologist from the London School of Economics, who did some research into the French presence in Senegal in 1966-67.[2]

She interviewed 250 French residents. One of the questions she put to them was 'Why did you come to Africa to work?' To this the most common answer (22 per cent)was 'I thought I would find an attractive position, money', followed by (19·6 per cent) 'to become acquainted with Africa'. 12·8 per cent of informants answered, 'I prefer to live abroad to get out of the "*cercle*" of France'; 8·8 per cent said 'life is more pleasant'. 50·8 per cent of these self-seekers and hedonists, when asked what were, for them, the most important advantages in Africa, replied 'Climate, sea'. 24·8 per cent said 'general material or

[1] Buluba Leper Centre is sponsored by a German charitable association in Wurzburg. It employed an ex-German Naval officer Beier who founded a fishing station and used to shoot bush buck to provide the patients with meat.
[2] *White Society in Black Africa: The French of Senegal*, London, 1972.

financial gain', 22·8 per cent 'life is easier and more agreeable', 12·4 per cent 'opportunity of accumulating savings'.

Almost half the informants (48·8 per cent) thought that conditions of work for the French in Senegal were better than those in France (26·8 per cent thought they were worse).

To the question 'Do you think that accelerated Africanisation in your type of work is advisable?' 68·3 per cent replied 'no', 26·7 per cent replied 'yes'. Those who said 'no' gave as their reasons 'lack of cadres, need for further technical training' (50·2 per cent), 'Africans work poorly, lack of enterprise, no sense of responsibility' (13 per cent).

We have not, I think, learnt anything new from Miss O'Brien. Her Frenchmen have come to Africa to enjoy the good life on attractive pay. They do not think Africans are capable of doing as good a job as Europeans – left to themselves, standards will fall. In the old days, we are told, Frenchmen often used service in the colonies as a way of fleeing creditors at home. Since then Tarzan in Senegal has become virtuous: a technician, but still, like his forefathers, convinced of his superiority.

Significantly Miss O'Brien also found that white women suffered more than their husbands or children from depression, the result of loneliness, boredom and lack of activity. Further, that 'hostility to Africans can be strong and occasionally obsessive among women with psychological difficulties'. Theroux, then, was shrewd to choose white women to express the nastiness of his Africans.

Poor white women. Why do so many writers on Africa (and India too) pick on them? Nadine Gordimer, herself a South African, has this cruel vignette: 'She has been out in the sun for twenty years. Smiled at him; teeth still good. Ugly bright blue eyes, cheap china. She knew she still had beautiful legs, nervous ankles all hollows and tendons. Her dead hair tossed frowstily. He thought: she's horrible.'

Perhaps the white man resents the presence of the white woman in Africa because she reminds him of nanny, interfering with his fun. If she too can motor through the bush, and photograph rhinoceroses, how can he pretend to himself or to anyone else that Africa is a place for he-men only? Joy Adamson, cuddling her lions and sketching tame chiefs, has done a disservice to that manly image of the white male in Africa. She has emasculated Hemingway's hairy-fisted heroes. After her, the Masai warrior leaning on his spear in an ochre landscape has become for ever a stage decoration.

Graham Greene, as one might expect, looked at his fellows in Africa with an imaginative insight that would not have suited Miss O'Brien's questionnaire.

Sitting in the humid solitude of war-time Freetown, he wondered insistently what he was doing there. 'The answer,' he concludes, 'was probably much the same as my companions in the City Bar might have given (they were failures but they knew more of Africa than the successes): an escape from school? a recurring dream of adolescence? a book read in childhood?'[1]

[1] 'The Soupsweet Land,' *Collected Essays*, London, 1969.

CHAPTER 20

Slumming

Paul Theroux: JUNGLE LOVERS, *London, 1971*

Having had fun with the English ladies, Theroux now chooses a blundering, good-natured American to express the dilemma of 'culture-shock' in a satirised African state.

Calvin Mullet is sent by Homemakers' Mutual of Boston and New York to sell insurance in Rwalawi. After some months he finds that he has collected but five clients, three of whom he keeps up to date by paying their premiums out of his own pocket. Disillusioned, he gives up. He had come to Africa with a charitable but deluded eagerness to help. But the feckless Africans didn't want insurance.

How indeed could it have been otherwise? 'Extra money,' he discovers, 'wouldn't help anyone – it would only make him more liable to theft. A person who appeared the least bit prosperous was nationalised and burgled; if he refused, he got his skull cracked by the Youth Wingers. . . . It was cruel to make them think that they could be saved by insurance.'

Africans, he decides, were both perishable and static. 'Nothing could or did happen to them, except death. . . . Some giant would have to snatch up the country, like a clogged ketchup bottle, and smack it violently on the bottom for it to change; but that would never happen either. And besides, the bottle might turn out to be empty.'

Amiable, frequently drunk, sweating and dirty ('he pisses on his shoes'), Calvin takes a room in a whorehouse in Blantyre, succumbs to squalor, marries a local slut, goes native. No longer recognisably American, disillusioned with Africa and yet 'practically an African', he surrenders to the greasy girls, the beer, the broiling hot nothingness.

His stay in the whorehouse gives him expert knowledge of the girls that is worth having.

'They were the dregs, either schoolgirls or badly mauled hags . . . they quarrelled over him, gabbling and pushing each other . . . they inspired dread and pity, they were awkward and fat and loaded with poisons. Some had ridiculous nicknames, Essy and Kitty, and others Biblical names, Abishag and Zipporah (Abby and Zip), or names of troubling irony: Comfort, Grace, Chastity, the missions' legacy. All of them had bruises on their shins, a badge of the profession; their hands were lizard-textured. They were very shy; they giggled monotonously, they smelled, they snored. Calvin had seen men drag out their breasts and begin biting them.'

When Calvin paid his fee, he felt he was being more useful to the girls than selling them insurance. He was not, like the do-gooders, offering salvation; only a little cash which could be turned into simple comfort. He was not ashamed. There was no guilt. His colour was no problem – 'in whorehouses there was complete integration'.

In the bar of the whorehouse we meet deaf Major Beaglehole who tells startling anecdotes for the price of a whisky. 'I killed my commanding officer as sure as you're sitting there,' is one of his openings. 'While I was fighting in the Western Desert that chap was tupping my wife.' (Have we not met the major before, in a Kampala bar, and listened to the same anecdote, or to one very similar? A small man with a hearing aid and a glass of waragi and water, pertinacious as a terrier, barking from time to time to attract attention among the lunch-time drinkers?)[1]

---

[1] Mr A. C. Duffield is now, to our sorrow, dead. Though frail, and in his seventies, he was brave. Savagely attacked by kondos not long before his death, he was back at the City Bar a week later. In his weekly letter to the *Sunday Nation*, Nairobi, he described the incident in a humorous way. 'I was slashed four times in the skull,' he wrote, 'and a surgeon has just removed my left eye. . . . Not much was missing – a leather case, a portable radio, a shirt, a cardigan and a pair of shoes; not much of a haul for so much violence. . . . I'm going to acquire a black eye-patch and see if Moshe Dayan wants another successful general for Israel. . . . Probably most of my blood is now new and I am deeply grateful to the unknown donors (perhaps African secondary school children) who built up the blood bank. Their good rich blood has transformed me, temporarily at least, from a cynical old curmudgeon into a man who believes in the essential goodness of most people (except kondos). . . . My assailants probably thought they had killed me (and they nearly did). The kondos kill to avoid being identified.'

Bailey (the manageress) and Major Beaglehole say this sort of thing about Africans:

'They're all nig-nogs, with arses for faces.' (Bailey)

'They're laughing at us now, they're putting the Union Jack on their knickers. We're down and they're laughing. But we won't be down much longer. I tell you, Bailey, we're coming back in numbers and God help them then. . . . We'll have it all back, from the Cape to Cairo. We may have been Wog-bashers, but by God we were fair.' (Beaglehole)

Calvin, once he has given up trying to *change* anything, is happy, dossing down with Mira on rainy afternoons, stumbling to bed drunk with her at night ('every time he made love to her he felt he would never go home, ever'). The room was a pigsty. But Mira was his blackbird, his cat; she had sharp little teeth; and she washed often. Calvin did not. He said that like an African he was happy dirty.

The theme of the white man who takes up with a black or coloured woman and goes native is a stock one. There is supposed to be something shameful as well as comic about it. The products of the liaisons are the despised half-castes, the mulattoes, the quadroons, the coloureds, the Anglo-Indians with their sing-song English and darkly pigmented elbows. The white renegade of earlier fiction used to die of drink or fever in a dirty bed. The myth of his degradation and squalor is a form of caste worship.

But Calvin Mullet, the white Tarzan who has let himself slide down the slippery slope, who has surrendered his status and his superiority and joined the jungle folk, has found happiness. 'The black race stinks in its poverty,' wrote Céline. He spoke of the 'obscenity of its resignation'.[1] Calvin, drunk on his verandah, sees angels in the black men's minds.

Still, he will be cheated in the end. To everyone's astonishment, when Mira bears a child – the child he has been dreaming of – it is coal black. We leave him cuckolded, wondering in his naïveté at its thick black hair and wrinkled face.

Disciplining Africans used to be the Western preoccupation. Understanding them is the current theme. Like Pavlov's dogs, we are bewildered by their unpredictability. A kick in the white

[1] *Voyage au bout de la nuit*, Paris, 1932.

man's pants from the local tyrant one moment, a smile and a gratuity the next. The old colonial servant could at least look forward safely to his pension. Today's expatriate may find himself bundled off to the nearest airport within twenty-four hours, leaving his dog behind.

When he left Africa Paul Theroux went off to teach English Literature in Singapore. Will he now make fun of gangling Englishmen who impose T. S. Eliot on yellow men?[1]

---

[1] His new novel (*Saint Jack*) is in fact about a pimp who works for a gang of Chinese girls. The style is the same ('Money changed hands in the bedroom when the feller was naked and excited; then the stunt itself . . .').

CHAPTER 21

Prospero and Caliban

F. Oyono: HOUSEBOY, *London* 1966; *O. Mannoni:* PROSPERO
AND CALIBAN, *London* 1956: *L. Barnes:* AFRICA IN ECLIPSE,
London 1971.

Oyono's *Houseboy* is the story of a young African boy Toundi
who runs away from his village in the French Cameroon to join
a white Catholic mission. When his patron Father Gilbert dies,
he is sent as houseboy to the local French commandant. At first
everything goes well. Then Toundi, because he is intelligent
and learns too much about the private lives of the commandant
and his wife, is thrown out and handed over to the police. The
police beat him, and he dies of his injuries.

One of my students, Yolamu Nsamba, wrote a review of
Houseboy in which he makes some interesting references to
Mannoni's *Prospero and Caliban*, a French writer's study in the
psychology of colonisation based on his experiences of the
Malagasy people of Madagascar and of the French colonialists.

I have tried to indicate a part of Mannoni's thesis below, but
first let us see what Nsamba has to say about *Houseboy*.

White Skin
Toundi (Nsamba points out) ran away to the mission station
because, as he wrote later in his diary, 'I just wanted to get close
to the white man with hair like the beard on a maize cob.' I am
going to suggest that this African boy was attracted to the white
man because of the colour of his skin.

The fair skin obsession is widespread among dark peoples.
'The life of a dark marriageable girl in Bengal used to be one of
unending humiliation,' wrote Nirad Chaudhuri.[1] We know that
the Ottoman sultans used to stock their harems with fair-skinned

[1] *The Autobiography of an Unknown Indian*, London, 1951.

Circassian girls. Similarly, to the simple African mind a white skin, corresponding to the relatively light complexion of some of his race, symbolises beauty. Among my people the Banyoro, a pretty girl is said to be as white as an egret, or as milk. To be dark complexioned is to be ugly. Young African women crave to lighten their skin through cosmetics, with the often grotesque result that girls whose faces are much lighter than their legs are common in Kampala.

According to legend a royal Cwezi dynasty once ruled for a short time over the Banyoro people. It was a dynasty of fair-skinned men. One day they mysteriously disappeared: it is thought they drowned themselves in Lake Albert. This fair-skinned dynasty has left behind a memory of legendary exploits, a cult of Cwezi spirits, and a fair-skin ideal that is associated with supernatural powers and is perpetuated to this day in folk tales of idyllic damsels and white goddesses.[1]

It is relevant to recall here an incident that befell Major Gaetano Casati, the noted Italian explorer, geographer, and agent of Emin Pasha. Casati was accused by King Kabarega of treachery. 'You have brought the Waganda into our country,' the Vizier told him, 'you are the cause of our children being ravished, our goods stolen, and our crops destroyed.' Casati was tied to a tree, threatened, and beaten by villagers. Luckily for him the king was not certain whether Casati may not perhaps have been some descendant of the Cwezi. So he spared his life.[2]

I am sure this 'light skin complex' will help us understand why Toundi 'just wanted to be near the white man'.

Wherever Europeans have founded colonies with colonised subjects, asserts Mannoni, 'there existed legends foretelling the arrival of strangers from the sea, bearing wondrous gifts. From the early 17th century any shipwrecked sailor was welcomed with open arms, and the chiefs quarrelled over possession of them'.

Well, the long-awaited white strangers did come! They

[1] J. Beattie comments on this in *Bunyoro: An African Kingdom*, New York, 1960, and in an essay in *Spirit Mediumship and Society in Africa*, London, 1969.

[2] See Casati's *Ten Years in Equatoria* (English translation), London, 1891. Casati's book is dramatically illustrated in the Italian style and shows him tied to a tree with naked spearmen threatening him. See also J. W. Nyakatura, *The Kings of Bunyoro Kitara* (vernacular).

penetrated deep into Africa. The African was ready to receive them. He served them with what seems to us incredible hospitality, faithfulness and loyalty mingled with reverence and with fear of the supernatural.

Ruthless types like Stanley had loyal followers. The men who carried Livingstone's corpse to the coast gave proof of an immense attachment to a man with a white skin.

The old soldier in *Houseboy* boasts to his friends (he was describing a visit to a brothel in Algiers): 'I chose a real white woman with hair the colour of the beard on a corn cob, eyes like a panther, buttocks like putty stuck on a wall.' His listeners made sounds of approval.

We are no longer surprised, these days, when African students return from Europe with white wives.

And was it not a historic event for Africans to see the corpse – *the dead body* – of Father Gilbert? Who could have believed that white men were mortal?

In short the African loved, admired, was loyal to and curious about the man with a white skin. He embraced him and allowed himself to be taken over by the white master. On his account he surrendered the roots that bound him to his own heritage. But the end was cruel disappointment. The white man's response to it all was indifference if not outright rejection. Under his rule the black man could rise only so far in the social scale, and no farther.

To the white man it seems that the African was merely a black savage, his blackness associated with the colour of mourning and of death, of bubonic plague, of ill omen, of witchcraft and of night. Writers like Graham Greene have been morbidly attracted to Africa because it symbolises for them superstition, violence, death, and disease. Dr Schweitzer said, 'It is impossible to rely upon the blacks.' He counselled white men to keep away from negroes. Their relationship with the latter should be summed up in the phrase, 'I am your brother, it is true, but your elder brother.'

Prospero and Caliban

To return for a moment to Toundi and the master-servant relationship: a relationship which is, I think, identical with that between Prospero and Caliban, or Crusoe and Friday, and psychologically typical of the colonial situation. 'The master has a servant, the servant likewise has a master, and though he does not compare himself with him, he nevertheless takes pleasure in the value of the thing he possesses' (Mannoni).

Toundi takes pleasure in Father Gilbert's motor cycle. 'I was happy. The speed intoxicated me.' Equally he takes pleasure and pride in the commandant's beautiful wife.

Father Gilbert, for his part, is delighted with Toundi: 'He presents me to the whites who visit the mission as his master-piece. I am his boy, a boy who can read and write, serve mass, lay a table, sweep out his room and make a bed.' Like Man Friday, Toundi is happy to be possessed by a master. His situation of dependence is psychologically satisfying; for he has a 'dependence complex'. To quote Mannoni again, Toundi 'takes possession of the person upon whom he depends and in that way values him and has certain obscure foundations'.

Now let us see what happens to Toundi's original sense of trust. Early in his career Toundi is happy to transfer his dependence bonds from a capricious father to the white priest. His mother gives him her blessing. In Mannoni's words, Father Gilbert assumed responsibility for him as absolute master, protector, and scapegoat, shouldering Toundi's burden of guilt for offences against the customs.

Yet when Father Gilbert dies, Father Vandermayer strips and searches him (he suspects the boy may have helped himself to the Sunday collection). Soon the white engineer accuses him of interfering with his African mistress. The commandant kicks him, and his wife nags at him. We now see the 'Prospero complex' in all these whites. Toundi is their Caliban.

Yet the masters are not satisfied with bullying Toundi. They are dismayed to find that Toundi (to use Mannoni's words) 'should claim to be a person in his own right, and from time to time show that he has a will of his own'. Toundi is not the creature on whom they can project their own vices. He is a real being. This outrages them. 'He fancies himself,' says Madame, 'he has been taking liberties.' 'The natives,' says the doctor's wife, 'are everywhere except where you want them to be.'

When the commandant himself turns against Toundi, treads

on his fingers, says he smells, refuses to be served by him, Toundi realises that his last refuge has abandoned him. He has been betrayed. He brings the commandant a glass of water that he has spat in. This is his gesture of revolt. What course, one wonders, would Toundi's defiance have taken had he not been arrested shortly afterwards?

To conclude, then, using Mannoni's phraseology, in choosing a colonial vocation Europeans had certain psychological satisfactions to pursue, e.g. the desire to dominate, to boast of superiorities. The story of *Houseboy* revolves round the unleashing of those neurotic tendencies on Toundi.

As for the workings of the 'dependence complex', when Toundi shows signs of having a mind and personality of his own, the whites think he is uppity. They throw him to the dogs.

In this moment of repudiation, cruel disillusionment is likely to provoke thoughts of hatred and revenge. As Mannoni puts it, 'Feelings of hostility are liable to arise when the bonds of dependence have been snapped.' Freud has written, 'When a deity lets down his people, they will murder him.'

This is exactly the tragedy to which the colonials – who assume so important a role in the African mind, 'shouldering so many offences against the customs' – are doomed. Such is the revolt of our era, the 'African Revolution'.

YOLAMU NSAMBA

Dependence Complex

Professor Bloom has called Mannoni 'persuasive but impressionistic'.[1] Another professor, though greatly attracted to Mannoni's 'curious notions', says they contain their share of solemn nonsense.[2] In the context of Nsamba's remarks, the

---

[1] Leonard Bloom: *The Social Psychology of Race Relations*, London, 1971.

[2] A. P. Thornton: 'Jekyll and Hyde in the Colonies', *For the File on Empire*, London, 1968. Professor Thornton has fun at the expense of the old colonial Englishman's odd, codefied attitudes, but makes the point (which Mannoni understresses) that his behaviour was in fact conditioned by his living among people who, if he lost face, would take advantage of it and challenge his authority. And so, says Thornton, 'a white man does not show fear. He does not show anger. He does not lose his dignity. He cannot relax. His efficiency can never be in question, or at least be seen to be in

relevant part of Mannoni's thesis, as I understand it, may be roughly indicated as follows:

In the so-called 'primitive' societies, people enjoy a sense of tribal security nourished by a social structure that affords everyone a place, and the emotional comfort of being attached to it. When a people loses its tribal security through colonial invasion, it transfers its strong need for something to depend on to the new colonial masters. The relationship may be reassuring and satisfactory for a time. But if these bonds of dependence – which are encouraged in the colonial situation – prove disappointing; if there comes a time when the subject people feels rebuffed or rejected; then the bonds are snapped, and the dependence complex turns into active hostility. The patron has betrayed his beneficiary and provoked his wrath: first training and educating him, and then, when he shows a will of his own, refusing to accept him as an equal.

Mannoni points out that this dependence complex, of which he has so much to say, meets exactly the psychological needs of the 'colonial' Europeans. Philip Mason, in his introduction to the book, puts it this way:[1]

'Everyone in a competitive (i.e. European) society is, to some degree, the victim of an inferiority complex, which may be expressed in a manly determination to make good, in a desire for perfection . . . in a tiresome aggressiveness, in a hundred other forms. To the spirit convinced of its own inferiority, the homage of a dependant is balm and honey, and to surround oneself with dependants is perhaps the easiest way of appeasing an ego eager for reassurance. M. Mannoni suggests that the colonial administrator, the missionary and the pioneer show themselves, by choosing a colonial career, particularly prone to this weakness, of which the germ is present in every member

---

question: one white man supports another. He must exhibit *sang-froid* and *savoir faire* in all normal situations, and also in those that are abnormal, a great many of which he himself creates: for what was "big game hunting" in origin but a need to draw attention to one's superior courage and skill? Native prudence retires from the presence of the tiger or the rhinoceros, but a white man must pit wits with him. And large beasts must be felled with a single shot.'

[1] Philip Mason was until recently Director of Studies in Race Relations at the Royal Institute of International Affairs.

of a competitive society and flourished with peculiar luxuriance in the warm broth of the colonial situation.'

'The colonialists,' says Mannoni, 'know of the need for dependence, for they exploit it; they live by it. They do not want it to be removed. . . . They do in fact foster it by instinctively adopting a paternalistic attitude, with too much affection and too much punishment.' He stresses that 'the colonial is not looking for profit only; he is also greedy for certain other psychological satisfactions, and that is much more dangerous.'

In short, the coloniser has got rid of his own inferiority complex by implanting an inferiority complex in the colonised. Henceforth it is the colonised who feels that his own skin colour is disadvantageous; who associates power, privilege and status with white. And it is this inferiority complex, says Mannoni, having its source in the impact of European culture on a native culture, that poisons the attitudes of all backward peoples and is the key to their psychology.

Among many shrewd insights, Mannoni points out that

'grave misunderstandings occur between Europeans and colonial peoples because we have certain moral prejudices which prevent us seeing things as they really are and but for which we should realise, for instance, that dependence excludes gratitude. That this is so is shown by the fact that we have to *teach* European children to be grateful, and even then there is an element of hypocrisy in it, for the child cannot really learn gratitude until he has attained independence'.

So now we know that those exasperated travellers who complain of the 'natives' lack of gratitude' are simply projecting upon the native their own desire for reward. The patron should not press his beneficiary for the return of a loan which the latter has accepted as a gift.

Finally, to illustrate the effects of the colonial relationship on the subject races, Mannoni quotes Caliban:

> '. . . When thou camest first,
> Thou strok'dst me, and mad'st much of me . . .
> . . . and then I lov'd thee

– and then you abandoned me before I had time to become your equal. In other words: you taught me to be dependent, and I was happy; then you betrayed me and plunged me into inferiority.'

Mannoni's psychological explanations are all very well. Most of us are probably unaware of these subtle thought processes and inferiority feelings within ourselves. When I confront Mr Tompkins in the City Bar with the phrase 'The negro is the white man's fear of himself' he tells me not to be silly.

None the less, the implications of Oyono's theme in *Houseboy* – the frustration and rejection of the black man's aspirations by the old colonialist reluctance to acknowledge his maturity – is easily recognisable. Relics of this attitude are still with us in, for instance, the noticeable caution with which expatriate heads of department Africanise staff for fear standards will drop; a tendency for the British and other Western governments to withhold aid if their protégé shows signs of defiance; widespread lack of sympathy with African 'Freedom Movements'. Bluntly, a reluctance to believe that Africans can run things either efficiently or honestly on their own.

But by and large Oyono's theme is already dated. It belongs to Bradley's day ('In so far as we DCs thought about ultimate independence at all, we did so in terms of two or three generations').[1] The contemporary obsession is with aggressive black self-assertion marked by bouts of outright harrying and rejection of the white man in Africa, and, on the latter's part, by a serious loss of confidence in his role in Africa.

Here in Uganda the old European patron and mentor, the missionary as well as the out-and-out business man, have been called imperialists, spies, and guerilla agents, and many have been peremptorily told to go.[2]

---

[1] Sir Kenneth Bradley: *The Diary of a District Officer*, London, 1966.

[2] Thus Dr Barkham, Senior Physician of Mulago Hospital, was accused by Amin's government of spreading 'political gonorrhoea' and given a fortnight to leave the country. Missionary societies have been charged with recruiting and harbouring military men and mercenaries. Like the Indian (and the Israelis) before him, the British in Uganda are denounced for 'milking the economy'.

Barnes

Leonard Barnes, who submits to no orthodox school of thought and has worked out his own ideas about Africa, gives serious attention to Mannoni's theory of the African dependence complex and its corollary – fear of freedom. I would like to cite some of his comments.

'The crux of the African psychological predicament at the present stage,' he says, 'is that the new rulers and their adherents are deeply immersed in a dependence complex, yet sharply challenged at the same time by political and social issues of great urgency and complexity, which only radically independent minds have a hope of solving.'

He goes on: 'Africa's need . . . is simply the universal need for men and women of mature, balanced, and independent personality. These are in short supply everywhere. . . . How can Africa multiply hers? The key lies in the wide dissemination of the experimental spirit.'

'The African aim of self-determination,' he concludes, is being frustrated by 'certain traits in the contemporary African-type personality which take comfort in dependence. . . . What the new Africa is in search of, whether it knows it or not, is some form of collective psychotherapy.'

The desirable new traits Barnes lists as follows:

1 Capacity to accept personal responsibility.
2 Capacity to decline the role either of *patron* to *petits frères* or of *petit frére* to *patron*.
3 Capacity first to limit, then to reduce, addiction to foreign aid, whether financial, technical, or military.
4 Capacity to accept it as a grace in sons and daughters to improve on the performance of their parents.
5 Capacity to keep the African-type personality intact by avoiding cultural contamination and assimilation, while at the same time selectively incorporating non-African personality-elements of a hygienic kind.
6 Capacity to stand self-critically aside from the routines of African culture, and to submit them to amending scrutiny.
7 Capacity to incorporate the scientific attitude and its conceptual equipment.

8 Capacity to collaborate in political campaigns aiming at social growth.

These capacities, if realised, would in their aggregate constitute a cure of the dependence complex. It is noted, for future reference, that advance towards any of these capacities is barely perceptible, if at all, in any spare-part élite country.

By contrast, steady advance towards all of them is going on in all the movements of peasant revolt. In his forthright way Barnes explains what he calls 'spare-parts élitism' as follows. It means:

'the replacement of non-Africans by Africans job by job, first in key positions, then with all proper speed in all positions of public authority'. But it is erroneous to think that 'African personnel can be treated as mere spare parts for the old colonial engine. All that occurs then is that one set of exploiters is substituted for another, while the engine either breaks down, or continues to run to the old tune for the old purposes.'

One disastrous consequence of this is that 'foreign aid is delivered exclusively into the hands of the urban élites . . . it only rarely reaches the peasantry at all. . . . The main practical function of foreign aid, is not to boost African development, but to nourish the theft-economy.'

This theft-economy (or, to use Professor Andreski's notorious phrase, 'kleptocracy')[1] Barnes considers to be a far more significant mark of new African states than the widely publicised trend towards the one-party state or to military dictatorship.

[1] Stanislav Andreski: *The African Predicament*, London, 1968.

CHAPTER 22

Encounters

I have read or skimmed through several hundred books in my garden. Lately I have read Graham Greene's *A Sort of Life*, J. S. Collis's *Bound upon a Course*, Naipaul's *In a Free State*, and Susan Hill's painful study of a child's misery *I'm the King of the Castle*. I name these books because they have left an impression on me – and so, too, did Ian Harvey's *To Fall Like Lucifer*, in which this former junior minister in Macmillan's government relates the story of his public disgrace (it is not easy, though, in the cruder atmosphere of Africa, for the reader to get seriously worked up about a gentleman's furtive act with a soldier in a London park).

What appalling things seem to have happened to some British authors in their childhood. Beverley Nicholls recently told us how he tried to murder his father. Collis says quite frankly that from the hour of his birth his mother hated him. 'There was no let up for forty years. The earliest years were so difficult to take that I have suffered virtual loss of memory. . . . Certainly I have no recollection of anything save shrinking from her and her shrinking from me, no word of endearment or act of tenderness.'

Graham Greene relates that as a child he was not ill treated. But bored and lonely (he speaks of his hopeless misery, humiliation and mental pain) he used to skulk and play truant: a manic depressive (as he was later to diagnose himself) with an early death-wish. His several clumsy attempts to commit suicide failed.

And from what awful private experience is Susan Hill writing when she so excruciatingly records how a young boy is bullied and tormented until he drowns himself? 'On the bank of the stream he took his clothes off and folded them in a pile. He

shivered and the water was very cold, silky, against his body. . . .
He began to splash and stumbled forwards, into the middle of
the stream, where the water was deepest. When it had reached
up to his thighs, he lay down slowly and put his face full into
it and breathed in a long, careful breath.'

As for Naipaul's book, which reviewers have called a master-
piece, his Africans are little better than animals. Their armpits
smell, they have paunches and clumsy feet, from time to time
one hears them giggling and screaming insanely in the kitchen.
Why does Naipaul fear and hate the black man?

Childhood

My own childhood, by comparison with the miseries recorded
above, must have been idyllic. I was generally out of doors,
dirty, muscular, wearing big dusty boots. No one flogged or
bullied me. In fights with street boys I could look after myself.
I played cricket in summer and football in winter, or watched
the grown-ups – club cricket at Moseley Ashfield where red-
faced stockbrokers muffed catches, the Hon. F. S. G. Calthorpe's
Warwickshire eleven (with Quaife, Howell, and Tiger Smith) at
Edgbaston, Moseley Rugby Football Club at the Reddings. I
trespassed in other people's gardens, in private parks, railway
cuttings and tunnels, crouching in a sooty manhole when the
trains came thundering through. I was fed on meat and heavy
puddings, and in winter threw snowballs at policemen.

Something bred in me at an early age the desire to wander
that has kept me away from home for forty years. Was it that
picture by Millais of the boy enraptured by an old seadog's
yarns? The prize edition of *Masterman Ready* I won at my
preparatory school? Those nineteenth-century German volumes
in Gothic print collected by my mother, with their fairy-tale
etchings of gabled and turreted cities, of Anabaptists who looked
like madmen from Grimm ('they took off all their clothes and
walked naked in the streets of Münster'), and of Prussian
Uhlans hunting Frenchmen with lances? Was it the claustro-
phobic monotony, the bricked-in skyline, of those Birmingham
streets of bolted houses? Or the gift, when I was seven, of a
bicycle which enabled me to escape to fields where horses
swished their tails?

The War, for me, with its visits to foreign cities (Baghdad, Damascus, Odessa . . .) and the constant bivouacking in a changing landscape, was the continuation of a meandering journey that I had already commenced in the thirties in Central Europe and much earlier along English lanes.

Now, in East Africa, when it is evening and I listen to the shrill of insects and for the thousandth time, before I go to bed, search among the stars for the Great Bear that is shining high over Europe and smell the heavy scent of mango blossom and moon flowers, I sometimes feel that I have been cooking here in the sun long enough, that I would like to go tearing again on skis over the frozen glaciers of the Silvretta, or let the cold November swell of the Black Sea burn my body with an icy electric shock. Clearly I have drifted into the dead-end profession of itinerant teacher because I have found it to be a convenient way of subsidising a journey. But what have my school friends done, who studied sixth form history with me under Ian MacMaster?

There were three of us and we each in 1931 started on level terms by winning an open history scholarship to Oxford or Cambridge. Roy Lewis until very recently was Commonwealth correspondent of *The Times*. His writings on African affairs, liberal yet realistic, have certainly influenced the opinions of a great many people. J. H. Parry, former Vice-Chancellor of the University of Wales, scintillates as a historian of maritime discovery and seaborne empires.[1] Myself, I have slipped away from office and desk into the open spaces and the sunshine. 'Madly singing in the mountains' has been fun. One day there will be no answering echo. Only, at the bottom of the last hill, the charitable institutions of the Welfare State and a bench in a public park.

Impressions

Let me quote from Roy Lewis's latest book *The British in Africa* an example of his insight:

[1] John Enoch Powell was two years my senior at school, and I had little to do with him. He was a white-faced, earnest boy who carried a Greek dictionary under his arm. He did not smile, or kick a rugby ball. In his speech-making and polemical journalism, which has outraged and fascinated Englishmen, I recognise the arrogance and sometimes crazy, arid logic of the brilliant book-worm.

'The encounter with Africa was an encounter with Africans. There was no empty space for settlement; even when there seemed to be, Africans in hordes appeared as soon as the settlers had jobs to offer or cattle to steal. European life in Africa was as deeply pervaded by the personality of the black savage as in India it was by the Hindu and caste. Discovering, misunderstanding, and rediscovering the African personality was a large theme in British historical experience in Africa. . . . British life in Africa was life with Africans – whether trading with them, fighting them or governing them. The black man was the module of all the natural marvels of the dark continent revealed to African eyes by explorers.'

In referring to the pervasion of European life in Africa by 'the black savage' Lewis is making a point that is too little stressed. The Europeans in Africa have tended to understate, if not deny, the effects that living among Africans has had upon themselves; for it is the mentor, conscious of his own superiority, who believes he dominates, not his pupil. Van der Post thought differently, even though the instances that he cites from his experience of Kenya settlers in *Venture to the Interior* happen to be somewhat discreditable.

'We hear a great deal about the devastating effect that the European has on the native in Africa,' he writes, 'but none has ever stopped to inquire into the effect of the native on the European. . . . One sees it in the records of European crime in the colony . . . conventional morality has lost some of its power, people's appetites are given an importance and a licence they do not have at home. . . . Nor is it an accident, I believe, that like his black neighbour the European leaves a very heavy, a disproportionate burden of the daily practical work to his women. These settlers' wives in Kenya are amazing. I raise to them a light, humble, European hat, officers' demobilisation pattern, without snake or zebra skin round it, with great sympathy, respect, and deference.'

We can all think of other effects in this interplay of influence. Africa knocks the Puritanism out of an Englishman. The black man's easy going attitude to work, the zest and the indolence, the capacity for quick emotional response and happiness, remind him that life is not so grim after all. He slows down, reassesses himself in unusual situations. He may expect too much of the African, in which case disillusionment can turn him sour. But the man in an English suit who was plummeted from London on to Entebbe airport will never be quite the same again. Egrets wearing tiny yellow spats greet him. By the roadside, the coffee blossom is like white lace.

In another passage, referring to the modern type of traveller ('the tourist') in Africa, Lewis says:

'Travellers changed their fashion too. Though some sought the remaining inaccessible places, most now explored the African community. It became the thing to travel on African buses or mammy-wagons, living in African homes or hotels, travelling third class, wearing short shorts or other modern leisure wear, and to come up with a fund of funny stories exactly as in Victorian times, but in a modern genre recorded on tapes. Travellers were no longer amateur explorers in Livingstone's footsteps; they were amateur anthropologists.'

So after those footslogging journeys in search of the Nile source, the trail-blazing through forest and bush, the hunting down of his animals and the planting of commercial crops in their stead, it is the African himself whom we have currently set out to discover; and if, when we are confronted with men such as Nkrumah, Lumumba and General Amin we curtly dismiss them as paranoiacs, hypermanics, it seems we are not getting very far in our researches.

Leonard Levitt of the American Peace Corps made his own private discovery of the school children of Ndumulu School in Tanzania – and of the local food ('Could I eat it without becoming sick?'), the beer ('a thick mushy gray-brown paste, with bubbles and foam'), the women's breasts ('very large and very black – ah, what mothers they must be!').[1]

Paul Theroux has told us what it is like to doss down in the dens of low-class African women.

[1] Leonard Levitt: *An African Season*, London, 1968.

Dr John Beattie, in quest of anthropological knowledge, took a hoe and dug his own food plot in a Bunyoro village.

My Danish neighbour, trying to discover and to understand, found himself groping, lost in the dark places and the hysteria of his young African wife's unhinged mind.

The number of white men who have photographed a circumcision ceremony among the Bagisu grows. Essays, monographs, and symposia on the African personality abound. What was Levitt's conclusion?

'It suddenly occurred to me,' he says, 'that we had been with these people nearly a year now, that we had lived in their village, had eaten their food, had taught their children. But what did we really know of them? Nearly a year, and what had we learned? If anything, that we weren't close to them at all, that we seemed to become farther apart the longer we lived there. . . . Nearly a year . . . and how little I understand.'

Encounter

Here now, taken from among the millions of words that white men have written about Africa, are one amateur's impressions of a minute fragment of that historic 'encounter' with Africa and the Africans to which Lewis refers:

'I looked at the jostling men: at their lip-plugs lodged like loose dental plates in the gap where incisor teeth had been rooted out; at their feathered coiffures, their lean, scarified bodies, their hairless bellies and dusty buttocks. They carried sticks and spears. Some had glazed and damaged eyes, one or two were blind. They brought with them a swarm of small, irritating flies. They wanted cigarettes.

'This, my first confrontation with naked tribesmen, was an unforgettable moment. I have had 500 Italian prisoners-of-war stripped for delousing in the Western Desert: they were merely white men whose pallor was stained with dark patches of hair; without dignity, bawling out in their high voices the names of their friends, grinning and scratching themselves. This sort of nakedness, though, had style. The Tepeth were not, in fact, naked at all, but they had subtly refashioned their nakedness in

a decorative way. In the virtual absence of clothes it was their
bodies they had cut, coloured, disguised, and pierced with bits
of finery. The dark pigment was a varnish, the beaded necklaces
and flashing armlets the skin's mosaic.'

On landscape, there is this passage:

'In Kigezi and the Congo border country, rain and mist
enfold forested tumuli in black shadows and a blue-grey wash.
The innumerable hills, piled one upon the other, enclose you
like tumbling waves. No sooner have you breasted the top of
one than you must descend into the trough of another. The
elusive view which you hoped to see from the next knoll is
likely to be blurred or lost in aqueous haze. Away from the
contour strips and the roughly cleared scrub where mosquitoes
buzz, forests of bamboo and trees swollen by creepers shut
you in.
'Karamoja is different. In its clear light and dry air you can
see for miles across immense tracts of grass and scrub. It is a
restless landscape, alive with the small moving figures of cattle
and herdsmen, of game and flitting birds. Even the cattle kraals
are transient. Here and there among the stones are the ashes of
a wanderer's fire; or a water hole trampled with spoor and
splayed footmarks, on which green scum is floating. It is a
country to set one's feet in motion. A twenty-mile trek through
the grass is nothing. The morning's landmarks, slightly altered
in angle and aspect, will still be there at night.'

Both passages quoted above represent, it will be said, the
romantic impressions of an outsider. I should apologise for
quoting them, for they are my own.

11a Atum resting; Turkana camp

11b Kalisto and family outside his bachelor hut
11c Kalisto with students, Adilang

12a Terraced fields, Kigezi

12b Kampala garden; flamboyant tree

PART V

EDUCATION AND TRADITIONS

CHAPTER 23

Teaching

Twice a year I and my colleagues of the National Teachers' College in Kampala tune up our second-hand cars and rattle round Uganda for six weeks to watch our trainee students temporarily in action at the dozens of secondary schools that over the years have sprung up from an original small nucleus of missionary establishments. We cover 2,000 to 3,000 miles. When it is over we wipe the red mud off our cars, hand in the reports that will decide the professional future of a hundred or so young Africans, and cash our mileage cheques.

After long months of theory and library study, teaching practice is the testing time for our students. They have been coached – perhaps over-coached – and they must now go out to face the bowling. The young man who has been concentrating on modern European history finds to his alarm that he has to give, immediately, a course of lessons on Ancient Babylonia. The cantankerous student leader who in his first two years slated the imperialists in debate but has since, with the promise of a posting and a monthly salary near at hand, cooled down, will conduct himself, temporarily, like a lamb under the eye of a strange and stern headmaster. Our Indian students are no longer with us. The shy Ismaili girl who cooked her own rice meals and curried sauce in her room and hid her legs in cotton trousers would have probably had to tackle a class of muscular African boys who seemed too big for their desks.

The travelling we do on these occasions takes us to many remote and fascinating places: private schools, windowless and dusty, hidden behind banana groves; old mission centres of weathered red brick standing in gardens of exotic shrubs; an American-built boarding school for girls with electrically operated kitchens and cement-covered walks; city day schools that teem with shifts of children.

There is Nyenga, a little cloistered refuge overlooking Lake Victoria where *mvule* trees hang dark bundles of foliage over cascading bougainvillea: Villa Maria on a steep hill above coffee and banana gardens through which the blood-red paths are cut like tunnels; Nyapea, 5,000 feet up on the Congo border, a place so cool that the priests (Americans of the Sacred Heart community) eat ravenously at breakfast and wear pullovers.

Africanisation

The ultimate aim of the teacher training courses is to produce enough African teachers to run Uganda's secondary schools. It was intended that they should reinforce, and gradually replace, the 800 mainly British expatriate teachers who were considered indispensable to the educational system especially at the higher levels. Now that so many expatriates have left under pressure of recent events, the immediate contribution of African teachers has become even more vital.

It is an ambitious and necessary programme that sprang decisively into life only half a dozen years ago when large grants were provided to expand secondary schools and teacher training on a national scale.

It should not be thought that Africanisation implies unreasonable antagonism towards expatriate teachers (though American Peace Corps teachers have sometimes been suspected of CIA connections). The fact is that expatriate teachers are expensive. We tend more and more to be birds of passage on short contracts, so that our contributions are erratic and incomplete. As representatives of a foreign culture we inevitably, whether by design or not, disseminate some attitudes, ideas, and beliefs that are not necessarily relevant to Uganda – a process which critics would call 'brainwashing African children'.

It is difficult, of course, for a European teacher to see African history from the inside: to teach it without arrogance or undue reference to Livingstone, Speke, Lugard, and the rest of those triumphant intruders with their askaris and their superior knowledge. (In Turkish schools, I recall, history and religion were two sacrosanct subjects that foreigners were forbidden to teach, with the result that Turkish history was presented to the nation – and why not, if it strengthened morale and patriotism in a vulnerable geographical situation? – as a scroll of victories in battle.)

It is difficult, too, for a foreigner without unusual gifts of insight and much special knowledge to recognise the true positive value of many basic aspects of African society – polygamy and bride price, the extended family, belief in spirits; and it is almost impossible for him to identify himself with the private background, the problems and joys, of an African village boy (still more girl).

Yet there is no easy or immediate prospect of finding enough African teachers to take over education completely – and with competence – at the higher levels. The sort of young African who can qualify at this standard will find better rewards for his abilities elsewhere: in scholarships and posts abroad, in politics, business, and the new parastatal bodies that are taking control of major sections of the Uganda economy. Bright young men do not want to rough it up-country with a bicycle and lantern and the awful boredom of the dead nights.

There are not many places outside Kampala even in Uganda's provincial towns, that provide the social and cultural amenities (books, theatre, intellectual stimulus, fashionable shops and good bars) which young graduates from the capital have grown used to.

Concurrently with the recent appearance of more and more trained African teachers in secondary school staff rooms (which, in the British tradition, tend to be happy, informal places littered with tea cups, football boots, and old magazines), much has been done to Africanise the syllabuses. In biology, students have been made to take far more interest in their own environment (perhaps a false sense of inferiority inclined them in the past to ignore or belittle their own flora and fauna as uninteresting, primitive or 'brutish').

Not only are the latest English language textbooks written by Africans. It is not enough nowadays to tell young Africans that they must read Rider Haggard. They want to know why; and they want to read their own African writers too. The scope of

English literature has been widened to include a whole new genre of prose and verse written by Africans– often with themes of protest against white colonialism or of corruption amongst the native élite – and made cheaply available by Heinemann and by local publishing houses in Kampala and Nairobi.

Above all, African history is now shown to have a past that antedates by aeons the arrival of the white man, and over vast areas has continued to evolve almost with indifference to his presence. The new version of African history, researched and rewritten from vernacular sources and from an African point of view, looks to the ancient links with Egypt, the Sudan, Ethiopia, and northern Africa, even China: examines the origin and migration of tribes, the age-old skills in metallurgy, art forms and medicine, the practice and development of religious beliefs that, despite early misinterpretation by missionaries, are far removed from 'paganism'.

The days when schoolmasters and textbooks taught that African history began with its 'discovery' by the white man, who in his god-like presumption bestowed European names on Africa's lakes and mountains, are over.

Schools

Wide differences in the style and quality of schools, both primary and secondary, in Uganda, though these have been diminished by the expansion and repair programme initiated under Obote, may reflect the old religious ambitions of their founders as well as discrepancies of prosperity between one district and another. In earlier times, when schools were strictly denominational, Protestant and Catholic missions often erected rival primary schools almost facing one another (an unnecessary duplication of resources), or so far removed that children obliged to attend the correct denominational school might have a ten-mile walk to the classroom.

In Acholi and Teso, where people are not ashamed of digging and children are brought up to respect authority, the thorn bush and cotton fields open up from time to time to show well kept schools with grassy lawns that are neatly shaved by pupils. Among the countless rounded hills of Kigezi, where education was started comparatively late and communications are difficult, rural schools are often ramshackle places hidden among quick-growing elephant grass.

In prosperous Buganda and Busoga you will see files of children in bright school shirts and skirts trotting along the verge of shining tarmac roads. Across the Nile, to the north, and in Karamoja, where the dirt roads quickly turn to mud or dust, the Verona Fathers have to cope with poverty and parental obstinacy.

In the east, Mill Hill Fathers have stamped their personality on solid buildings of red brick, with arches and cloisters that put one in mind of Germanic Europe. Uganda's best-known school, producer of an 'élite', associated with cricket, the education of sons of chiefs, and a certain aura of public school snobbery, was founded by the CMS.

Private schools (there are many) cannot easily be categorised. The pupils who attend them are a mixed bag. The owners charge heavily. Yet boys frequently sleep on makeshift beds in overcrowded dormitories, and they may have to grow much of their food on neighbouring plots of land.

There are the big-town day schools, busy as sausage factories, which used to overflow not only with African boys and girls but with the children of local Indian businessmen and shopkeepers. Indian children rarely boarded. African food would not have suited them (no chapattis, no rice curry, or coast mangoes), and they would not have been able to practise their religion. Indian parents, as we know, are even in exile among the most conservative in the world. They insist that their children grow up observing the social rituals and taboos that in effect keep them apart from other communities, yet are the secret of their survival.

Indian boys used to play cricket and hockey, Africans excel in athletics, football and boxing. In the classroom Indian children are bright, noisy, inquisitive; African boys (unless they have been got at) are generally soft-spoken and serious, the girls, if they are not prodded, and especially if they are in mixed classes, shy and silent observers (a girl is traditionally trained at home not to voice her opinions in public).

The African boy is extraordinarily teachable. His parents have sacrificed to scrape together the fees (1,000 or more shillings a year to board, an enormous sum for a small cotton farmer).

He comes into the classroom to learn. Success in exams will revolutionise his life, lift him out of the village into the dream-world of the twentieth century.

For the Indian schoolboy there was rather less at stake. He had more money behind him. There was probably an Indian shop or business to absorb him.

Yet the present system of education in Uganda, despite all that has been done, has serious flaws that have attracted increasing criticism. True cultural independence, it is often argued, requires that Swahili or a vernacular language should be introduced as a medium of instruction to supplement English. The present overwhelming stress on academic subjects ought to be offset by a stronger national drive to train more young people in technical and agricultural skills.

There are not enough office and white-collar jobs to absorb the expanding host of school-leavers, the thousands of young people who having had schooling up to primary seven, reject the idea of working on the land, overflow the labour market, and imperil the social stability of towns.

As for the expatriate teacher, his rewards are not to be measured solely in material terms. In the strange, dynamic, and unpredictable environment of Africa he can take time off from the rat race to reassess himself. He counts as a real person, his craft is necessary, and it is respected. He can identify himself with the exciting aspirations of a developing country.

He is, or ought to be, whatever the nature of political government, an optimist: for what would be the point of teaching if the results were negative? Finally, it is not too late, if he happens to be travelling up country, to see an unscheduled lion come out of the grass and cross the red earth road.

Literature

A decade ago the English literature syllabus both in schools and in higher education in Uganda consisted almost entirely of British authors: adventure tales and Biggles at one end, Shaw and Eliot at the other. Whatever their merits, none of these books had any direct relevance to an African situation. When I started teaching at the National Teachers' College in Kampala

I got permission to introduce books that had an African background or were written by modern professionals. The mixture is still in use.

The African student's response to his reading reveals interesting insights. His sensitivity to sleights or criticism makes him feel unhappy with Graham Greene's picture of Africa in *A Burnt Out Case*, with its lepers and droning mosquitoes and the superstitions. 'A white man's distorted view of "Darkest Africa",' he says. In Camus's *The Outsider* it is not the senseless killing of an Arab that offends him but a young man's inconceivable refusal to 'show grief' at his mother's death, an insult to his own emotional family mourning and death rites. For him, Scobie's guilt feelings about adultery in Greene's *The Heart of the Matter* are the scruples of a weakling. Oyono's *Houseboy*, set in the French Cameroon, confirms his worst notions of white colonial rule, though he readily concedes that such brutal behaviour was not typical of British rule in Uganda.

Europe's cult-image of the 'noble savage' as described in Moorehead's book on Captain Cook's Tahiti he finds amusing and implausible: utterly alien to his own experience of the white man's attitude to the 'black savages' of Africa.

No African student would want to emulate Gavin Maxwell (*A Reed Shaken by the Wind*) who voluntarily, at great expense, in gross discomfort and for the sheer fun of it, spends weeks exploring bilharzia-infested bogs among the Marsh Arabs of Iraq. In all probability his own village childhood will have given him a surfeit of bog and bush.

Tournier's reconstructed Robinson Crusoe (*Friday, or the Other Island*), who draws up a constitution for his desert island, invents a water-clock, works madly to keep himself sane, stocks up with huge quantities of food and masturbates against trees, he joyfully recognises as the conventional West European: worried about tomorrow ('for us Africans, time is what is *present* and what is *past*'), possessive, compulsively busy, sexually perverted.

Writing
One thinks of the background landscape to mediaeval European

paintings as stylised chaos: black forbidding mountains, ravine and forest lowering behind the cloisters and the frail Madonnas. The only acceptable piece of nature was a tamed enclosure: a garden with fountains playing, an arbour.

The African writer, too, seems to turn a blind eye on the realities of nature. His fictional or poetic landscape is the village clearing with its granaries and cattle kraal, its squabbles over land and bride wealth; or the towns with their bars, corruption and women. It takes a middle-aged white man, a Hillaby, to walk some hundreds of miles through the bush and to *describe* it; or a retired Dutch gentleman, a Van der Post, to give us a meticulous description of a mountain. No black African seems to think that nature in the raw, or the birds, animals and plants that inhabit it, are worth the effort of close descriptive writing. His sunset, or the shimmering plain, if they are described at all, are done so cursorily or in clichés. The African writer has his reasons. He has probably grown up in the bush. He has seen enough of wild grass, prickly trees and crocodiles. He does not like them. His parents have had to struggle against them for survival.

When the rescue ship arrives at length at his desert island, Tournier's English castaway refuses to be taken off. It is Friday, the black man, who deserts – running back to the civilisation that is going to enslave and put him miserably to work in the plantations.

The town dweller in Europe, looking through his window at the suburban asphalt, longs to walk in a copse with toadstools and small animals in it. Blackamoors are no longer brought to England as pets and servants. Instead, with the approaching extermination of our own wild life, we import African lions to prowl behind English hedges.

So it has been left to Hillaby (*Journey to the Jade Sea*), not to the indigenous writer, to note that 'a spiral of birds turned like tea leaves in the sky'; to Van der Post (*Venture to the Interior*) to describe roan antelopes 'with horns like Saracens' swords', 'a great bronze leopard sunning itself, and drying the dew off its whiskers', 'aloes like scarlet candelabra', and those 'immense piles of rain wheeling over Mlanje'.

African hunting songs praise human bravery. It was Hemingway's red-faced Mr Wilson who reminded us of the courage and pain of the hunted animal.

My own African students find it difficult to paint a landscape in words. For them it is either too obvious to merit description; or too unsympathetic to identify with. Since Africa consists largely of unmolested nature, they are ignoring one of the main experiences in their lives.

Whatever his academic shortcomings in some fields – in the enormous field of European and world history, for instance – the young African is mature in things that count: in matters of birth, death, illness and human suffering, of which he has much private experience. He believes in political democracy but accepts that in an African society, conditioned to put tribal loyalties first and to fear and follow chiefs, it is not workable. He is always ready to protest against institutional rules which, he thinks, infringe his rights as a 'human being'; yet he is easily cowed by the barrel of a gun.

He has wit and zest. He is delightful to teach, to know and to befriend. But the ghosts and fears that emanate from an antique background and an elemental struggle to survive still haunt the depths of his mind.

SCHOOLS

During the long dull hours I spend in hotels while visiting the schools where our students of the National Teachers' College are on teaching practice, I sometimes make notes of the day's experiences. I cite some of these entries below, not because they record anything unusual but because they are typical of the daily round.

July 1969: Mbarara

I am staying at the old Ankole Inn. Few guests, empty sauce bottles, chicken feathers blowing in from the kitchen. Most people prefer the new Agip Motel which has an ugly view of a petrol station but good food. Mr Hall, who built and for many years managed the Ankole Inn and gave it style, has lately sold out to Indians. He has retired to a hut near the servants' lines and champs his meals (no lower dentures) alone in a corner of the dining room. An Israeli military instructor from the barracks, with paratroop wings and thick hairy arms, glowers at me over a piece of fish. Village girls smeared with Lifebuoy soap still wait among the bushes at night to catch guests going to bed. Last night two drunken Indians in sports jackets and with Ronald Colman moustaches made a great noise in the bar. At 2 a.m. I got out of bed and asked them to shut up. After some argument they left. As they drove off (not before) they shouted 'White bastard!' The local honky-tonk is run by a Goan. Half-hidden behind the barmaid's breasts I can see in his living room a big picture of Jesus with a Bleeding Heart.

July 1969: Masindi
Every day zebra-striped mini-buses serving Murchison Falls Game Park bring package tourists for lunch at the Masindi Hotel. The tourists are mostly elderly American couples (some Scandinavians and Italians). They are enjoying the adventure. Cameras hang round the men's necks like stethoscopes. Men (in Bermuda shorts) and women, as they bend over the cold buffet (they are rather greedy about food), expose big round bottoms and white legs streaked with blue veins. Denied service, I wait grumpily in a corner till they have gone.

The young African headmaster at Hoima gave me a rocket for smoking my pipe in the laboratory. A very good student teacher did his best with the geography lesson (the Andes, their salt lakes and rain belts), but the class had been at it since 7 a.m. and as the clock approached 1.30 p.m. their heads sank lower and lower on the desks.

At Kabalega School, another poor history lesson; a few bare facts taken from the textbook ('Charles the Great wore a Holy Crown blessed by the Pope').

February 1972: Lira
There were at least 150 men but only a dozen women at the hotel dance last night. The girls look terrible this morning, bashed to skin and bone. The music (played by a regimental jazz band) was so loud that Remy Oler told me today they could dance to it at Boroboro five miles away. At Comboni College

the term has just started. The boys are in clean shorts and shirts (which they wash, but do not iron, once a week), some already split over arms and shoulders. They have long tapering legs and large feet. A plaster crucifix hangs over every blackboard. The student teacher whose music lesson I observed (excellent rhythmic drumming) has spent his lodging allowance on a new pair of Terylene trousers and asks me for a loan. The white priests, as they always do, keep the school gardens in splendid condition. Along the country roads men are lugging bags of cotton on bicycles; fallen cotton fluff spatters the verges like scraps of snow.

Driving to Gulu I pass through tracts of bush scorched by grass fires. Coral trees stand among soot and blackened ant-hills; the scarlet trusses flaring from their leafless branches look like flames, as though the trees were still on fire.

March 1972: Kampala

Four of the schools I am due to visit have been on strike: Kigezi High School, Wanyange (Jinja), and two in the Mbarara area. Strikes seem to flare up from single incidents (a disappointing film show, a meal of rotten potatoes) that bring to a head and are symptomatic of long-standing irritation. Strikes are often violent (stone throwing, car burning).[1]

March 1972: Aga Khan School, Kampala

The children at this Ismaili-founded school used to be almost all Indian. They are now very mixed (Indian, African, some white). The Irish headmaster – a former priest who married and has children by a Kenya African girl – sees to it that the school has tone: pupils wear school uniform, blackboards shine, the zebra crossing is supervised. During the English lesson some

---

[1] A bad incident involved a stone-throwing attack on J. B. Stenhouse, an expatriate arts teacher, and his wife by pupils of Mvara School, Arua, on the night of 20 February 1970. Stenhouse fired his shot-gun and wounded a 19-year-old student who bled to death. The following October a Gulu chief magistrate (Patel, an Indian) sentenced him to seven years imprisonment for manslaughter. Stenhouse's appeal against his excessive sentence was turned down by the High Court, Kampala (the Acting Chief Justice said he was a man 'without respect for human life'). But it was later upheld by the East African Court of Appeal, and Stenhouse was released and sent back to Britain.

Indian boys and a Ghanaian (son of a diplomat) showed off
and laughed at the student teacher's mistakes. Our trainee
African teachers always find Indian pupils a trial; they are too
bright. The Indian girls smelt strongly of hair oil.

March 1972: Old Kampala School, Kampala
Old, rather tumbledown buildings. Blackboards are grey. There
are separate staff rooms (an Indian custom) for male and female
teachers. On a patch of grass surrounded by a hedge Indian
girls were doing gymnastic exercises that resembled a rhythmic
dance. An African gardener was grinning and spying on them.
Many sunbirds and purple starlings.

March 1972: Kitante School, Kampala
Founded as a day school for Africans (no Indian connexion).
Buildings are new but overcrowded (two shifts a day) and already
dirty. Many of the boys have to live and sleep rough in servants'
quarters or on mats with friends and relatives. The English
head (a TEA man with a fine beard) and his wife are glad to
have left Moroto, where they saw the soldiers run amok last
July.

January 1973: Arua
The headmasters of Ombaci and Koboko secondary schools
are Italian priests who for many years, through many ups and
downs, and despite some prejudice against their nationality,
have stuck to their job of educating Uganda's tough northern
tribes. The headmaster at Ombaci was too worried to talk to me.
During the night the sum of 11,000 shillings in newly paid
school fees had been stolen from his office. I went into the school
chapel. A handsome painting over the altar depicts the two
stages of a successful Christian life: the schoolboy with his
books (and a typewriter); the grown man, in a suit, with his
happy family. The figures are looking up at heaven.

Between Arua and Koboko I drove through General Amin's
country. His people the Kakwa, a small Nilotic tribe from the
Sudan, were walking to markets: men in round Moslem caps,
their women tall and ugly, covered in vivid headcloths and
long orange-patterned skirts and gowns.

The two recently recruited Egyptian doctors staying at the hotel in Arua are elderly (both are retired) and they are not happy. They have no house, no transport, a food problem (no fresh salads), and the heat drives them to their beds in the afternoon. 'Most of my patients have vd,' one of the doctors told me. 'About 25 per cent have bilharzia. It is a special sort of gonorrhoea. There's only one drug – which I haven't got – that will cure it. The discharge has a very bad smell.'

'The extra money I earn in Uganda,' he added, 'pays for my son's education in London. By the way, if you want to get on with Africans be polite to them. The real reason why the Asians were kicked out was that they spoke rudely to black people.'

'What about the economic war?'

'In a year everything will be normal.'

A sleepy young soldier detailed to guard the Nile bridge at Pakwach crawled out of a small tent (he was sharing it with a girl whose legs I could see sticking through the flap) and asked me apparently without malice to repeat after him, '*Uganda mazuri* (Uganda is good), *Uganda mazuri, Uganda mazuri sana* (Uganda is very good)'.

January 1973: Mbarara

I have just heard that Mr Hall died (peacefully) in his bed at the Ankole Inn two or three days ago. I had tea there yesterday but no one told me of his death. Mr Hall (fifty years in Africa) was one of the pioneers of modern Uganda. 'I used to be in business,' he once told me, 'buying up property for a song and selling it at a large profit for companies. Uganda is a rich country – minerals, soil, fish. But the people running it lack know-how. Children twenty years ago were in a terrible state – eyes oozing pus, runny noses, swollen faces – very different now. Mothers are very good.'

In the garden of the Ankole Inn I watched a monkey in a cage defend a heap of rotting food scraps. Crows and marabou storks were trying to get at the scraps through holes in the wire. When the storks approached, the crows pulled them back by their tail feathers.

In Mbarara town I saw a Jaguar, a Wolseley, and an MG

sports car, all dented and beginning to rattle, being driven by private soldiers. Opposite the barracks is a hideous row of hovels where greasy women crouch over basins.

Mr Hoyle and his wife no longer run the Agip Motel. I said good-bye to them some weeks ago in Kampala, where Mr Hoyle had just spent two days in a police cell. They told me that General Amin had called at their motel, looked round with a scowling face, and sent them an expulsion order within twenty-four hours. Soldiers in army lorries stripped their house.

NATIONAL TEACHERS' COLLEGE

Under Richard Poskitt (1966-71) the National Teachers' College, Kampala, recruited good teachers, expanded (with British aid) its buildings and modernised the syllabuses. By 1970 all seemed set for a highly effective teacher training programme. But in this excellence there was a fatal flaw; of the fifty-five teaching staff, only six were Africans – an intolerable disproportion and an unrealistic one; for we white expatriates did not only teach and examine, we had to administer, discipline and regulate the college lives of 400 black students. True, the Uganda educational authorities had trust in us, the students appreciated the skill of white teachers in the classroom, and we, for our part, tried hard and not without success to understand our students' personal relations and problems.

Nevertheless as the days of the Protectorate retreated farther into the past, the existence of a white enclave at the heart of Uganda's educational system was becoming an aberration and a target for criticism.

In the event Amin did not tell us flatly to go away. His calculated rudeness and hostility towards the British, the spread of violence (which affected morale), and Mr Heath's retaliatory decision to withdraw aid to Uganda (which hurt our pockets), were enough to persuade the bulk of the college expatriate staff to cut their roots – some to their surprise found them shallower than they had thought – and leave Uganda between the closing months of 1972 and mid-1973.

Looking back on these events we see (April 1974) that the staff ratio at the National Teachers' College has been dramatically reversed. The six African teachers have become forty-two, the fifty-five white teachers have dwindled to three.[1] Fear and shame have knocked some of the spirit out of the students. As one up-grader student put it to me, 'We are walking through a dark valley and we dare not stumble.'

[1] The African Director who succeeded Poskitt felt obliged, after some months under Amin's military government, to flee for safety to Zambia.

CHAPTER 24

Writings

In my previous book on Uganda I noted the educated young African's talent for writing and gave examples of his work. I have encouraged students to be interested in their own traditions and culture. The contributions that follow have significance because they throw some light on the old customs that, though the outsider knows little at first hand about them, are the key to an ordinary African's behaviour, influence his prejudices and account, among other things, for his contempt for celibacy and the childless, his feeling for ancestral spirits, his fear of witchcraft, his zest for drinking and dancing.

AN ETOSOT WIFE GIVES BIRTH TO HER FIRST-BORN

The first symptoms of pregnancy may be digestive disorder or loss of appetite. The woman's husband may not suspect anything at this stage. But older women will notice. Later, when she starts to get plump, and her skin unnaturally delicate and sensitive, her husband will realise what has happened and village women will begin to gossip. But they won't mention her pregnancy in so many words for fear the 'thing' may disappear.

After three months the woman's condition is made public. As this is going to be her first-born, an older clanswoman will instruct her in the rules she is expected to observe. The rules vary somewhat from one locality to another. She may be forbidden to enter her father's house until certain ceremonies have been performed. She may be told not to eat the internal organs of animals or to hold a bone in her hand while biting the meat off it – someone else should separate the meat from the bone for her. (A bone is associated with choking, strangulation – difficult delivery.)

The pregnant woman and her husband are repeatedly warned against having sexual relations with anyone else for it is believed (apart from the risk of catching a venereal disease) that the sperm of a man other than he who has 'made the womb' may cause the woman to abort.

Advanced stage of pregnancy

Shortly before she is due to deliver the woman shows obvious signs of the impending crisis. She moves very slowly and she is tired. Her lips are parched, dry, and open. She sits with her legs stretched wide apart. She looks gloomy and apprehensive, as though she were under sentence of death. Her belly is greatly swollen, and the flesh has redistributed itself over her body, so that her lips and cheeks grow thin, and the dry, wrinkled skin hangs loosely on her bones. The size and shape of her rounded buttocks have changed. They are flatter. Her waist has thickened. Her whole appearance arouses sympathy.

At this advanced stage of her pregnancy, the husband stays for most of the time at home or near at hand. He is worried. He is alert for her slightest complaint of pain. At night if she seems unwell he massages her waist to ease the discomfort.

Meanwhile the woman will have prepared some of the things she will need when she delivers her child. She stores some millet flour to brew beer (*ajono*) with. She collects and washes scraps of cloth, ties them in a bundle, and puts them away for use immediately after she has given birth. She shells some groundnuts and puts them in a gourd.

Labour Pains and Delivery

One day the woman is suddenly gripped by labour pains. She feels so uncomfortable that everyone with her gets nervous and uneasy. The woman will certainly have been worrying for some time whether she will have a safe delivery or not. But when the labour pains come on, her fears are communicated to the others as she cries, grits her teeth, grimaces, and puckers her eyes with pain. Her husband feels that it is all his own fault. He feels guilty. If she is going to die, he will be to blame for her death.

But it is action that is needed now. The husband rushes out to fetch the midwife. Women place the patient in what is thought to be the correct position, with her back pressed against a wall and her legs spread open at about sixty degrees. Once she is in the required position, she is told not to change it.

A watery liquid sometimes mixed with blood eventually bursts out of her vagina. Now she is told to hold her breath and strain, like a person working to evacuate a hard stool. Her position is slightly altered. A woman gets behind her and makes her lean back against her legs till she is almost sitting on her waist. Another helper kneels directly in front to await the baby. Meanwhile everyone is urging the woman to go on forcing hard.

As soon as part of the baby appears, everyone presses hard on the patient to help expel it. But if the baby doesn't come out for some time, the midwife inserts her fingers into the vagina to check its position, which she may try to alter a little. Usually the head comes first, and when it does, the midwife gets her hands ready to receive the baby.

This is the critical moment. A careless or unskilled midwife may not catch the baby properly for it is coated with a slippery slime. It is also vital for the mother, despite the pain, to go on forcing the baby out, for if she desists, the baby may be strangled at the entrance to the vagina. So the helpers exhort, shout, even slap the mother.

Meanwhile her husband is waiting outside the house. He can hear everything. He hears the midwife urging his woman 'Do it! Do it!' He may get so worked up that he runs in to urge her himself, though the helpers won't welcome him. He will know, at length, that the child has been safely delivered when he hears the midwife and the helpers laughing softly. The suspense is over. Everyone is asking if it is a boy or girl. The midwife may be too busy to confirm this till she has blown into the baby's nostrils ('opening, or cleaning, the nostrils', as we say).

The umbilical cord is cut with a sharp piece of dried elephant grass, and the baby is cleaned with warm water. It begins to cry almost immediately. The midwife formally announces its sex, and names it before handing it to the mother to suckle. Meanwhile the midwife has been waiting for the afterbirth to come out. This may be delayed, in which case a herbal medicine may be given to accelerate its expulsion.

The mother is then washed, and the afterbirth is buried in the house together with any blood that has escaped during delivery. She is given millet-flour porridge to eat, and she will eat only this food for the first three days. Beer is brewed the same day, to be drunk when the three days are over. The mother must stay indoors all this time.

Ceremony after Birth

On the third day clanswomen come to clean the house. They smear it with cow dung, and prepare food. Millet bread is made, and a sauce of pounded ground-nuts, sour milk and water. When the meal is ready the mother and her baby sit at the door of the house. None of the relations and others present may eat until the mother and her infant have first tasted it, a little of the sauce being put on the baby's lips. The same procedure takes place when the beer is served.

Once these formalities are over, the mother must keep to the same food for at least three weeks. Only then can she eat normally with her family. But she will not resume sexual relations with her husband until the baby has begun to toddle – i.e. for about eight months. It is believed that if this taboo is not observed, the child's physique may suffer. It may, for instance, be very slow learning to walk.

Such is the traditional manner of child birth among my people, the Iteso. Today, of course, most women prefer to go to hospital if they can. The fee is small, and delivery will be safer.

JOHN OKIROR

CIRCUMCISION AND MARRIAGE AMONG THE BAGISU

Imbalu

The circumcision rite is known among the Bagisu as *Imbalu*, which is the name of a double-edged knife. Medicine-men once used this sort of knife when identifying evil-doers. If a man had been sick for a long time, and his relatives suspected that someone was bewitching him, the medicine-man would line up all the suspects, heat his knife till it was red hot, then pass it over the feet of each suspect in turn. Whoever suffered burns from the knife was the guilty one. He was beaten or hanged. The same type of knife is used in circumcising boys. This operation, too, causes a sharp 'burning' pain to the initiate.

Preparing for the Rite

It used to be customary to hold the circumcision rites only in good harvest years, so that initiates would be well fed, and there would be plenty to eat and drink during the celebrations. Nowadays the rite is performed in every even year, irrespective of the size of the harvest.

Isonja, the old custom of dancing before the ceremony, is still observed. The youths sing, dance, beat drums, blow whistles and make a terrific din, which the Bagisu love. They trot in procession from one house to another, collecting gifts, chanting and jingling their bells. Merrymaking lasts for some months. Initiation is usually performed between July and September. In the weeks before circumcision, the lives of the initiates are held to be especially precious, and people try to guard them from accident (someone, for instance, may carry a boy on his shoulders when crossing a stream). Yet modern car and bus drivers, speeding recklessly along the roads, have been known to plough into processions of dancing boys and to maim or kill them.

Initiation Day

It is usual these days for parents to put up a simple enclosure for the circumcision ceremony. Each initiate on entering knows where to stand (this has already been rehearsed). An egg covered in banana leaves has been placed on this spot. Underneath it are buried the herbs that will make him brave. Each boy jumps three times. At the third jump he lands on the egg and breaks it. He then has to stand still. A great crowd will have assembled by now, and the operators arrive. Meanwhile the mothers of the boys are expected to be sitting inside their huts, holding firmly to one of the supporting poles. It is said that if a mother moves or talks before the knife has cut, her son will take fright and run away.

The operator now does his work. He pulls the foreskin as far forward as it will go, and cuts it off. He then holds the penis at its full length and cuts off every piece of remaining skin, except for that on the underside. The bloody pieces of severed skin are thrown at the boy's feet; his father will collect and bury them in some secret place unknown to witches. During the operation the boy must not show the slightest sign of fear or flinching. Even the twitching of an eyelid is counted as cowardice; and cowardice must be heavily paid for.

When it is done, the boy jumps three times to show his joy and courage. He then sits on a lump of wood, a cloth is wrapped over his shoulders, and people press forward to congratulate him. His mother runs up shouting with happiness. There is dancing and drinking. The boy's father now takes him – the 'new man' – into a special hut and attends to him that night. In the old days the wound was treated with ash; now hospital medicine is used. The youth is given an attendant to look after him, clean and cook for him, till the wound has healed. Only fellow initiates, parents, and old people may visit him.

Before the operator leaves, he will have washed the boy's hands in a ceremony known as the 'cleaning of hands', so that he can touch food (if this isn't done, he will have to use a stick). During this ceremony, the operator will confirm that the initiate has now attained manhood and is a full member of the clan. He blesses him and wishes him success in founding a family. The initiate receives a spear as a sign that he is a warrior, and a knife and axe to indicate his job in the community.

It is a most shameful thing if, during the circumcision ordeal, a boy shows fear, trembles, loses control of his bladder, or collapses, so that people have to hold him up while the operator does his work. The boy's parents will feel let down, and he will go on being teased and taunted till his age-set forgets the incident. Moreover, his parents will have to compensate the operator and those who helped him with additional gifts. Parents hate this kind of son. They will tend his wound. But even small children will mock him.

Circumcision is honoured among the Bagisu. They are proud to have undergone this test of courage – the more so, as the other Bantu tribes of Uganda do not circumcise, which makes the Bagisu feel they have a special status. Indeed medical authorities recommend the operation for hygienic reasons (the stripped penis is easier to keep clean). Some Bagisu, it is true, especially educated ones, prefer to have the operation done in a hospital. But this defeats the main purpose of the rite: which is meant to be a collective experience as well as a test of bravery. Formerly no marriage was held to be valid until the young man had been circumcised. Our neighbours, the Sebei, still hold this view. But the Bagisu have changed somewhat. Present marriages are accepted on condition bride price has been paid.

Nevertheless, popular enthusiasm for the rite is such that boys are under very great pressure to submit to it. When it is circumcision time, a boy who shows unwillingness to face the knife will be caught, beaten and cut, to teach him the 'good manners' of the tribe. Men who are suspected of being uncircumcised may even be stripped naked in public – in shops, buses, on the road, anywhere. Sometimes the police have to intervene to prevent trouble.

Our custom may seem cruel. But I, as a Mugisu, support the custom. And the Bagisu don't dream of giving it up.

Marriage

Once they have been circumcised, the youths have joined the adult community. They are entitled to take part in clan councils, and to get married. What of the girls?

Bagisu girls, unlike neighbouring Sebei, do not circumcise. But it was the tradition that girls should show themselves to be adult through the painful process of cutting keloids on the abdomen and head.

The complete scarification took a long time to do. When they were about ten, girls had to buy a special needle from an iron-smith. They pinched the skin of their bellies into a fold and drew the needle through it till they had made a deep hole. They filled the hole with wood ash and waited for the wound to heal. These scarification marks were cut in lines running down the abdomen. On the forehead two lines were cut, running down the temples. When the keloids had healed, they stood out as hard as peas. They are commonly seen on old people. They were thought to be decorative as well as being proof of bravery. Some girls used to pierce holes in the lower lip. Into this they

fitted a plug of polished wood. The lip-plug was both orna-
mental, and prevented the saliva from dribbling out. When the
mutilations were finished, a girl was ready for marriage.

Clan exogamy was strictly enforced. Marriage was traditionally
arranged by the parents, generally at harvest time. After bride
price had been paid, the girl's parents would prepare her carefully for marriage. They instructed her in her new duties,
fattened her on a special diet, and smeared her with fat or oil to
give her a smooth and glossy skin.

A bride was customarily escorted to her new home by her girl
friends. They carried hoes, as they would have to help prepare
new fields for the bride during their stay. If the bride was
found to be a virgin, her husband and his relatives rejoiced.
They would send her parents special gifts. They took the bedding
to show them the blood.

Bride price used to amount to four to ten head of cattle,
plus goats, fowls and other gifts. Nowadays the local government authority has ruled that bride price should not exceed
three head of cattle, or a cash payment of 900 shillings. Some
parents, of course, demand more than this. The church in my
area supports the principle of bride price. The Bagisu are still,
on the whole, polygamous. But economic pressure and the
spread of education increasingly discourage the polygamist.

(MRS) GRACE MOLLI

A GIRL'S TRADITIONAL PREPARATION FOR MARRIAGE

African parents naturally prefer to beget sons. But among some
tribes, such as the Iteso, where bride price is high, girls are
more welcome than in others. A brother can spend his sister's
bride wealth on acquiring a wife of his own.

Traditionally African girls are brought up by their mothers
with the assistance of aunts. They are instructed in house work
and prepared for marriage. This preparation differs among
tribes. Thus Sebei girls (like the Nandi and the Kikuyu of
Kenya) undergo clitoridectomy.

In some Bantu tribes (e.g. the Baganda, the Banyoro and the
Banyaruanda) girls have traditionally prepared themselves for
marriage by pulling the clitoris to a length, varying according

to custom, of from three to six inches or more. Girls used to collect in age groups and go into the bush to do this in private. When the Christian missionaries came they discouraged such practices as 'sinful'. The result was that men were no longer pleased with their wives, and divorced them. Such men blamed schooling and education for interfering with the old customs. It was not simply a question of girls being encouraged to break taboos on eating chicken and mutton. Girls who had not been prepared for marriage in the old way, by lengthening the clitoris, were considered imperfect. The prejudice is still widespread. Girls who have been mainly educated away from home at boarding schools have to suffer the consequence of not conforming with tribal tradition.

A girl would inform her mother when she first started to menstruate. She would be kept at home for a few days, and be well fed. She was not allowed to move about, or to cross a road – especially at a point where roads meet. Her parents would give the girl a piece of new bark cloth and underwear. The Baganda had special terms associated with menstruation. It was referred to as *okwekoona akagere* (stubbing one's toe) or as *okuzza omukono emabega* (to turn one's hand behind). During their seclusion girls would be warned against the sexual designs of men. Henceforth they were forbidden to play with boys – only with girls. And they were stopped from climbing trees; they were told that if they did so, the mangoes and oranges would turn tasteless.

MARY KAMPI

Surely Miss Kampi exaggerates the length (she says it is three to six inches or more) to which the clitoris is pulled. Not all educated girls practise this custom; but even the educated ones are still under pressure from older women to continue with it. Many men, including educated men, are in favour of it. Women who have conformed are considered wise. They are always warm to their husbands, and husbands find joy and satisfaction in such women. But I think it hardly likely that men will divorce wives who haven't conformed. They simply look for a 'better woman' and practise polygamy.

In short, a girl whose aunt has neglected to instruct her in the proper preparation for marriage will suffer when she grows up to be a wife.

(MRS) W. M. LUBEGA

MARRIAGE CUSTOMS OF THE KIGA

Betrothal

Much of what I know of the traditional marriage customs of my people the Kiga I learned from my grandfather Rugiirwa, whose marriage connexions – his fifteen wives came from twelve different clans – gave him a wider range of information than most men had.

Traditionally a betrothed couple were forbidden to have sexual intercourse before the wedding night. A girl's conduct was subject to strong taboos. If she became pregnant before marriage, her parents had no alternative but to drown or spear her.

A go-between (*kiriima*) appointed by the young man's parents was responsible for negotiating the bride price, which was paid in cows and goats. It was a tense moment when the livestock were brought for inspection to the girl's parents' compound, for the marriage depended on the elders' decision. The moment they declared to the groom's party (*Bakwe*) 'We now accept you as our son-in-law and take your gift' everyone clapped, danced and sang, and there was much boasting. All were happy, except for one lonely person, the bride.

While the rest danced and sang, she sobbed. For soon she would have to leave her home and live among strangers, and she did not even know the man she was going to marry. Was he old, young, lame? Would he ill treat her? And there was another fear: would she be fertile, able to bear children? A childless woman was not a woman at all. No one believed that a man – unless he was impotent – could be sterile.

So the young girl couldn't help crying. Yet her crying was artistically done. It was beautiful, and it was intended to evoke sympathy. Some of the words she would utter ran:

Hm, Hm, my mother, my father,
Hm, Hm, my uncles, my brothers,
If you eat these cows know that you're eating me,
If you see vultures pecking the ground at the new homestead
Know they are eating me.

Her tears only encouraged the groom's party to rejoice more. They would call to her:

> Don't fret, dear one, don't weep!
> You are going to the land where digging is cursed,
> To a land so flat that the eagle has no landing place
> To a land where women neither draw water nor fetch firewood.
> Welcome to the heavenly land where you need not support
> your skirt with a belt!

(The last line meant that she would be treated like a queen. She would be spared heavy work, so would not need to tie her skirt – she could secure it with her hand.)

The more they sang, the louder the young girl cried. This was the ritual response expected of her; and she cried even more in the night, when her girl friends started their farewell song:

> *Kare kare owieshemwe.*
> Farewell, beloved one and friend,
> We shall stay behind.
> Obey your husband,
> Don't let our clan down.
> When he beats or scolds you
> Tell him 'You shouldn't beat me,
> It's your cows that incite you!'
> If you see your mother-in-law with her clique,
> Avoid them, lest they call you names.
> A husband is inconstant,
> Inconstant as the sky.
> When he turns against you
> Remember your clan has men.
> The cows will return
> To preserve your life.

Next morning the *Bakwe* ceremoniously presented a hoe and the bride, having been washed and smeared with clarified butter (*amajuta*) to make her skin smooth and slippery for 'the journey ahead', was formally handed over by her father-in-law.

The *Bakwe* now went home, and were soon followed by the girl and her bridal party. The girl was not allowed to walk. She was made to sit astride one of her brothers' shoulders (they took it in turn to carry her), with her legs dangling on his chest. Her head was hooded, her skirt parted in front so that her legs were visible, her private parts being shielded behind her brother's head. Though it was not customary for women to use underwear, she was not embarrased to ride thus on her brother's shoulders. It was the custom. It was in any case unthinkable for a Kiga to have lustful feelings for a sister. We have a saying '*Enyama y'otalya ogisiira embwa.* – The meat that you don't fancy is better given to a dog.'

The bride was not only forbidden to walk, she could not even step on the ground. Her escort carried a mat which they spread whenever she dismounted or took a rest. When the party started off again some grass was plucked by an aunt from where the mat had been spread and put into a basket. People believed that if some malicious person could pluck grass from the spot before the aunt did, that person would be able to use black magic to prevent the girl from bearing children. The grass was to be kept in the bridal couple's sleeping place till after the birth of their first child.

Arrival
At the gate of her father-in-law's compound, the mat was spread again, and there she rested. She had come at last. The groom's heart would be beating hard; the prize was within his reach. He gathered courage, and taking a small stick (*omusinga*) to which the silky hair of a maize cob was tied, he went up to her and gave her three gentle taps on the arm, saying 'When I speak twice, I expect you to speak once. If you dare speak more than you are allowed to, I shall beat you harder than this.'

We have to bear in mind that this was the first time the groom had ever touched his bride, or perhaps set eyes on her. Even now he could see only her arm, for she was hooded and covered. The token strokes he had given her were intended to convey the message that as a woman her role in life was to obey, while the man's prerogative was to give orders.

Dusk had fallen, and there was feasting and dancing to welcome the bride. Knowing that her 'ordeal' could not be much longer delayed, she was expected to burst into renewed sobs as she said farewell to her brothers and to all she held dear.

Urine Ceremony

A Kiga wife joined her husband's clan and had close bonds not only with her husband but with his brothers and lineage kinsmen. The 'urine ceremony' that now followed was meant to make this clear.

At cockcrow the groom and his brothers had to urinate collectively on a slightly concave stool. If one of the participants had an empty bladder, he was to force himself until he produced at least a drop. The stool, with the urine on it, was placed in an empty room. Then the groom had to dip his hands in the urine and sit waiting by the stool, in the dark, as quietly and expectantly, if I may use the analogy, as a bed-bug waiting for its victim in a crack of the bed-frame. Meanwhile her aunt and the *kateramucucu* or Dirt Beater (an elderly woman whose job was to ensure that the bride was clean and to comfort her till it was time to leave her on her own), having stripped her naked, carried her struggling into the room. She was made to sit on the wet stool in such a position that the groom could touch her genitals with his urine-drenched hands. Immediately he had done so he dashed out in triumph. The first part of the marriage had been completed, and there was much boasting and dancing to celebrate it.

Here I must explain that a newly married bride was not supposed to sleep with any man but her husband, lest she should forfeit her chances of ever bearing children. If, however, she were to sleep with any of the brothers in whose urine she had sat on first arriving, it was not thought that this would hinder her from conceiving. Indeed, even after she had borne children, a brother was not considered culpable if he made love privately to his sister-in-law. If they were discovered, there would still be no cause for scandal and alarm. But if a wife was found making love with a distant clansman, it was a very serious matter.

After the urine ceremony, the bride was dressed again in her skin skirt, with another skin above it. This time the skirt was tied very firmly. Her aunt and the Dirt Beater used a rope belt which they secured with a great many tight and complicated knots. The object of this custom was to cool the groom's ardour; for he was not supposed to start any real sex play until he had unravelled all the knots in the belt. If he neglected to do so, or skimped the work, it was thought that he would never be able to father children with the girl. Her womb would remain as tight and knotted as the knots in the belt. So, even if he had to struggle all night, he was compelled to unravel the belt. As we can imagine, the result of this might be that a boy would temporarily lose interest in sex. By the time he had undone the knots, he had no proper erection. Some bridegrooms were so affected by the hard labour and psychological strain that they remained dormant for a day or two.

Consummation

The bride's escort now fetched their sticks and spears, drank a last pot of beer, and left for home. The young bride was alone among strangers. She was given some millet which she had to grind together with the groom and his brothers and sisters as a sign that there would be a fair division of labour within the family. Then the groom's sisters led her straight to the bedroom where a grass mat was laid on the floor. The groom followed.

Now the wrestling began, and I can assure you that it was the survival of the fittest! The man had to accomplish three things. He had to unravel the knotted belt: to show the woman that he was stronger, by putting her down; and to retain his erection. The bride would defend herself like a wild cat, scratching and pulling her husband's hair. He had to fight his way to the fulfilment of his marital duties.

If he was too small to master the bride in the wrestling – and girls were not expected to sympathise with or surrender to weaklings – then his big brother had the right to settle matters with the bride first: that is, to have sexual intercourse with her, before the husband could claim his due. Once a woman had been penetrated she was not supposed to show any further resistance to him. As in everything else connected with the marriage ceremonies, there was logic behind this custom. It originated in the fact that some fathers married their sons before puberty or while they were still physically undeveloped and weak.

Now that she was a 'proper woman', the bride would pretend

to be shy. She would refuse food until her husband bribed her with a copper bracelet. The youth – now a man – had his penis examined by his uncles to see whether he had found 'problems' in penetrating – a sign that the girl had been a virgin.

It was the rule for the bride to stay secluded with her husband for four days. She then paid a short visit to her parents, who were anxious to know whether she had been a virgin; if this was the case, they would have something to boast about. There was a formula for telling the parents of a girl's condition. If a virgin, the husband presented his father-in-law with a brand new hoe. If not, he gave him a hoe-handle with the end pierced. He would not consider divorcing such a wife, but her father would be expected to return some of the livestock he had received as bride wealth.

Seeing the Sun

The bride now started her month-long period of seclusion proper. She was kept busy cooking, serving food, sweeping the house and compound (she did this very early, at dawn, before people could see her), making raffia baskets, fetching grass to spread on the floor. Efforts were made to lighten her skin. Her sisters-in-law smeared her with red earth mixed with bleaching fruit juices, which would be washed off at bed time, and renewed each morning.

Once her seclusion was over – by which time it was not uncommon for the young wife to be pregnant – she went out with her husband to show herself off. There was no more weeping, no more mock modesty, as she and her party made their way to her parents. She laughed and chattered, and looked beautiful. Her skin colour would be deep orange – due both to the bleaching treatment and to keeping out of the sun. She was ripe and appetising. She excited desire in the hearts of men, envy in the eyes of girls. They saw that after all marriage was a wonderful thing.

'Seeing the Sun,' as the ceremonial reception at her parents' home was called, lasted about four days, which were filled with dancing and feasting. On the last day the young wife's father would fix a hoe-blade (the one he had received as bride wealth) in its handle and give it to his daughter, saying 'Go and dig,

a *Euphorbia candelabrum*, Mount Zulia
(aramoja)

13b Wild date palms, Mount Zulia

13c Giant groundsels (Karisimbi summit, Congo)

14a Teuso woman fetching water   14b Adequately covered?

14c Suk girls, Kachagalau

and be a good wife in every way to your husband and a good woman to the clan. Be a good representative of your old clan, so that your sisters will find suitors.'

And so the wedding ceremonies were ended. From now on the young couple would have to face the world on their own – though the husband's father would continue to shelter them while they were preparing their own home and cultivating their first crops.

Things, of course, have changed nowadays. Kiga parents have much less to say in their children's marriage decisions. Wedding parties are less elaborate – young people consider them a waste of time and money. Sexual morals have become slack. The old people go to their graves groaning and cursing modern ways.

VERICE BATAHI

ELOPEMENT AMONG THE ACHOLI

Reasons

There are various reasons for elopement: a young couple's unwillingness to wait for the often protracted marriage negotiations to be completed; defiance of parental objections; the man's inability to pay the required bride price.

In the case of elopement it is the girl's parents who have most to lose. Once their daughter has run away, she is 'spoiled'. Even if they compel her to return home, she is 'second hand', and who will want to pay a high bride price for her?

Moreover, by compelling their daughter to leave the man who wishes to marry her, her parents may offend public opinion. If the matter is brought to court, they may be accused of encouraging prostitution among the Acholi, and the girl's father is liable to imprisonment. The court in any case will authorise the marriage.

Parents may object to their child's choice of marriage partner for a variety of reasons. They may assert that the suitor or the proposed bride come from a family that practises witchcraft, or that they are lazy and of bad character. The suitor may be too poor; the parents want their daughter to marry a rich man.

Impostors

Because elopement has become more common these days among the Acholi it has tended to become a fashion that attracts imitators. The young man who runs off with a girl is admired for his 'toughness'. If she is beautiful and well mannered his parents, relatives and friends congratulate him. He has brought off a successful coup.

The practice, for which there may be valid reasons, naturally gets abused especially by the type of Acholi who is employed away from home in the army, the police, or the prison service. These men have an advantage over the many youngsters who stay in their villages without money or jobs. They earn regular pay and they can offer not only social security but a more sophisticated personality.

During their service outside Acholi they can save money, acquire property, accumulate possessions such as sofa sets, radios, modern bedding, cars. When they come home on leave they build brick houses that are admired by villagers who sleep on a skin or a reed mat in a thatched hut and own scarcely anything of value.

On leave these fellows swagger about like rich men. Their lavish spending impresses the girls. They boast that money is no problem. They buy drinks for everyone, and the girls think they are wonderful. The soldier on leave breaks the earth with his heavy boots. It shakes when he treads on it.

Soldiers and policemen are notorious braggarts. The private soldier claims to be an officer, the simple policeman an inspector. Where then is the car they boast about? They have had to leave it behind through unavoidable circumstances. The girls giggle in admiration and fly to them like bees to honey. They are 'men among men'. The impostors take the beautiful girls and leave the ugly ones behind to solace the villagers.

I know of a soldier – he claimed to be a lieutenant – who ran off with a well educated Acholi girl who took him to be the 'progressive' type of husband. He turned out to be a cook in the barracks. The girl was heartbroken. Her virginity was gone. Her parents nearly hanged themselves in their anger and disappointment.

Married Women

Though there are many exceptions to the rule, the majority of Acholi girls who elope with a man subsequently marry him. To achieve this end, the runaway girl must prove during the trial period before marriage that she will make a good wife. Her lover and his parents will observe her carefully – her manners as well as her skills. If she fails to pass the test her future is gloomy. She is the leftover after a meal. People will despise her. Men without wives will exploit her, help themselves to her; she is nobody's wife.

Among the Acholi it is rare for a married woman to elope. It takes a bold man to run off with someone else's wife. He will have to protect himself and her against the husband's wrath. His life is in danger. He must go into hiding. Not only the injured husband is after his blood. Every other husband feels he has been insulted in his own marital status. They are likely to ostracise him.

As for the injured husband, people despise him. He is branded as a man 'whose knife isn't sharp' – so his wife had to look for a keener weapon. Other wives will admire the man who eloped with her. He is the hero who rescued a fellow woman from a useless and impotent husband.

Fine

Eloping can be an expensive matter. It will cost the man 150 shillings as compensation to the girl's parents (*luk* or fine). If he makes her pregnant before a settlement is reached, he will have to pay an extra 400 shillings. Since the fine is in proportion to the 'damage' done to the girl and to her parents, a stupid or careless fellow who gets more than one child during the elope-ment period must pay accordingly – a situation that the girl's parents naturally welcome. Every child is worth 400 shillings to them in *luk* money – and this holds good even if a child does not live. It is the custom, and custom cannot be altered. Some men find themselves paying a fine of 1,200 shillings!

Such men have landed through their own folly in a trap. They look gloomily upon the world, and no wonder. For in addition to the *luk* they must still, one day, raise the bride price with which to legalise the marriage.

No Acholi can visualise marriage without the payment of bride wealth or elopement without *luk*. If, however, a man runs off with a married woman he is responsible for his action not to the woman's father but to her husband. He must be prepared to repay him the amount of bride price which legalised the original marriage. If his offer is turned down, then he knows that he must pay with his life.

ABUJERE

THE CASE AGAINST POLYGAMY

Polygamy reflects, among other things, a desire to have many children, to be head of a large family, to be able to practise the ancestral cult on a big scale. Africans generally assume that the more women a man has, the more children he will beget. This may sound a truism. Yet it by no means necessarily follows. Polygamy in fact may have an adverse affect on a society's birth rate, since plurality of wives favours dissipation of sexual effort, thus reducing the potential fertility of wives, especially if there is no rule of cohabiting in rotation.

I know of some polygamous families with fewer children than monogamous families. The reproductive powers of several wives are wasted, for instance, on a husband who is sick, or ageing. If one of a man's wives contracts a venereal disease, the husband will catch it and pass it on to all his other partners, who may be rendered sterile.

Polygamy is not society's answer to more children. The average total of children born to a troop of co-wives is likely to be less than they would have delivered had they been single wives to monogamous husbands.

Reasons for Polygamy

In Africa, polygamy has been closely connected with the traditional status of women as mere material goods. Women in fact commonly approved of polygamy. Not only was it culturally accepted. They saw nothing wrong in having an additional person to help with the chores and field work. An only wife needed company at home, since her husband would be away for most of the day. A woman did not feel it was an indignity to be one of several wives. A senior wife might even insist on her husband taking other wives to enhance the family's status and prestige.

European psychology, as I understand it, differs sharply here. The European has an inbred possessive attitude not only to material things but to the marital partner. Each partner expects and claims sole marital rights over the other.

Now let us take a closer look at the background of polygamy. In the past, partly in consequence of wars and slave-raiding, and because of men's greater exposure to physical accident, women in a traditional African society outnumbered men. Women depended on men both for protection and economic support; numerical excess weakened their bargaining power.

Again, in traditional African society an unmarried woman was considered a freak. People would suspect she had something wrong with her. There were no 'spinsters' retiring gracefully from the race to make way for the luckier ones.

So with proportionately fewer males available, polygamy was inevitable if all women were to get married.

Now for another interesting explanation of polygamy. There is in Africa a widespread belief that 'there should be no sexual intercourse during lactation'. A man is traditionally supposed to abstain from sex with his wife while she is expecting a baby and to continue to keep away from her while she is suckling it. The suckling period may be very long, up to two years or more mainly because of the lack of suitable food when the child is weaned. Certainly the Banyoro and Baganda traditionally abstained from sexual intercourse until weaning, in the belief that if they did not do so, the breast milk would disappear and the baby would die. No wonder husbands looked for other sexual outlets – and to polygamy – in such a situation.

The practical reason behind this taboo would be, I assume, to prevent a second pregnancy and birth coming so soon after the previous one that the older infant would have to be prematurely weaned and put on a less healthy diet. With education and better child-care facilities, this custom is losing ground, though *kwashiorkor* (literally 'first-second', the disease the first child gets when the second is expected) is still quite common.

Again, after he has lived with a woman for some years, a married man tends to lose interest in her. He casts his eye on younger and prettier girls. He will, perhaps, to begin with, keep another woman unknown to his wife. Later, when she gets pregnant, he will take her to wife.

It is generally believed that marriage is for life. So when death intervenes a widow may be encouraged or even expected to marry her late husband's brother or some other suitable relation of his. Under the levirate system (common amongst the ancient Hebrews and familiar to us through the Biblical story of Ruth), if the widow then bears children they will belong to the dead husband. This practice also involves polygamy, because the dead man's heir may already have his own wife or wives. It is a practice commonly found in societies where every woman is expected to have a husband, and where the role of wife is the only one open to her once she leaves her father's house. Without polygamy to take care of them, such women would be condemned to lives of prostitution.

It is interesting to note here that the Hindus used to solve the problem of surplus widows by practising *suttee* (Sanskrit *sati*, 'true wife'). When her husband died the widow had to join his corpse on the funeral pyre, and she would be burnt together with him. Despite Hindu resistance the British stopped the custom in the early nineteenth century.

Organisation of a Polygamous Family

The family structure associated with polygamy is known as a compound family. In my own village in Bunyoro, under this system each wife lives with her children in her own separate hut in the compound. The husband stays in his wives' huts, visiting each by rotation. The time he spends with each wife will vary according to circumstances. His visits may be weekly, fortnightly, or once a month. While he is with her, the woman is expected to cook and care for him.

In another type of compound family, the husband has his own

hut and visits his wives only to have sexual intercourse. His food and drink are brought to him in his own dwelling. The husband expects to be given a share of each of his wives' dishes.

In some polygamous societies, the husband cannot afford to build a separate hut for each of his wives. One large house is erected in which each wife has a separate room or space to herself. The wives can still take it in turn to cook and care for their husband, and each woman will usually have her own cooking utensils. In short, the specific form of a polygamous African household varies from one society to another.

Wives of polygamous households, it is often said, are generally on friendly terms with each other; and it is true that if society has accepted this custom, they have no right to grumble about their lot – an atmosphere of quarrelling and jealousy would defeat the ends which polygamy was designed to achieve. There may be discord when the husband dies: disputes, for instance, over whose child should be the dead man's heir. Usually, however, there is a senior or first wife, and the other wives are expected to respect her wishes.

In some societies only the first wife has the title of 'wife'. The rest are considered to be concubines. In others, there may be several wives as well as concubines. Jacob, son of Isaac and Rebecca, married two sisters Leah and Rachel, each of whom gave him their handmaidens as concubines. In Uganda today, especially among the Banyoro, the Batoro, the Banyankole and the Baganda, the 'senior wife' is known as 'the wife of the ring' whilst the rest are merely 'wives'.[1]

Relations between Co-wives

But to return to the frequently held belief that relations among co-wives are generally friendly. I dispute this. My own observations are that there is more often jealousy and rivalry between them. True, I know of instances where, ironically, co-wives co-operate to the extent of forming a common front against the husband! Basically, though, co-wives find them-

---

[1] The Banyoro have adopted under missionary influence the phrase 'wife of the (wedding) ring' for a legal wife on whom bride price has been paid. She used to be called *omukazi ow'ensimbi*, literally 'a woman for whom money has been paid' (*omukazi*, woman; *ensimbi*, cowrie shells).

selves competing for a husband's attention and affection. Some other students of African society have noticed the same thing. Dr Beattie quotes Professor Maquet's observation that the 'very word for co-wife means "jealousy" among the Ruanda people' (in Luganda, *mugya* means co-wife and *bugya* means jealousy).[1] Professor Schoeck tells us that among the Lovedu of Bechuanaland, the term for fellow wives is to be translated as 'people who roast one another'.[2]

Certain psychological attitudes among Africans foster bad blood between co-wives. In a typical African society, where a woman's main role is to bear and bring up children for her husband and his lineage, and where barrenness is thought to be caused by sorcery and witchcraft inspired by one's enemies, if one of the co-wives stays childless whilst another bears children, suspicion will poison the atmosphere. Co-wives will accuse each other of doing evil, and the result may be persecution, assault, murder, even suicide.

Many such tragedies occur in the villages of Uganda. Jealousy is at the root of them. If a polygamous husband fails to hold the balance between his wives, he can expect trouble. To succeed in his domestic life, he must be well off. If he has three wives he must provide them with three sets of cooking gear. He cannot buy a new dress for one wife, he must buy for all; and the dresses must be equally smart. Competing for his attention, they will seek to outdo each other by demanding personal luxuries that must then be given to the others.

Strife may occur over children. The husband is expected to treat all his children equally. If he doesn't, the mother of the less-loved children will make trouble. Problems arise amongst the children themselves. Half-brothers quarrel over disparities in inheritance, and over rank. A father's apparent favourite arouses bad blood between them; and jealousy amongst sons can be even more serious than between co-wives.

The Zulus have a saying, that 'the love of sisters overcomes the jealousy of polygyny'. These people approve of marriage to two sisters. Yet the Lozi say exactly the opposite: 'the jealousy

[1] John Beattie, *Other Cultures*, London, 1964.
[2] Helmut Schoeck, *Envy*, London, 1969.

of polygyny spoils the love of sisters. It will break up their family.'[1] I think the Lozi are right. Sisters who are vying for the same husband's love will forget they are sisters. They may even murder each other.

Objections to Polygamy

I can list many objections to polygamy, which must occur to anyone who keeps his eyes open. Thus, a polygamous father will see less of his children than he ought to, since each mother tends to live in an isolated circle within the family. Such children are likely to fear their father. He will be something of a stranger to them, and they risk growing up to be maladjusted in later life.

True, the spread of Christianity in Africa has induced a great many Africans to marry in church and to set up monogamous homes. This does not necessarily stop them from pursuing the attractive women they meet in bars and night clubs and in the office. Many such husbands get illegitimate children by these women, and have to pay a large slice of their income to support them. In many parts of Buganda, in fact, the traditional type of polygamy has been replaced by what is called 'vertical polygamy'.

Under this system, a man marries a woman according to local custom, in church, or simply by agreeing to live with her. They produce children, and when a man tires of his partner he dismisses her and takes another. He may repeat this process several times. The children of each successive 'wife' are usually separated from the mother. They may stay with the father, or he may pack them off to a grandmother. Such children are bound to suffer a sense of insecurity. They do not know who their next 'mother' is going to be, and she may ill treat them.

Polygamy also poses a problem for young men who want wives but find that polygamous husbands have cut the supply. Not only does a polygamist monopolise several females for his own benefit; the richer and older he is, the larger will be his flock of women. So the young man, who is probably poor into the bargain, cannot find a wife at all; or he is obliged to marry

[1] Quoted by Gluckman in *African Systems of Kinship and Marriage*, ed. Radcliffe-Brown and Daryll Forde, London, 1950.

an older woman, or a widow, for whom bride price payment will be less. This is a situation which obviously reduces the birth rate.

Let us admit that the conditions which once made polygamy possible in Africa are vanishing or no longer exist. A brood of co-wives and children used to confer prestige on the father. Today they are a burden, and in an urban environment impossibly expensive and inconvenient to house, feed, and educate. The polygamists are on the retreat. Religion, economics, and psychology are against them. And yet, how curious it is to note the confusion into which Christian beliefs have led us.

The early missionaries to Africa insisted on monogamy, and committed Christian converts accepted this principle. Nevertheless a great many people suspected that monogamy was a European invention, an accretion to the Christian faith that lacked Scriptural authority. Were not the kings and heroes of the Old Testament polygamists? Even the New Testament appeared to proscribe polygamy only among the clergy. So people assumed that the Europeans in Africa arbitrarily forbade polygamy for no better reason than that they themselves did not practise it.

Non-Christians can oppose stronger arguments to the monogamist. Monogamy, they may claim, is an infringement of the law of nature by the stupidity of man. Monogamy breeds prostitution; for the unmarried woman still has her sexual drive, taboos on intercourse during pregnancy and lactation demand that a man finds other sexual outlets, and husbands, imperfect as they are, and tiring of the same daily diet, will always relish a change.

Sooner or later, though, I believe that in Uganda the expense of polygamy, the growing self-respect of women, and wider education will combine to rout the polygamist. There may have been good reasons for polygamy in the past when people lived in primitive and static societies intent only on survival. But polygamy today is an anachronism. I appeal to every African man to forget and forego this small part of our African tradition. And let all those conservative African women who still believe that to be one of several wives is the normal human condition, realise that their sex is being trodden on. We are not cattle, to be ringed, counted, and herded into a pen.[1]

(MISS) F. A. ISOKE

SONGS AND DANCES OF THE ACHOLI

Many of the old Acholi customs are dead. Some were suppressed by foreign missionaries and administrators; some have died a natural death; others are even now giving way to imported ideas. Lifebuoy soap and coloured head-wraps have replaced traditional ointments (such as shea butter-nut oil) and decorations. The only occasions when 'picturesque tribesmen' shout their war-cries today are at beer parties and funeral ceremonies.

Extraction of incisor teeth is no longer widespread – the younger, educated generation has other ideas about beauty. Scarification (*kedo*) is less noticeable. It is a painful process, and women who submitted to it were admired for their fortitude. There are mocking stories and songs about girls who ran away from the *kedo* ceremony. These days women say that a scarified face makes them look old before their time.

Not everything, of course, has gone. Some of the dances, for instance, and the religious ceremonies, vigorously survive. The Acholi indeed excel in traditional dancing. An Acholi who can't dance is made fun of. Let us look at some of these dances, starting with Larakaraka, which was, and still is, the dance for village youths.

[1] The following judgment may be cited as relevant to Miss Isoke's comment on polygamous attitudes: The Chief Justice of Uganda, Benedicto Kiwanuka, passing an exemplary sentence of fifteen years imprisonment on a man who had killed an unfaithful wife, said in the High Court (20 June 1972), 'This man already had three other women when he decided to take this one on. Four women is a bit too much for one man, and if the dead woman found herself dissatisfied and sought her own pleasures elsewhere it was this man more than anyone who was to blame. To be lenient to this man,' he said, 'will be giving licence to other men to kill their wives or lovers just as they please. The time has passed when a wife was considered to be nothing else but a mere piece of property owned by the husband.' Mr Kiwanuka, a distinguished person who had been the first Prime Minister of Uganda, and a political detainee under Obote, was dragged (during the Tanzania invasion scare) from the High Court in Kampala by armed men and – like, for instance, Kalimuzo, Vice-Chancellor of Makerere University – has never been seen again. It was on the day he was seized that panic struck Kampala; the entire population started to run, as though practising for sports day (21 September 1972).

Larakaraka

The dance starts in the early evening and ends about midnight. Each neighbouring village provides its own team of boys and girls. Boys wear nothing but a strip of cloth over their genitals and ostrich or cock feathers on the head. In the left hand they carry a calabash, in the right old bicycle-wheel spokes. They also carry small axes, clubs or knives to defend themselves with in case a fight breaks out during the dance. The girls wear skirts and a cloth round the breasts. They tie a mass of beads round their waists, and strap rattles to their legs. The leader of each girls' team has a whistle.

The teams from various villages meet in the arena, which is a clearing outside the home of the Larakaraka organiser. As each team arrives, its leader silences the big drum in the centre and starts a new song. Most of the songs are short, repetitive, and deal with love and bride wealth. Here is a typical song:

> Laliba has taken the wealth
> To buy meat in the market.
> With what shall Kolo marry?
> Behold the child of Aol's mother,
> Laliba has spent the wealth.
> With what shall Kolo marry?'

Laliba had a married daughter, Aol. But he wasted the bride price, neglecting his son Kolo, who also wanted to marry.

In the arena the boys form arcs of circles, with their legs interlocked. The girls line up facing them, in the centre. When the song starts the boys take it up, swaying from side to side and strumming the spokes hard against the calabashes. The girls dance silently; only the team leader's whistle sounds. One of the latter's duties is to arrange with the other leaders for one set of dancers to take turns with another. Girls may not dance in front of their own brothers.

While the boys sway in unison, the girls shake their breasts and twist their hips. The climax is reached with the 'moko (getting stuck') stage – for which reason the Larakaraka dance is also known as *moko*. Each girl singles out a boy and pushes him out of the arc. They run to a quiet spot and make each other's acquaintance (nothing sexual). After a while they go back to dance again. Sometimes later in the dance a couple may run for good. A good dancer may get 'stuck' many times in the course of an evening.

Bwola Dance

The Bwola (Royal) Dance and Otole (War) Dance are rare. They are performed only on important occasions, such as the visit of a national leader. The Bwola was traditionally organised at the call of a chief. It is performed by mature men and women. The songs tell of historic persons and events. They praise (or rebuke) the deeds of chiefs and warriors. Here is an example:

> *Alero opong i Langwen ye*
> *Lagem konya ki lweny*
> *ii! ii!*
> *Paibwoo ye! Oneno tong Lango?*
> *Tong Lango tero paco*
> *Tong pa Lango tek macalo man*
> *Macalo Panyagira!*

> The people of Alero are away at Langwen
> You, Lagem, help me in the fight
> O Paibwoo! Have you seen the Lango spears?
> This battle will never end
> Lango spears drive me back home
> The Lango spear is deadly
> As deadly as Panyagira's.

The people of Bwobo are a minority clan to the west of Gulu. At one time they fought the formidable Langi, hence this song. It seems from the song that the Bwobo were overwhelmed. '*Paibwoo ye!*' is their common war-cry, dating from the time of their ancestor Obwogo.

There are three stages to the Bwola dance. First the dancers advance, closely packed in rows one behind the other, stooping close to the ground and humming the song with a buzzing noise. The men have small drums and sticks. They wear antelope skins round their waists and leopard skins on their backs. Ostrich plumes decorate their heads. The women are grouped in the centre. The men move forward with the big mother-drum leading. Inside the arena they form a circle round the big drum and the second stage begins. The men now circle the big drum sideways, stooping and straightening up, playing their small drums to the rhythm of the mother-drum.

During the last (*Labala*) stage the small drums no longer sound. The men don't move sideways but in file round the big drum. The women change their positions but stay inside the circle, joining in the men's songs. Occasionally when a man leaves the circle to blow his horn or perform a mock fight, a woman will run after him to gyrate and excite him still further. The Bwola dance is complicated and thrilling. It is often included in the repertoire of the Heart Beat of Africa dancers as a show-piece for visitors to Uganda.

Otole Dance

For the Otole War Dance the men wear the same dress as for the Bwola, but they carry spears and shields. The Otole is less intricate but more strenuous and tiring. The men run into the arena with the women behind them. From time to time they regroup and engage in mock fighting. One Otole song goes:

> Son of Anyala,
> Olebe, lead on to the front.
> Olebe, your courage equals the whites'
> O son of Anyala,
> The spear that was blessed by the elders
> Heeds not the dangers!
> Son of Anyala, Olebe,
> Lead on to the front.
> O the spear that was blessed by the elders!

Another song – an elegy for a dead warrior and hunter – is:

> *Tong man butu koyo ye!*
> *Aligo ye! Ladwar!*
> *Tong ma yam ageno*
> *Tong man butu koyo*
> *O! Aligo ye, Ladwar!*
> *Maa tong ma yam ageno*
> *Tong man butu koyo.*

Alas, this spear lies cold
O Aligo! O hunter!
This spear that I once trusted
Now lies cold
O Aligo! O hunter!
The spear that I once trusted
Now lies cold.

The historian has only to look at the Bwola and Otole songs of the Acholi to learn a good deal about their past.

Funeral Dance
When the Christian missionaries first came to Acholi from Europe they taught that the dead would live again, not only as spirits but as respectable people, in Heaven, or as condemned villains, in Hell. The Acholi found this a strange notion. A corpse never rose again among the Acholi; only its spirit lived on.

When someone dies, relatives hurry immediately to the funeral. *Ringo Koko* (running to cry) is meant to console the family of the deceased. People burst into the compound showing great anger with death. They sing songs describing death as an invincible enemy who is ubiquitous. Nothing can be done about death. There is no reference to the will of God. Men perform the mock fight in imaginary confrontation with death. They blow loudly on their horns, leap high and come down with a thud. But they are helpless. Death is implacable.

Their songs express this impotence in the face of death. One song goes:

Death has no home,
No man knows where death's home is.
You boys would have fought death bravely
But no one knows death's home.
We lay an ambush for death,
But death does not come.
We would have fired our guns at death.
Even women would have fought this battle,
But no one knows where death's home is.

Another song (in Bitek's version) is:[1]

[1] Quoted from Okot p'Bitek's 'Concept of Jok among the Acholi and Langi', *Uganda Journal*, Vol. 27, No. 1, Kampala, 1963.

Behold Oteka fights alone,
The Bull dies alone.
O men of the lineage of Awic,
What has the son of my mother done to you
That he should be deserted?
Behold the warrior fights single-handed.
My brother is armed with bows and barbed-headed arrows.
He fights alone, not a single helper beside him.
My brother fights alone,
He struggles with death.

The traditional funeral ceremony (*Guru Lyel*) is so deep rooted in traditional religion that it will not easily be ousted from our customs. Even so, one can detect the influence of modern times in some of the new funeral songs:

Brother, there is death in the kettle.[1]
What can we do?
A! Brother, I warned you in vain,
Where did the child get death?
He got it in the beer.
O brother, too long you were roaming the villages.
What shall we do?

This sort of song would be used at the funeral of some delinquent, who has ignored warnings of friends.

Apiti Dance

The Apiti is a dance for mature women, and is traditionally performed for older people. Nowadays women dance it at political rallies. Apiti songs are generally praise songs, or they express concern for men who are loved. Here are two such songs:

O our Odai!
Our only child
Odai is like a European
Odai!
When he stayed away
The village was silent
O our Odai!

A kettle is used as a vessel for *pombe*.

The phrase 'Odai is like a European' is meant in praise. For the European, who had 'conquered customs', was all-powerful.

> The only son of my father,
> The only one,
> My brother is gone.
> The war has called him away.
> It was because of anger that he went.
> The war called him to Gil-Gil,
> The war called him to Nairobi,
> The only son of my father,
> War has taken him away.
> It was anger that took him.

The reference here is to a young man who because of some personal row or anger, decided to enlist as a soldier.

In the Apiti dance the women stand in a ring. When the drums play they dance round the drums. A woman with the sweetest voice leads each song. The women wear their best skirts. At the climax of the dance they stop singing and begin to murmur, and to stretch their long necks like giraffes.

Nanga Dance

The Nanga is a wedding dance, spectacularly revived of late. Even I know how to play some of its tunes on the *nanga* instrument, from which the dance takes its name. Acholi men love playing this harp. They play it to themselves, brooding, thinking of a girl. They play it while strolling about. They play it in company, round a fire at night, to entertain guests.

To play the *nanga* well, one must first carefully tune it, then rest it on a calabash, and if one is expert one will produce beautiful music. The *nanga* really comes into its own at a wedding. During the wedding dance, the girls do the '*teke*' (rhythm of the waists), of which there are two main variations: the La-pa'laro and Anginya. In the La-pa'laro the movement is violent and faster. The girls cover much ground quickly, and it is tiring. So the Anginya is preferred, with its slower waist rhythm (just visible in the shaking of the dress), and the girls move much more slowly. This is a chance for the boys to join in. They interlock their legs as for Larakaraka, facing the girls. Instead of strumming calabashes they clap their hands.

When a girl approaches too near with her 'teke' a boy rushes up to raise her hand. It is embarrassing for a girl if she cannot perform the 'teke'.

Nanga songs may also take the form of friendly insults or banter between in-laws. For instance:

> Behold the owner of the cows,
> His ears don't suit the copper rings,
> O mother!
> You want to have your own way,
> You arrange marriage by tricks,
> But behold the owner of the cows,
> His ears don't suit the copper rings.

This is a familiar theme: a young girl complaining about her parents' choice of a husband for her. In this case, she is being given to a rich man, whom she finds ugly – even his ear-rings don't fit. Bride wealth was not a mother's direct concern, but she could influence it by bringing pressure to bear on her daughter or husband.

Jok Dance

By 'Jok' we understand various spirits, both good and bad. Young girls are often said to be seized by *Jok anyodo* (the spirit of birth), and the diviner expels it in a ceremony that includes the Jok dance (Myel Jok). This is done at night. The diviner wears black goat skins, people assemble with gourd rattles, and the young girl is sat on a stool with a black goat skin round her waist. The people begin to sing Jok songs and to shake their rattles. When the girl trembles it is a sign that *Jok anyodo* is ready to dance. The songs are intensified, the rattles shake louder, the girl jumps up to dance. It is said that the girl is not aware she is dancing, for it is the Jok in her that dances, being about to leave the girl. When the girl is in the throes of her dance, other girls are asked to help her.

The Jok drum is small, and only one note is played, repeatedly, on it. Three major spirits are exorcised in this way: *Anyodo* (spirit of birth), *Urongo* (spirit of wild beasts), and *Kulu* (spirit of the river). There is a special song for each spirit, intended to incite it to dance. Here are some examples:

Anyodo Song

Laboke has crossed the Pajule sea
He has gone to seek bride wealth
How he suffers and dies!
But the girl walks with flat breasts.
O the earth has defied me,
There is no one to help me.

Urongo Song

The hunter trembles,
O the hunter fears.
You elders, grip the spears,
The beast hides under the *cwaa* tree.
You boys, grip the spears,
The beast hides under the *cwaa* tree.

Kulu Song

O the spirit of the river,
The spirit has killed my house,
The spirit has killed my child,
What can I do?

A new spirit, called *Jok munu* (the white man's spirit), also
seizes people who have travelled outside the district on government service. A typical *Jok munu* song will show how foreign it is:

O the white man drops bombs.
It is one o'clock, one o'clock.
The white man drops bombs
It is two o'clock, two o'clock.
The white man drops bombs.
It is three o'clock, three o'clock.
Now the white man takes tea.

The words are an obvious satire on the white man's habits:
love of routine, making war, and tea drinking.

Jok Rut

Of all Jok dances, the Rut (twin) is the most important. *Rudi*
(twins) are believed to be the special gift of *Jok anyodo*, and
the wish of the ancestors. Jok Rut is performed before the
ancestral shrine (*Abiila*). The ancestors are thanked and food
offerings are made to them. People abase themselves before

Anyodo, smearing ash on their bodies and singing songs intended to persuade *Anyodo* not to call away one or both of the twins. For twins are more vulnerable, more likely to die, than normal infants. When a twin dies, it is said to have 'escaped', and no one weeps, for the surviving twin may get jealous and decide to die too. Here is a Rut song:

> Behold the mother of twins lies on her back.
> O twins,
> O Ocen and Opiyo!
> The mother of twins lies on her back,
> Her body is covered with ash-dust.
> O twins,
> O Ocen and Opiyo.

Other Dances

Other dances that are popular today – the Rumma, Lukeme, and Dingi-Dingi, are youth dances copied from elsewhere. The Rumma and Lukeme are corrupt versions of the rumba, but whereas the Rumma is danced to guitar music or to a record player, the Lukeme is danced to a local instrument and the songs resemble those of Larakaraka. The Dingi-Dingi is a girls' dance based on the movements of physical drill at school, said to have been invented by Palabek ex-servicemen of east Acholi.

Missionary Attitude

The missionaries at first rejected African entertainments as 'black' or 'Satanic'. Their 'black list' included native beer and spirits (kwete, aragi, lacoyi), dances (Larakaraka, Bwola, Otole, Apiti), and games (Lawala, Dini-Dini). They later accepted certain dances such as the Bwola, Otole and Apiti, and allowed them to be taught and performed at mission schools. But these were dances for elderly people which did not have much appeal to youth. The real youth dances like Larakaraka were forbidden to native converts. Missionaries considered them symbols of diabolism and African ignorance.

Islam

Islam has been the least successful, the most rejected, of religious faiths among the Acholi. To start with the Arabs and the Nubians who introduced Islam were hated on account of the role they played in the old Acholi slave trade. Worse, Islam insisted on circumcision or *yom* (absence of the foreskin), which the Acholi detested and found embarrassing, not because of the physical mutilation itself, but because the Acholi used to be scantily clothed (they wore small antelope skins) and it was thought indecent to walk about with the skinned head of the penis exposed.

When the Nubians came to circumcise people, they were greeted with mocking songs, such as:

> The Nubis have hereditary caps,
> The Nubis have read Islam,
> They wear red caps
> They shake the caps,
> O Nubis!

In this song, there is a dual meaning to the word 'cap'. It refers both to the red Muslim fez, or other headgear, and to the exposed *glans penis* without the foreskin.

Islam also wanted everyone who accepted the faith of Mohammed to abolish many of their traditional customs and 'to live like Arabs'. This was not acceptable to the Acholi. Nor did the Nubis and Arabs dress as impressively as the white man; and they did not bring medicine and education. Arab dress – the long *kanzu*-type gown – in the 1920's was, it was thought, only suited to 'chiefs with big stomachs'. Acholi women refused to adopt the Arab fashion of completely covering their bodies as though they were corpses. They did not want to wear trousers and to squat carelessly on the ground with their legs apart like frogs.

OKUMU PA'LUKOBO

ACHOLI PROVERBS

1 The monkey behind will laugh at the tail of the monkey in front.
2 One hand isn't enough to open the vagina.
3 A single frog can spoil the well.

4 Only an elder can borrow the selfish man's axe.

5 It is the beautiful one whose teeth smell.

6 He who defecates by a path will do so again. (Bad manners persist.)

7 Even the proud man must one day eat his vegetable with the dew still on it.

8 The tender hooves of the calf follow in the spoor of the older ones.

9 A man does not praise his brother's bull.

10 The guinea fowl can't cure its baldness.

11 The cock in a new home won't crow.

12 The kite can offend with impunity; for he can fly away.

13 The smallness of the dik-dik does not spoil the taste of its soup.

14 When the others are being taught, the orphan must listen at the door.

15 The European went *pole pole* (slowly), and didn't fall.

16 One chicken will run off with the intestines of another in its beak. (Thieves prey on each other.)

17 The weak must rely on mercy.

18 The lion that roars hasn't caught its prey.

19 What is delayed will turn to stone.

20 The loss of a single reed won't make the roof leak.

OKUMU PA'LUKOBO

HUNTING THE ELEPHANT

Do you know how our Langi ancestors killed elephants? I will tell you.

To kill an elephant there must be a thick forest, a hundred spearmen and ten runners. The tactics are well defined.

The spearmen squat behind trees, shrubs, ant-hills and tufts. The runners provoke the beast, by piercing him with the javelin, into chasing them. They lead him among the hidden spearmen. Each spearman rises and spears the elephant as he chases the runners. The runners take it in turn to relieve each other. The elephant is at length confined within a closed place. The blood from his wounds pours on the ground. There comes a point when the beast staggers and slips in his own blood, and falls. It is said that once an elephant has fallen down he cannot rise again.

The elephant is not cut up the same day as he is killed for the hunters are tired, having fought him from morning till sunset. They start cutting up the carcass next morning.

It is hard work. The hunters struggle for the soft internal organs – the heart, liver, lungs and intestines. Each hunter digs a tunnel into the carcass to get at these delicacies. Cutting up the elephant is a race. So one must be careful.

Otyeno once had his testicles severed from his body. He had crawled deep inside the elephant. Another hunter, Abongo, who had also worked his way into the elephant seized Otyeno's testicles and cut them off, mistaking them for part of the elephant's liver.

Since then men have learned to be careful. A man now takes his wife to hold his testicles behind him as he burrows into the elephant.

T. C. LAWRENCE

A KARAMOJONG FOLK TALE

The Unfortunate African

When the world was young, God had three well-loved sons. They were almost identical, and they were all brown. God wanted to know who was the fleetest runner among them, so that he might reward him with more knowledge and more privileges. So one day he chose a pool of very clear water and added to it a purifying oil known as *akimyet*. Then he summoned his three sons and said, 'Listen, my children. I want to see which one of you can run the fastest.'

'You will all toe this line.' God pointed to a mark on the ground. 'I shall go to that pool over there, and when I give the signal you will race to it as fast as you can, and dive in. I will give the winner a prize.'

When God gave them the signal the three boys ran as fast as antelopes to the pool. One after the other they leapt into its clear and shimmering water.

When they came out they were astonished to find that two of them had changed colour. The first to plunge into the pool had turned white. The second had stayed brown. The third had turned quite black.

God explained to his sons that the winner had been purified by the lotion he had added to the pool. The second boy had not changed colour as the lotion had already been exhausted. The last boy had turned quite black because the pool was dirty by the time he had plunged in. Each boy accepted the result happily, and they were proud of their differences.

God now gave the boys names according to their colour. The first boy he named Ekakwangan, meaning 'the white man'. The second boy he named Ekarengan, meaning 'the brown man'. The third boy he named Ekiryonon, meaning 'the black man'.

From Ekakwangan's children, the white race descended. Ekarengan's children fathered the brown race – the Arabs and the Indians. Ekiryonon's children formed the black races of Africa.

God, according to his promise, also favoured Ekakwangan with the gift of greater knowledge and with a sense of superiority over the others – especially over the black man.

My maternal grandfather told me this story. It is meant to explain how the different skin colours of the human race, and the white man's inventiveness, came about.

P. R. ODEKE

WIZARDS IN LANGO SOCIETY

Night Dancers

One type of wizard known among the Langi is the night dancer. In the past when houses had no strong doors this wizard was believed to put the inmates into a deep sleep, and then enter, urinate into the sleepers' mouths, and escape unobserved.

The night dancers caper about, sing evil songs, knock and rub their buttocks against walls. When they are tired of dancing they drop down and swell to an enormous size. While they are unconscious it is possible to slaughter them like sleeping monsters.

Worse still, the night dancer is believed to poison innocent people, especially fat lovely babies, by throwing poison on the shadow of the victim. This may sound incredible, but such is the amazing power of a wizard that many people have lost their lives in this way.

Among the Langi wizards are recognisable by their dirty clothes, dark eyes, shaggy unkempt hair, and long filthy nails. A harmless stranger who happens to look like this will be treated with suspicion. Parents warn children against wizards. When I was a child there used to be a witch in our village. She had to pass through our compound when she went to fetch water. When we saw her coming we used to bolt indoors. We thought that even the sight of her was deadly poisonous.

Ajok Ading

The *ajok ading* may be man or woman. He does not dance at night. He moves silently and envies people their possessions; he wants to destroy them. The *ajok ading* is most dreaded. He can, for instance, prevent young women from giving birth. It is said that if he can get hold of a piece of cloth that any young woman has either worn or used for sanitary purposes, or simply as a head-pad when she carries water, the wizard will hide it in a hole dug inside a fireplace so that whenever the young woman menstruates she suffers a severe disorder which will prevent fertilisation from taking place. Since to bear children is the prime object of marriage among the Langi, one can imagine how hated and rejected this sort of wizard is.

Young women, as soon as they marry and go to a new neighbourhood, are warned against all the wizards in and around the village. The *ajok ading* not only makes young women barren. He (or she) is notorious for killing babies. The wizard waits until these innocent creatures are blooming with health and then destroys them. This is a dreadful blow to the Langi who so love and cherish children. A fine child is the pride of the whole clan. See how our women enjoy holding and playing with their babies. A mother is proud when people say it resembles its father. She feels that her fidelity to her husband has been established and acknowledged. A woman doesn't fuss when another woman's baby pisses on her lap or stains her with its stool. Why should she? For if he is a boy, people look to the baby as the future burier of the clan dead; if she is a girl, she will fetch cows as bride wealth.

It is a favourite baby, loved among the village women, that usually falls victim to an *ajok ading*. He makes every effort to get hold of a thread from the baby's nappy or a piece of its stool, or a hair from its head, and use the object for his cruel sorcery. Soon the doomed baby loses its happy smile. It gets a high fever, then acute diarrhoea which no medicine can cure, and is quickly dead.

Crops

It strikes me as significant and sinister that there are always certain hard-working families in a village who despite every favourable circumstance get a poor harvest. This misfortune too is the work of a wizard. Motivated by envy and malice, the wizard hides a destructive charm in the centre of the victim's field or in each of its four corners. The charm will stop the seed from germinating properly. Or the wizard may wait until the crop is doing well, then blight it. It is a fearful thing to see the young crop wilt and die over a whole field. A poor harvest means famine.

To make matters worse the wizard generally chooses to persecute a large family, thus multiplying the disastrous consequences of hunger. The underfed children droop and go thin. Those of school age are tired and dull and cannot profit from their lessons. All this is the work of the malicious wizard.

Our society measures a man's greatness in terms of children, food, and livestock. A man usually marries more than one wife in order to produce more children. He then feels secure. No wonder the wizard who strikes at babies and at the family food supply is detested.

By our standards a great man is he in whose home many people can feed – the ne'er-do-well, the elders, and visitors. They can drop in at any time to eat and drink. A man feels small if he has no granaries. He is ashamed if there are no cow-pats and goat droppings in his compound. These would be signs of poverty, laziness, or ill-luck.

Cattle

Jealousy and envy choke the wizard when he sees someone who has more children, food and cattle than he has. If a man has a large herd of cattle, he yearns to kill them all. He uses a magic charm which he may hide in the kraal. Soon the cows begin to grow weak. They lose appetite. The milk dries up in their udders. The calves die, and then the cows and bulls. If the local witch-doctor cannot stop the evil quickly by discovering and removing the charm, the whole herd will perish. This is a disaster. For if a man has no cattle, his sons cannot marry. They will die without an heir, and this is a mortal blow. It means the clan cannot expand.

In the old days, when villagers were enraged by the loss of children, crops and cattle they would round up (under the leadership of the elders) all the notorious wizards in their area, take them into the bush, and torture them to death. Society approved of such a punishment. It was a just revenge for suffering. A whole family of wizards might be exterminated in this manner. It was the fairest and quickest way of getting rid of anti-social elements. There are still some wizards at large in Lango. Regrettably society can no longer take the law into its own hands and exterminate them. People curse the government laws that tolerate wizards and protect them against ruthless punishment, as was once the custom.

N. OPIO-BUNGA

DEATH AND BURIAL CUSTOMS AMONG THE BANYORO
Death
Our old burial customs are dying. Before they disappear, I would like to record how my people the Banyoro traditionally bury a family head (*nyineka*). Custom decrees that when he dies he should be buried as soon as the various burial rites permit (not, though, on the day of his death), for people fear death, and the smell of decomposition is offensive.

When *nyineka* sickens and seems likely to die, he is laid on the ground (not on a raised bed) in the sitting room of (generally) his senior wife's house where all his people, relatives and friends can gather to hear his last words. The dying man is placed with his head pointing towards the main door – for everyone knows that he is on his way out. When he dies, he is left in this position.

Fried peas and *simsim* are placed in the dead man's right hand and his children come to eat for the last time from the hand that used to feed them when he was alive. The children pick the food with their tongues only. This – the first rite – signifies the loss of the family bread winner. Close male relatives and friends (they must all be men with families) are summoned to wrap the corpse. They handle it with great care, for it is bound for a last resting place among its ancestors, whence its spirit will watch closely over the bereaved relatives, especially over wives and children and over friends united to the dead man by the ceremony of blood taken by incision from the belly and mixed with coffee berries. The men who handle the body must also have lost their fathers; death can be transmitted by touch from the dead man's home to others, and no one wants to imperil the life of an aged father who is already likely to be on death's waiting list.

Women naturally take no part in wrapping the body. They are inferior; and it would be improper for them to see the dead man's private parts.

Meanwhile a fire is lit in the centre of the compound, where a growing crowd of mourners gathers. Men will spend the night outside. Women, in consideration of their sex, and to keep them separate at this time from the men, shelter inside the dwelling.

People must not only grieve. They must be heard and seen to grieve. Men who would ordinarily pride themselves on self control do their best to force out tears. They tie strips of cloth round their bellies to support them, as they will have to go without food for several hours. It is the women who are most prominent in the lamentation. When a woman arrives she can be heard grieving some distance away; and the noise she makes sets off all the other women again.

This, the first stage of mourning, is known as *okuganya*, and it involves some hardships. The men and women who keep vigil outside in the yard and in the sitting room may not wash their bodies; and they must sleep rough, without covering, on dry banana leaves as a reminder that the master who used to see to the comfort of his family and of visitors is no more. No one eats during the night. People may smoke, and drink banana beer, but not *waragi*, which is too strong for a solemn occasion.

Beer and tobacco are permitted for they soothe the nerves and help people forget their sorrow. Indeed, in Bunyoro and other parts of Uganda, it is usual at a time of mourning for the elders to call for their pipes and start drinking beer as soon as possible. Thus they 'nourish their minds' and chase melancholy away.

Burial

Nyineka is buried on the second day. The body is measured, and neighbours, friends and relatives dig the grave. It is generally sited in a banana grove near the house, and it must be deep enough to make it difficult for night dancers to get at the body. Night dancers are believed to be cannibals, and many people who are suspected of being night dancers have been accused of deliberately causing death so that they can have a meal of human flesh.

Wrapped and tied in bark cloth, the body is carried on a mat to the grave amidst lamentation. Traditionally no funeral speeches are made, as is the modern custom. Two men stand in the grave and the body is lowered to them. They untie the ropes and make sure the body is properly placed.

The senior wife throws some soil into the grave, thus 'burying her husband', which is her privilege alone. The other wives and their children do the same, followed in turn by all the other mourners, using their hands only to drop soil into the grave. The grave diggers then make sure that all the soil is returned to the grave, so that it forms a raised mound.

The corners of the grave are marked by stakes driven well in, and stones are heaped on the edges of the mound to keep the loose soil in position. Some of the dead man's possessions, e.g. mattresses, clothes, bowls, are either buried with him or thrown on top of the grave. This is done because it is feared that anything used by the dead man may spread death. I have, incidentally, never heard of anyone who believes in, or even discusses, the after life. It seems that the psychological reason for burying the dead man's property with its owner is to get rid of what would otherwise be a constant reminder of his death.

Women bring water for the grave diggers to wash the dirt off their legs and hands, which would otherwise carry death to their homes. The pots in which the water is carried are broken and the fragments thrown on the grave, likewise the baskets that were used for hauling the soil to the surface. The act of burial is over.

Ceremonies

All the mourners now assemble in the yard. A widow, related to the deceased, takes a burning reed and passes it across the backs of the widows of the dead man. This is meant to signify that they have lost a husband, and the widow who performs this ceremony is initiating the others into the 'widows' club'. The ceremony also indicates that they have lost the man who used to provide the fire wood that kept them warm on cold days. The ceremony is called *okukanga*, meaning 'to roast the body a little'.

That night, the three stones are removed from the senior wife's fireplace and put outside to signify that no more food will be cooked for the master in any of the huts in the compound.

In the morning everyone who took part in the burial has the head shaved in front. This ceremony is strictly observed, for it is believed that if any of them neglects to be shaved, and later walks through a garden, its crops will die.

Beer is served, while the deceased's biggest and oldest crowing cock, he-goat, ram and bull are slaughtered. These were the dead man's property and they must die with him (note that they are not only males, but masters among their fellows). The meat is cooked and served to the mourners.

The dead man's basket and the bowl from which he used to eat when he was in his senior wife's hut are thrown into the courtyard upside down – a sign that the things that used to stand upright when their owner was alive are now upset and turned towards the soil which he has entered. An unmarried daughter takes the spear which he inherited from his father and which symbolised his authority, and stands it upside down against the wall facing the main door into the yard. These things stay upside down till the funeral rites are over.

Food is served to the dead man's wives in baskets without bottoms. Like the baskets, the wives have lost their foundation and their families are in danger of breaking up.

Early on the third day, the same unmarried daughter fetches a big bunch of bananas from the garden and cooks them unpeeled in the yard. This is done 'to inform' the banana plantation that its master is dead; and it is for this reason that these bananas must not be touched by the knife.

The girl then goes to all the master's gardens, crying out, and roughly snatching samples of his crops – this again is to make the gardens feel the impact of the danger that threatens the homestead.

The girl also goes crying to the well to inform it that the master's water pot will never return there. The water she now fetches is spilt and the pot broken on the head of the grave so that the water 'goes to the deceased'. It is the last water he will get and his pot perishes with him.

The food which the girl has collected is cooked beside the grave. It is served crudely, on banana leaves only. The dead man's children come to eat it – their last meal with their father's spirit. They don't swallow the food, they bite at it and throw it at each other. When their father was alive he enforced strict discipline at meals. Throwing the food at each other signifies that his firm hand has been removed. This token meal is also the last one that the dead man's children will eat together in a family atmosphere, for some of his wives are likely to leave the homestead and go back to their original homes or to other places.

The Heir

The fourth day of the burial ceremonies, known as that of *ekyera* (from *okwera*, cleanliness), introduces the final cleansing rites. It is the second major stage of events. Rites of darkness and grief are succeeded by those that mark the return to normal bright life, and the formal appointment of the new heir.

Early in the morning the dead man's wives and children have their heads completely shaved, thus cleansing them of the death that has lately surrounded them. They remove the strips of dirty bark cloth they have been wearing, wash their bodies, and put on fresh clothes. As the head is master of the body, it is cleaned with special care.

Having at last 'got rid' of death, the wives and children, led by the heir, walk back in procession to the yard under an arch of reeds. The spear that has been propped upside down against the wall, now freshly washed with the juice of two creeping plants (*orweza* and *orwihuru*) to rid it of any elements of death, is handed to the heir. He is led to a new house that has been built for him and for the dead man's senior wife who can, if she consents, become his wife if she is not his mother.

The master of ceremonies then formally declares the heir to be the new head of the family. 'The heir's word,' he says, 'will be his father's word.' He ends his speech with the words, 'Now eat, drink and dance for the heir. The death and burial ceremonies are over.'

The feast is now served and people start dancing. For four days there have been misery and moaning, the dirt and darkness of death. The shadow has lifted. The guests get drunk, and some men and women make love in the small shelters they have erected. At such a time many new babies are conceived, as though to replace the dead.

At cockcrow the dead man's widows and children strip the thatch from the house where he died and throw it on the grave and on the ground. All this is done amidst loud crying. Using pangas they cut the roof and pile the wood and reeds around the grave. They leave the house walls standing. Without a 'head' it will in due course collapse.

It now remains for the dead man's property to be formally shared among his family. The heir normally gets a sum of money. All his father's daughters are put under his care. He will receive their bride wealth, and he must distribute it among the relatives. The heir receives cows, goats, and other property. The land is also his and he can distribute it, if he wishes, among his brothers. The other children also take their share. Daughters normally get money, sons livestock. The stepmothers are given to the elder sons.

The senior wife, followed by her co-wives in order of seniority, now go to their new places. Each of them receives one of the dead man's spears (a man keeps a spear in each of his wives' houses).

It will be clear from what I have written that the traditional burial ceremonies among my people the Banyoro are heavily

15a Teuso girls outside Pirre village stockade

15b Teuso carrier on Mount Zulia
15c Old Teuso man

16a Wagisu carriers on Mount Elgon

16b Victoria lakeside (Entebbe)

loaded with symbolism: a symbolism reflecting deep rooted attitudes to death that were inevitably resistant to the new beliefs preached by Christian missionaries. Nevertheless a European may find among our burial customs some echoes of his own ceremonies. For death is feared everywhere. The spirits, or the God, of death must be placated, repelled – and yet in the last resort accepted. Life, for the survivors, must go on. Knowing that their own day of doom is inevitable, they must still safeguard themselves against it.

The Banyoro ought to ask themselves these questions: What is now happening to the old customs? Are they worth preserving? Did the various rites and ceremonies help to sustain unity among our people? If they did, how shall we preserve what was good in them?

ELISHAMA KATEBALIIRWE-AMOOTI

PROVERBS FROM TORO AND BUNYORO

1 When his hoe breaks the lazy man feels relieved.
2 A child that never visits other homes will think his mother the best cook.
3 The creeper that will break the machete first coils round it.
4 It's foolish to dream of sauce at the sight of one white ant.
5 He who has a mother doesn't laugh at the old woman who has died by the wayside.
6 Wisdom, like fire, is obtained from another's hut.
7 If people refuse you food when you are present you won't expect them to keep any for you when you are absent.

J. KARUGABA

PROVERBS FROM KIGEZI

1 If you disturb excrement you get the stench.
2 An old woman was made love to at a well, and when she returned home she said, 'My children, in future you will not fetch water. I will fetch it.'
3 An inexperienced bull kisses the axe.
4 If you must eat a toad, then eat a juicy one.
5 The earthworm is slow, but it gets to the well.
6 The inexperienced lover excuses his clumsiness by saying the mat is slippery.

7　A woman farted against a pot of beer, and excused herself by saying, 'In my family, new beer is taboo.'

8　The one who is left behind says 'They are waiting for me.'

9　A chameleon, carried away by flood water, thought to itself, 'Such love-making is indeed rough.'

10　Another chameleon swept away by flood water said 'Well, we might at any rate get as far as Kampala.' (In a desperate situation one seeks some consolation.)

11　A woman farted at her mother-in-law's funeral, and excused herself by saying, 'Even the living are half-dead.'

12　A woman fornicated with a visitor, and said 'Homes that get visitors are useful.'

13　If they throw shit at you, it's better that it stinks. (A secret enemy is more to be feared than the one who declares himself.)

14　When his mother-in-law was about to be buried, the hyena said 'Bury her deep'. (We know only too well our own weaknesses and temptations.)

15　The old woman who knew you as a lad should die when you grow up. (It's embarrassing to be reminded of our childhood follies.)

16　I would have killed you if the Europeans hadn't come. (A recent saying, in reference to the law and order which Europeans introduced.)

17　A fool pounds grain in a calabash.

18　The dog fled when a bone was thrown to it, thinking it was a stone. (Ability to recognise an opportunity is the key to success.)

19　He who brews alone, brews bad beer.

20　The child who's always crying, will call in vain when a snake bites it.

21　The spectator at a wrestling match cries 'Just throw him down, and let's go.' (The observer won't appreciate a problem that he's not involved in.)

22　An old woman crushed a ripe banana and boasted that her strength would be the death of her. (Don't boast of trifling achievements.)

F. KWESIGA

The White Pumpkin

His gun on his shoulder,
A hat pulled like a basin over his head,
The white pumpkin came over the hill.

His shorts looked like a woman's skin skirt,
His gun like a baking stick,
He resembled and was taken for
A woman.

Crying in terror
The naked children fled,
Followed by their mothers
With babies dangling on their backs.

'An evil white spirit!' men cried,
'A white monster!'
And within the blink of an eye
The village was empty.
Far away they fled
Into the deep forest's breast,
Among mosquitoes and potholes of elephant.

Expecting a roll of drums,
The white pumpkin wondered
To find the village so empty and still.

Then stooping, long-nosed,
He went into a hut.
O horror! O stench
Of turds!

He stood there amazed and fascinated.
This was revelation. This was discovery.
This was the true heart of Africa –

A fire compact and living
That licked three spherical stones
On top a fat pot
Simmering and spitting.

In the hut's shadow,
A huge wooden bed
Behind it, goats.

The black pot coughed and belched
With its load of beans.
In the roof rats wrestled.

He stood there
His breast thumping
Unwelcomed,
And furiously he cried,
'Where have these savages gone!'

Then from a small rectangular box
He drew a flame
And set the village, the whole village, afire.

I saw it. I saw it all.
And I saw him wash himself
Behind a grain bin.
I saw his chest
That was hairy as a dog's, and pumpkin white.

ENOCH TINDIMWEBWA

Poor Man, Rich Man

Pity the poor man,
Surely he's bewitched.
His clothes are torn,
He is soaked when it rains,
Scorched when the sun shines.
He is always ill,
He can't even afford tea,
He sleeps naked among bed bugs.
When he yearns for meat
It's the intestines he must buy,
And if there's no offal he gets the bones.
The gown he buys a thief takes.
When he prepares a beer brew,
That's when the plantains don't ripen.
If he rears chickens in his yard
The jackal says thank you;

And when he would trade in fish
There's no market.
The goat he has bought
The hyena eats.
When he has a heap of cotton
Its price goes down.
Alas, if he gets some money
He loses it.

Yes, a poor man's lot is hard;
If he gets ten shillings he boasts,
He orders things in haste,
Meat for two shillings,
Beer for three,
Plates for two;
O and he must get his trousers mended –
Another three.
The ten have gone.

The poor man knows no happiness
He is not counted among the literate.
When he washes his shirt
He goes down to the river
And is caught by the tax collector.
He is considered a thief,
Also a brawler.
His mouth is always watering,
But the spittle runs in vain.
He smells but does not taste
The roasting meat.
Indeed, he is bewitched.

Now let us look at the rich man.
When a man gets riches
He turns self-willed, stubborn;
He spreads out his coat
With buttons unfastened,
His appearance changes
And his speech,
His belly swells
(This alters his way of sitting).
He no longer seeks friends,

His deeds are applauded,
For he is now a councillor.
He no longer wakes with the first cock-crow.
A hired *dhobi* does his washing.
He ceases to notice the poor,
He pushes them away with his legs,
They don't exist.
Yes, the food bursts his belly
And he erupts
More dung than a cow.

S. BYANSI

Butternuts and Ivory

I followed a path
Where the small birds
And spotted butterflies
Flew in and out of the *odugu* trees.
They flew with ease,
Never getting entangled,
Nor a blade of grass cutting them,
Nor thorns piercing their wings.

In a wood I heard a ringed dove
Calling like an old woman grinding millet,
And the *lakwal* ordering his troops
To wash the cooking pots quickly.

I came to a stream
Whose spray hung like ghosts
Over rocks where lizards basked.

I wanted to take off my clothes and shoes
To lie on the rocks among the lizards,
And when they tired of the sun
To glide with them in the shade.

How is it
That so many happy creatures
Abound here in the cursed torrid zone
Where heat, they say, dulls the brain?
Why don't they run to other places,
Places that are cool and civilised?

I know the reason.
For though you burn us, sun,
You give us millet, rain forests,
Butternuts and ivory.
Men and lizards rejoice in you.
We do not want to lose our paradise
To change our sun-split rocks.

OKUMU PA'LUKOBO

The Agwara

When the Alur dance *agwara*
A hill high among homesteads
Is their arena:
A circle cleared of bush and stumps.

Hanging from posts are the drums;
And when the sun has cooled
The drummers send their first echoes
Far among strangers.

Soon *agwara* trumpets vibrate the woods,
Calling youth to dance:
Along field paths they hurry,
Through thorns,
Hastening like *moro* ants
To the sounding drums.
Their blood is hot
And when they have arrived
And the leader starts the song they want
The drums take up its music,
The drums begin to chatter,
Yes, the dance is on:
Fever in young limbs,
White teeth and flashing eyes,
Heels that tear the grass,
Pounding earth to dust,
Legs that leap
Till even the old men feel fever in their blood:
See how they jerk their heads
Now dance with their arms
Now hum the *agwara* tunes

Hoarsely and softly recalling days
When their legs too were sleek and light
As oribi's.

When dance alone cannot express
Their joy and pride
Youths raise each other's arms high in the air
For the world must know how they exult.
It is a signal:
Seated ones rise
Old men crowd the ring beside the youths
They point their walking sticks to the sky
Like guns of soldiers:
In their mouths
The worn teeth gape like rusty stones
Even the students and the teachers
Even the élite from the mission
Even those who have watched it all
With feelings of conceit, of superiority,
Sense a fire in their veins
That jerks them,
That sends them into the ring,
And they find themselves dancing,
Dancing to the drums.

Round and round they dance,
To the gallop of drums
More tireless than crickets,
And the arena is full
With ten rings of dancers,
With sweat of dancers,
With voices of youths,
With their songs,
Till breath fails.

Now there is a stir among the trumpeters
Who have lined the arena's edge.
Lying on their backs
Like rowers pulling at the oars,
They aim their trumpets at the sky
And utter such a thunder clap
As though the heavens were rent:
It is the climax.

The youth who has performed best,
Who has sung well,
Who has not tired easily,
Whose arms have been raised most often,
The youth whose muscles lie like snakes
On the bone of his legs,
He is acclaimed the hero of the day.
Yes, he is one of the elders:
And everyone will say,
'That boy, is he not a true son of his father?
Truly, he is a real Alur!'
Indeed, he will have fame.
Many girls will love him.

OKUMU PA'LUKOBO

Epilogue

Expatriate Exodus

The immediate reaction of white expatriates to Amin's campaign of 1972 for a 'black Uganda', a campaign directed in particular against the Indian and British communities, was to wonder whether to stay or to quit. The British Government's retaliatory and arguably wrong decision of December 1972 to withdraw further aid to Uganda helped many British expatriates make up their minds. Those who chose to stay would not only have to put up with the probability of threats and insults. An expatriate who wished to renew his contract with the Uganda Government would be obliged to do so on local terms without benefit of the substantial London-paid salary increment.

So in the wake of the evicted Indians a great many expatriates left hurriedly to eat their Christmas dinners in Britain. At about the same time the Scandinavians also withdrew. Americans and Canadians followed.

Expatriate attitudes under pressure were revealing. People who quitted early took the realistic view. They were not prepared to be harassed as spies, to gamble on an unpredictable future. They feared for the safety of their families, and no wonder if they had been roughed up by soldiers, arrested, or assaulted by thugs. In this frame of mind it was to their interest to get quickly to the front of the queue for a new job elsewhere.

The arguments for staying were mixed. Breaking one's contract, despite the British Government's promise to pay compensation, would mean financial loss. Some expatriates had personal commitments in Uganda. Some were obstinate ('I won't be kicked around'). Many felt it would be wrong to desert a sinking ship: to abandon their students, their hospital patients, their congregations, their projects and their African friends at a time when it could be said that ordinary Africans needed their presence more than ever. 'Governments', it was argued, 'come and go. Any good will we can continue to generate will be a bonus for the future.'[1]

By October 1972 all the residents (about a dozen) of my block of flats had gone, leaving me alone, like an unpaid janitor, to check the locks. How black and quiet were the nights! No more overflowing dustbins to attract dogs; uncut grass, the buzz of returning mosquitoes. Jobless servants, now excessively polite, knocked at my kitchen door for water.

Mrs C was one of the first to leave. The school where she taught, following the loss of its Indian staff and pupils, had temporarily collapsed. She had been held up one night by a bandit with a pistol. She felt vulnerable.

Miss G, head of a child care society, elderly, ladylike, timid, feeling she was no longer wanted, transferred herself and her cat to Swaziland.

Mr S, who had served in the Ministry of Works for a dozen years, was expelled with his English wife because he was a non-citizen Indian. He left in good order, his belongings packed in splendid crates made for him by one of his department's carpenters.

Mr O, my Danish neighbour, and the whole of the Danish

---

[1] An English child care specialist told me he thought the British Government had been 'immoral and stupid' to withdraw that part of aid to Uganda which was in Britain's long-term interests, i.e. salary supplements to doctors, teachers, university lecturers, and technicians. Dr D. W. Barkham, after being expelled from his post as Senior Consultant Physician at Mulago Hospital (he was accused of spreading 'political gonorrhoea'), anticipated another consequence of aid withdrawal in a generous and eloquent letter to *The Times*. 'The losers,' he wrote, 'would be the people of Uganda. But they cannot be held responsible for the actions of their "government". . . . However much the plight of the Asians deserves our immediate sympathy and help, in the long run it is the Africans in Uganda who need all the understanding and support we can give them.' Dr Barkham's letter may have given some expatriates fresh heart to remain in Uganda. But High Commission officials whom I spoke to had not read or heard of it.

voluntary service team in Uganda, were withdrawn by their own government, who feared it could no longer guarantee their safety.

Mr and Mrs H, both teachers in middle age, anticipating after careful calculation the eventual eviction or withdrawal of all expatriate teachers, had decided to resign before the rush started. This was sensible of them, for they were able to sell all their property, turn it into good English pounds, and collect their gratuities, their air fares and other emoluments down to the last penny.

Miss O did not return from leave. She feared the authorities would make trouble with the documentation for her small half-caste daughter. Amin's soldiers had of late been showing their dislike of black-white liaisons and of their offspring ('half-castes are crooks').[1]

A H also left early. He was devoted to his students but resented the ill will generated by the government against the British. Nor, as breadwinner for four children, could he risk staying in a leaky boat.

Mr W sent his daughter home within twenty-four hours of her having been struck in the face by a soldier. (Yet Mr K, who was seized by soldiers in his own house, stuffed into the boot of a car, and dumped at Makindye military prison, had forgiven the authorities, and was staying on.)

Some missionaries accepted more readily than others that the time was ripe to hand over to native clergy. Teachers were torn between a conscientious desire to see their pupils and students through an impending examination, and their own self-interest, which was to get out quickly. A decisive factor for all expatriates was quite simply that life in the 'Pearl of Africa' had ceased to be free and enjoyable.

One of my own motives for staying was curiosity. Uganda was going through an exciting phase. How would it turn out? Though, to Africans, Amin's 'revolution' looked to be a grandiose affair attracting world attention, it was but a tiny

[1] Since the Indian exodus some half-castes in Kampala have tended, rather as the Indians did, to make themselves conspicuous at social meeting points. In a recent speech (20 January 1974) Amin has warned 'this breed of people against whose mothers non-Africans committed a mortal wrong' not to give themselves airs or 'look down upon black Ugandans'.

moment in history. The upheavals and the pressures could not last.

Consequences

With the turn of the year the exodus of expatriates continued, its momentum encouraged by increasing exposure to theft and robbery with assault. John B, a teacher with a notable reputation for goodness and charity to young Africans, was savagely slashed in bed. Two senior English inspectors of education were assaulted in their homes. Expatriates' cars continued to be seized at gun-point.

The departure of the Indians and of many Europeans had immediate consequences. In education the abrupt loss of teachers meant that courses at the higher levels could no longer be adequately covered. In the country's economic life, the wholesale take-over by Africans of Indian shops and businesses was accompanied by soaring prices and by shortages of staple commodities resulting in part from the disruption of the distributive system and of factory production. Many premises stood empty for some months till they were reallocated to black citizens (in Kampala the applicants, a mixed bag including housewives and men in threadbare collars, had to queue with their bank statements outside the vacant businesses and be interviewed on the pavement by soldiers attended by military police). The flight of skilled Indian mechanics, the absence of supervision (no Indian foreman to make sure the roof of the cement factory at Tororo didn't cave in under the weight of accumulated dust) and growing scarcity of spare parts affected the maintenance and repair of every type of machinery.

The expatriate found this initial process of disintegration painful. He saw something he was proud of – a well stocked Indian shopping centre, a hospital department, a promising school class, a motor repair service – begin to break up. Meanwhile social life had deteriorated. Mini-skirts (in deference to the Prophet) had long been banned, bars closed at 10 p.m. (worse, they did not open till 12.45 p.m.). The young, and the ambitious among us, and the children, seemed mostly to have taken flight, leaving a high proportion of duds behind: people with no prospects elsewhere, ageing school teachers, a few sad

Italians whose African Odyssey had commenced years ago in Mussolini's Ethiopia, the soured remnant of what had been a delightfully happy and varied foreign community.

Watching the looted cars rattle by, joining the queues for a pound of sugar, walking past what had been sophisticated shops that had sold jewellery, cameras, and souvenirs now filling their half-empty shelves with pawpaws, old tins of curry powder, and skin lightener, we in Kampala grumbled and were angry. The removal of King George V's statue from outside the law courts by city council workmen which, as I saw them hammering at it, filled me with a gust of rage, seemed to symbolise the end of one phase in Uganda's history; the invasion of Kampala's hotels and bars by Libyans, Somalis, and men in Moslem caps, presaged the start of another.

We, a community hitherto cossetted and respected, had of a sudden been threatened and made to feel unwanted. To the added chagrin of some, neither the British authorities at home nor in Uganda seemed willing or able to stand up for us – indeed, they clearly considered us to be a nuisance; they would have preferred us not to be in Uganda at all.[1] Hysterical newspaper reports by flitting journalists – skull-crushing by hammer in Makindye military gaol, the rehashing of old butcheries – did not help. It was pointless to mock the 'black Nero'; he enjoyed the publicity. *Punch's* satirical series on Amin, which has him talking like an Alabama negro, is off the mark.

Reflections

Let us admit that on their home ground black men are entitled to Africanise whatever they like, from God to Barclay's Bank and women's skirts; and that whatever they perpetrate in the alleged name of anti-colonialism or indigenous culture, there will be a strong body of non-African opinion ready to defend if not to applaud them.

It is the way these things have been done in Uganda that is most in need of justification. Amin's methods of economic war

---

[1] As potential hostages we were an embarrassment. In fairness to the British authorities it should also be pointed out that (*a*) the High Commission in Kampala had its hands full processing the evacuation of Indians, (*b*) Amin's aims were unpredictable, (*c*) it is probable that Amin himself was not fully in control of the soldiers who were harassing expatriates.

('I am a bulldozer') have brought instant distress. The ex-patriate's lament, that they would cause a drastic lowering of the standards which it had been his concern to introduce and to maintain, is proving to be a legitimate one.

But we touch here on a vital point of misunderstanding. It is arguable that those standards – *our* standards – were too high, if not irrelevant, for a tropical society whose political independence is but a few years old and which is unused to total responsibility. For a great many Ugandans, enmeshed in a European system yet with the African's powerful urge to relax and his delight in a windfall, they had been an incubus. Free now of coercion and of the naggings of auntie, he can 'fall into things', mislay the office files, park his car at roundabouts, bounce cheques, tether his spotted goat to the neat municipal hedge left behind by Mr Tompkins, enjoy himself.

Efficiency geared to the precise hands of a clock, intolerant of gaiety, is a Western concept perfected in the logistics of a railway timetable or in Hitler's crematoria. On a reasonably full stomach, it is the moment of emotional happiness and not at all the disposal of his sewage, or probity in public places, that the ordinary Ugandan really wants: something that the houseboy has the gift of achieving more easily than his white employer. In Uganda, thanks to Amin, many Africans occupying premises and selling off stock left behind by Indians have been reaping an undreamt of harvest of cash. The current euphoria of a favoured few who have come into possession of houses, cars and jobs is Amin's gift. The bill for it has yet to be presented.

Amin is fond of calling us 'spies' (a white man seen bird watching in a sugar cane field or changing a wheel within a mile or two of a barracks had better watch out); and though the European bridles at the charge, there is some truth in it, for we foreign residents whether we like it or not are the eyes and ears of a wider world. Our presence in Uganda must have some inhibiting effect on the excesses of government. The African feels less isolated and less vulnerable while there are white faces around. Corpses may be dumped in swamps, prominent individuals disappear. But the word spreads. It reaches the news media, and a Nairobi or London newspaper, though they may not always get the facts right, will announce their obituaries.

The humiliations inflicted on expatriates in Uganda have set a precedent that must erode respect for the white man in other parts of Africa. The Indian community, once they had shown signs of panicking, were done for. Amin has demonstrated that he can bully Englishmen too. The British, still more the Indians, in neighbouring Kenya know that their own position has been weakened by events in Uganda.

Because of Amin old prejudices against the black man have risen again to the surface ('What we have taught the African is but dust sprinkled on his arm,' I have heard a grumpy Italian, already bankrupted in the Congo, tell his friends. 'When it suits him he brushes it off'). Amin has done harm to his people and to the cause of Africa as a whole in that, governing by fear, he has reimposed on Ugandans old habits of submission and servility that one hoped *Uhuru* was eroding, and that in the past have been one of the black man's dominant character weaknesses – the secret of his survival, perhaps, in a cruel continent constantly overrun by predators but a prime cause of the Western (and the Arab) world's historical disrespect for the negro (and of their successful exploitation of his sinews).[1]

Many liberal minded people I know are now tempted to agree

[1] Two authorities for these statements, which may seem to be contentious, can be cited here: Professor C. D. Darlington's reference (*The Evolution of Man and Society*, London, 1969) to what he calls the 'genetic docility' characteristic of enslaved Africans – which he relates to the 'fatal abundance of tropical root-crops promoting the too-easy progress of agriculture'; and Professor Bernard Lewis ('Race and Colour in Islam', *Encounter*, August 1970) who quotes a great many references from early and mediaeval Arabic literature to demolish the 'myth' that, unlike Western society, the Moslem world has been free from racial prejudice and discrimination. ('Your mother is a black Nubian woman / With fingers like dung beetles': 'When he is hungry he steals, when he is sated he fornicates' – of an Ethiopian, attributed to the Prophet – are typical of the numerous insulting references to black Africans that Lewis has spotted.) Lewis admits that the Islamic world has never practised the kind of racial exclusivism which we find now in South Africa or which has existed until very recently in the United States. But he points to the cruel fact that, before black male slaves were permitted to enter Arab lands, a large proportion of them had to submit to castration. Now, of course, under General Amin, it is no longer safe for teachers in Uganda schools to draw attention to the role played in African history by Arab slave traders.

with those old timers who used to say 'The African is a nice fellow. But don't expect too much from him or you'll be disappointed.' The mistakes and excesses of a governing élite are one thing. The abandon with which so many ordinary Africans have joined the race to rob and cheat their fellows, and with the breakdown of supervision to shirk their work, is another.

The old timer's view is of course the sort of pulpit judgment that is coloured by personal irritation. It ignores, for instance, the mass of rural peoples whose long-standing and positive values remain uncorrupted by government conduct. It points, though, to an underlying difference in attitudes. Where we Europeans, in our clockwork world of acquisitive materialism, are doggedly and often drearily preoccupied with getting lifelong security for ourselves and for our families, one watches with envy the zest, joy and fatalism with which a Ugandan can forget his troubles in response to a bit of luck, the pay packet, an emotion.

NOVEMBER 1973-MARCH 1974

England

From August to November 1973 I was in England, at first in London hospitals, then convalescing with my brother in Dorridge, Warwickshire. Amin had long dropped out of the British news except for an occasional item chosen for its entertainment value.[1] One TV news flash showed him, huge and black, telling a group of Arab staff officers in Damascus that 'In Uganda millions of womens (*sic*) have volunteered to fight for their Arab brothers and sisters against the Zionists.'

The surgical ward of University College Hospital, London, was for me a painful experience. I felt I had been cut in two by a sword. But Manson's Ward in St Pancras Hospital for Tropical Diseases was a jolly place, more like a rest camp. Portuguese women helpers brought us tea and fruit cake. The windows looked on to an inviting churchyard where fallen plane tree leaves were blowing against a few elegant tombstones. The adjustable beds harboured delightful specimens: an old Welsh gentleman, eighty-eight years old, who spoke almost with

[1] Two recent items in *The Times* are headed 'Scotland urged to secede by General Amin' (14 February 1974) and 'Former Model is Uganda Minister' (21 February 1974).

affection of the ailment, sprue, which had attached itself to him in Ceylon forty years ago; an ex-army boxer who brewed his own tea; some wan, gentle youths with pigtails, dhotis, and chain necklaces who had collected Oriental parasites on the drop-outs' road to Katmandu.

I became a TV addict. I saw West Indies cricket fans beating tins at Lord's, and it struck me as Arnold ran up to bowl that the animal grace of the West Indies players made the Englishmen look by comparison like lumbering policemen. I found it embarrassing that the great leaders of Britain spent so much time quarrelling over the price of a sausage. Mr Heath boomed away like a Territorial Army colonel irritated by complaints about the rations. Only John Enoch Powell was different. He had a text, and in splendid phrases he preached.

Since the Uganda Government had failed to reply to my application for re-engagement on local terms, I flew back to Kampala at my own expense on a cheap Sudan Airways flight. At the Grand Hotel in Khartoum I found myself back in an Africa I had not visited for a long time. The bedrooms had punkahs, there were spy-holes in the doors. In the lounge large men wearing turbans, slippers and gowns stared at the legs of our two mini-skirted passengers over tiny cups of coffee.

When at length I threw my English raincoat into the back of a taxi at Entebbe and propped my two bottles of duty-free whisky between my legs, familiar warm air scented with humus and blossom blew in from a black night.

In my Kololo garden the termite mound had overflowed like a huge chocolate pudding into the drain. A car had run into the frangipani. But the robin chat was still singing away, a paradise fly catcher was flitting like a wraith round the mango tree, and a new ground squirrel had dug a hole by my pagoda. White moonflowers were out, casting their spent trumpets like paper spills among the grass. My dustbin had not been stolen, no one had broken in. I put on my white colonialist shorts and was glad to be back.

Return to Uganda

In Uganda meanwhile the internal situation had quietened. There had been fewer desertions of Africans in high places,

fewer murders – they were due in March (see p. 318). There
were queues for milk and bread as well as for sugar, not
enough beer (unless the bar-owner was a military man) to
last over the government-extended week-ends, and serious
inflation. The import of forty rather small new buses made in
Jugoslavia, the opening of an up-country sub-hospital with an
Egyptian doctor or two to keep it going, were being publicised
as triumphs.

Few of my European friends were left. Volkswagen's works
manager, an irascible but helpful Bavarian who for years had
given Beetle owners an efficient service, had fallen foul of an
African diplomat, and Amin himself had driven his Citroen-
Maserati SM to the workshop and personally handed Herr
Winklmeyer his expulsion order. Roger Counihan, one of the
last of the British lawyers, had decamped to Malawi ('It was a
wrench to leave Uganda after all those years,' he wrote to me,
'but the blow was softened by the continued deterioration of
everything in that country').

No one had matches (cigarette smokers kept a candle burning
in their homes). Grumbling was widespread.

The General himself seemed for the time being more
interested in cutting a heroic figure in Middle East military
affairs than in the scandals and failures of his policies at home.
He was exhorting the Arab armies to march on Tel Aviv. The
Israelis, he warned, were scheming to capture Mecca and
Medina. They would have executed a plan to poison the waters
of the Nile had he not expelled them from Uganda. Kissinger
was a murderer and spy. Mrs Meir, that 'murderous woman',
should 'pack her knickers' and go back to America. In a
telegram (8 January 1974) to General Dayan he announced
his intention to sponsor Palestinian suicide squads to liberate
their homes. 'I am one of the strongest men in the world,'
the message concluded, 'who fears nobody except God.' A few
days later he awarded himself the VC (Victory Cross, in Amin-
speak), DSO and MC.[1]

---

[1] In line with these posturings, and his talk of a projected 'Operation
Tel Aviv', Amin soon afterwards changed the name of the 2nd Simba
Mechanised Battalion, Masaka, to the Revolutionary Suicide Mechanised
Regiment – 'to be equipped with the most sophisticated weapons' (7 February
1974), the 'gift of Russia' (7 March 1974).

Criticism

Africans had grumbled under Obote. But the grumblers then were mainly the Baganda, whom he had alienated, or citizens (often Indians) whose lives and property Obote's police had failed to protect against kondoism. The magazine *Transition* had been banned, Luzira prison (known as 'the University' on account of the intellectual quality of its top inmates) had its distinguished political detainees. But student bodies, taking inspiration from Makerere professor Ali Mazrui, still met to debate the merits and demerits of Obote's policies. People weren't afraid of being stuffed into the boot of a car and instantly killed.

It is impossible and would probably be fatal to criticise Amin directly. Yet there has to be a safety valve; and complaints, addressed to the *Voice of Uganda* newspaper (whose editorial staff are from time to time harangued by a minister in combat uniform), or made to the great man himself by elders and spokesmen at open meetings (where he likes to strum his accordion), use the technique of first praising Dada and then belabouring the miscreants who are said to be scuppering his good intentions.

Foreign imperialists (Americans), colonialists (the British), Zionists, the new African businessmen and shopkeepers, civil servants, taxi and bus drivers – all take their turn as scapegoats for muddles due in the first instance to impulsive government decrees that are instantly imposed yet in practise allow the ruling caste itself to flout them.

'Long live General Amin!' runs a typical newspaper letter. 'Thanks to our beloved President many of us took up Asian flats, the gift of the President, in the city area with enthusiasm. But rogues have doubled the rents. Let our gallant soldiers step in and help the poor man. Please help!' (*Voice of Uganda*, 12 November 1973.) Or: 'The Asians were milking the economy. Thank God our President got rid of them. Our own brothers have taken over what used to be their businesses, many of them without having to pay a cent. Yet it is these brothers who are now sucking the blood out of us. O Dada, help!' (*Voice of Uganda*, 7 January 1974.)

Newspaper letter and leader writers do not mince words

('The tycoons have lost shape due to increased heavy drinking,'
complains Hummy Bob (*Voice of Uganda*, 13 December 1973).
'Some cannot even tie their own shoe laces. SAVE! SAVE!
SAVE!') Their cries, in an idiom that shows strong feeling, are
the record of a traumatic national experience. Here are some
excerpts from letters to the *Voice of Uganda:*

'If you peep through the windows in Kampala shops you
find that everything is priced but the price is totally threatening.
I don't see why our true black Ugandans should prove to be
ticks in cattle. The businessmen should be tolerant to their
fellow blacks by charging them fairly, for our old Babas and
Mamas have began again living like long ago, walking naked
with a piece of cloth to prevent only his/her bottom, because
of the threatening prices.'

MC.Y.M.K.K. Kanga Kukobo, Kampala.

29 October 1973.

'Those traders who overcharge – 35/- for a teapot in one shop,
while the same pot is 25/- in others – say "Supplies are short.
So what to do? The things cannot walk into one's shop." Yet
these traders were given *mafuta mingi*[1] loans in thousands of
shillings by the government to run their businesses. You find
that someone got a loan of sh. 30,000/- but if you value the
articles in his shop, they total to only sh. 1,000/-. In his shop
you find six bitenges[2] (which he charges at 600/- each), a
telephone, a chair and a table where he sits all day long yawning,
with a minimum of sh. 20,000/- cash in his pocket. He closes
his shop at 5.00 p.m. to go hunting for women and boozing
(an average of 30 bottles of beer alone daily). It is high time
these *mafuta mingi* people put in effort and started hunting these
goods that are scarce while we people in the offices are busy
collecting money for them.'

Freddy Kit. M., Mbale. 3 December 1973.

'Everybody jumped at his feet when General Amin announced

---

[1] *Mafuta mingi* (lots of fat), i.e. government loans to the new traders and
businessmen who took over from Asians (and Europeans).
[2] Lengths of printed cloth.

the transfer of our economy over to indigenous Africans without paying even a single cent, just only on a gold plate. But it is very surprising to see that our new businessmen have turned out to be worse exploiters than the expelled Asians. Our President's effort is being abused. Worse still, we are now creating a small group of only 8,000 people to sit on the rest of the population and exploit it. Only 8,000 people benefit from the economic war. In order to avoid all this, every business be it big or small should be nationalised by the state.'

S. Kato, Kampala. 31 May 1973.

'I strongly support the President and the Defence Council to punish the hoarders and overchargers. They want their tumbos[1] to bulge out so quickly like an expecting hydra and they have already proved their incapability within a few months by drinking and speaking big of themselves, leave alone ordering fleets of modern cars from abroad, and they call this *mafuta mingi*, a word which they misinterprete. I pray the government to take over all these businesses and employ school leavers of all grades to work in them. This will be creating employment for learned and able Ugandans instead of individual relatives of businessmen who simply sit in shops just to show off without any knowledge of its running. The State Trading Corporation will distribute the commodities to the government shops and hence no hoarding or overcharging since it will be the property of the government.'

Ssemugenyi, Kampala. 28 September 1973.

'I celebrated my 25th birthday in August. It has been long enough for me to learn that education is one sure way to poverty while *mafuta mingi* is one sure way to a fat tummy. With 20 years of school behind me my gross salary per month is 1330 shillings. Take away taxes, debts, etc., some shameful amount is left. When I find that the average *mafuta mingi* man makes two times my month's salary in one day, I start wondering why I wasted 20 years at school. What is the meaning of these unbelievable prices? Is *mafuta mingi* daylight robbery without violence? Is it a licence to cheat? Economists, please help me.'

Charles Kanyarusoke, Mbarara. 7 January 1974.

[1] Bellies.

Missionary hospitals in Uganda, despite the untidiness of patients, are clean, others often less so. Listen to this cry:

'Allow me space in your esteemed paper to write about the health conditions in Lira Hospital. I was admitted for a serious case of peptic ulcer. I woke up just to see most patients awake and seriously scratching themselves; furthermore leaving their bodies bare in the cold night. I asked my nearest neighbour for what was wrong and he answered that there were very many lice and bed bugs. I turned round to find mine even full of these organisms. From that time until daybreak I never slept due to the disturbance of these parasites. The pain of my ulcer increased very tremendously. When I asked one of the nurses to change the beddings, she looked at me with the eyes of a hungry watch dog and proudly walked away with her duck-like feet and swinging her about one ton buttocks. When the doctor came he found that my case was getting worse. Lives must be saved from dirt in hospitals. The President constantly emphasises to keep Uganda clean. Furthermore he frequently repeats his slogan: TALK LESS ACT MORE.'

G. Opio-Opio, Lira. 17 January 1974.

Bus journeys have their hazards.

'On several occasions passengers have fallen victims to heavy rains solely because some buses bear no window glasses. The hollow windows allow into the buses plenty of rain and very sadly passengers often find themselves not only wet but even in a sort of swimming pool. This is more pitifully true with buses on long routes. Remember: "Uganda needs us alive but not dead." '

Majembe-Magembe, Mbarara. 17 January 1974.

Taxi drivers endanger lives:

'We asked the taxi driver why he stopped to squeeze in three more people when the taxi (15 passengers) was already full. He said he was trying to recover what he had lost for replacing a burst tyre (on the way one of the behind tyres burst). I therefore wish the police would check on these people so that stuffing passengers like bags of sugar is stopped.'

Oswuban Okwerede, Kampala. 11 June 1973.

The new businessmen and traders, initially admired and envied for their good fortune in 'falling into things', have been reaping an ominous harvest of hatred. But it is not possible to know exactly how much of the blame for shortages and high prices should be apportioned to them. Producers and distributors are certainly at the root of much of the trouble; likewise conspicuous consumption by the armed forces (and seizure, for instance, of civilian transport vehicles). Amin launched his economic war against non-citizen Indians and Europeans. Ironically his war has turned into a family quarrel between native Ugandans.

Finally, on the subject of murder, a cry of despair set off by a televised interview which the General had with local newspaper men; Pressed several times by Mr Mukasa of the *Voice of Uganda* to account for a series of murders being committed at night in Mengo-Kisyeni ('My neighbours,' stammered Mukasa, 'come to my poor room and ask me as a journalist why these murders are never reported in the newspaper. . . . The relatives of the deceased not only want the murderers to be arrested, they want to see with their own eyes that they have been executed. . . . They beg, sir, to speak to you personally'). Amin stalled at first ('You are my friend, because you are telling me true things', 'Let all Ugandans love one another'), then finally agreed to reinforce military police patrols in the affected neighbourhoods. The irony in the General's reply was of course that in effect his military police were being told to arrest themselves or at any rate their own agents!

Commenting on this interview in the *Voice of Uganda*, a letter writer said;

'Bravo to Mr Willy Mukasa, one of the pressmen, who was very bold, the other day, to bring this particular question to the attention of the President. These cruel bandits who are slaughtering the innocent people are not kondos, they are not guerillas, but something else we demand to know. Innocent people are being killed like cocoons and no one seems to care who has killed who and why. As I write this letter, many of us are waiting for their turns, you never know who will be a victim tonight.'

Bagambi Amooti, Kampala. 28 June 1973.

Sayings of Amin

For journalists General Amin himself is a constant delight – for local radio announcers, with his string of titles and decorations (General Al-Hajji Idi Amin Dada, VC, DSO, MC, President of the Republic of Uganda), none of which may be omitted, an embarrassment.

For three years he has been spouting non-stop except for two or three brief intervals when he withdrew to Mulago Hospital for a medical check-up and rest. From his Command Post ('If Mr Heath wants his money, he must report to me here'), or sitting under the portraits of Bokassa and Colonel Gadaffi at State House, he is ready to pronounce on anything, at the highest and the most mundane levels. One day he advises Nixon by telegram how to handle Watergate. The next finds him telling American and Caribbean blacks to adopt one national language – Swahili; or railing against bell-bottoms, dirty compounds, and women's wigs (they are made, he has said repeatedly, from the hair of American negro soldiers who died on the battlefields of Vietnam). Many Africans see, of course, the funny side of Dada's posturings and laugh at them.

Amin's most boastful, boorish, and ludicrous utterances (he has quoted the spurious Protocols of Zion as evidence of Jewish villainy) may be combined, however, with homely good sense. In his homilies to the common man he is sometimes at his best: patently sincere, the old soldier, wise Dada, telling his people how to behave.

'Fear God and report spies,' he says. 'Keep your compounds clean, slash the grass or it will grow into a big forest and invite snakes and rats.'

'If you are drunk, for God's sake park your car and rest till you feel all right.'

In an address to Makerere students: 'Many of you have

gonorrhoea. This is not right. As future leaders of our nation you must have clean bodies.'

On abortion: 'Whoever practises abortion is a first-class murderer. The practice does not only kill the child alone but also the parent. This means that the country will have lost two citizens at the same time. If one does not want to get pregnant, she should not exceed her usual enjoyment. Experience has shown that several pregnant women get it through over-enjoyment and, therefore, whoever does not want children, should restrict herself.' (*Voice of Uganda*, 30 July 1973.)

A rebuke to his officers: 'I have discovered that when some officers are promoted they run for big cars like Mercedes Benz and stop buying suits, thereby dressing like cowboys in bell bottom trousers. This is shameful.' (*Voice of Uganda*, 11 January 1974.)

Amin

Like any other tyrant anxious and in a hurry to change a society that is set in its own ways, Amin in his efforts to stir things up collides with the dead weight of popular inertia or of sly defiance. The impossibility of finding a reliable let alone permanent apparatus of servants to enforce his numerous decrees largely nullifies the good in them and at the same time encourages inherited tendencies to law-breaking.

Local chiefs do not like being made to go on cross-country runs before breakfast. Uganda girls, whatever Dada says about the African race's 'natural beauty', want to wear wigs, miniskirts, tight trousers and slit dresses.

Young bank employees impatient to buy a car, cashiers and public servants who handle other people's money, can have less compunction about taking some of it for themselves when their own leaders have blazed the way on a huge scale by property seizure and division of spoils amongst themselves.

Shopkeepers are in business to make a profit, not to lose money by giving away scarce and desirable goods at government controlled prices – and in paper bags provided at their own expense.

Nepotism – the promotion of one's own extended family's interests – is a moral duty.

The soldier who has just learned to use a rifle, like any youth promoted to his tribal warrior set, will want to bully people with it.

Poor men and youths who hang about towns steal.

Despite the abuse he pours over us ('the English are the most hopeless'),[1] and his delight in Britain's 'economic collapse' ('no toilet rolls', reported the *Voice of Uganda*),[2] Amin in his heart likes his earlier patrons and military tutors – kilted Scotsmen ('the best fighters in Britain – they ought to become independent and leave the English to suffer')[3] appear to be his favourite British type, while the non-commital diplomat from Whitehall, shaking a small grey head, is his *bête noire*.

In his hatred of the Israelis (Nile water-poisoners, milkers of the Uganda economy at the rate of one million shillings a day, and thieves, he calls them, for Israeli contractors skilfully contrived to salvage much of their equipment during the expulsion process), there is clearly admiration; though he woos the Arabs for political ends and quotes the Prophet, he has a poor opinion of their fighting qualities ('If I had commanded one of the Arab armies during the October war, the situation would be different now').[4]

Amin wants very badly to be recognised and accepted by the respectable. Nyerere's coolness, blamed on the malign influence of Obote, and Britain's persistent ostracism, have hurt him. The more this approbation is denied him, the more extreme his reactions in favour of rebels like Gadaffi and the Palestinian guerillas. Eager to be praised by his betters, he laps up the flattery of minions: a congratulatory letter from some unknown Londoner, the gift of a club tie from a New Zealand rugby player,[5] will be publicly announced side by side with an adulatory note from the People's Democratic Republic of

---

[1] *Voice of Uganda*, 13 February 1974 (interview with French journalists).
[2] *V. of U.*, 12 February 1974.
[3] *V. of U.*, 13 February 1974.
[4] *V. of U.*, 24 January 1974.
[5] When Mr Kirk, the New Zealand Prime Minister, declining to reply to two telegrams from Amin (one asked that the All Blacks rugby football team visit Uganda and the other that New Zealand erase the Union Jack from her flags), said he had not passed the message to the New Zealand Rugby Football Union ('If he wants them he has their address'), he was, for a change, using language the General understands.

Korea. Sadly he has failed to win the esteem of countries that really count.

It would not be fair to blame Amin for everything that has gone wrong in Uganda. A great many ordinary Ugandans believe that the President is a good man doing his best: '*Bantu mbaya*, it is people who are bad,' they say. Dada may stop to help one injured child in a Kampala street. But he cannot be present at every street accident, or take every shopkeeper by the scruff of the neck and force him to unlock his sugar hoard.

In truth economic affairs, whose complexities he cannot be expected to understand – though at the height of his form during the Asian exodus he announced that he was one of the world's leading economic brains – bore and bewilder him, and he has virtually ignored the appalling deterioration of Uganda's economy.

What the General is really after is glory. True, he has lunched at Buckingham Palace. But it seems he can hardly wait to win a real medal in battle against white men. There are no more timid 'browns' to kick out. There is no glory to be acquired among the quarrels of Kampala shopkeepers. The black Nubian hero must spear, not a spider, but the lion.

Amin, however, is capable of startling *volte faces*; they can be easily explained away as revelations that like the Prophet's (and Mao's and Napoleon's) come to him in dreams ('My dreams are like the voice of God and not my own'). When the moment arrives he will no doubt expect to be forgiven by those whom he has scourged: 'We were enemies, but now let us slaughter a bull and be friends' – the instant magnanimity of the bully who has had enough. The British Government might forgive him (provided he promises to pay up the money he owes the British taxpayer); not so those of his own people whom his regime has murdered or wronged.

Hot tempered yet ponderous, driven by urges whose origins must partly lie in the obscurity of his childhood, Amin is a man in a hurry ('I predict that the end of the world will come in five years' time'), the barrack room sergeant who constantly exhorts us to double up. One marvels at the energy, the farce and the horror of his performance. As his physical appearance deteriorates and his head sinks lower into the great neckless shoulders, one wonders, too, how long he can keep up the pace.

It is widely believed in Uganda that a counter *coup* within his own army will one day finish Amin. This is not to say that Ugandans are looking forward to such an event with its inevitable reprisals and bloodshed. 'Amin, whatever his faults,' many say, 'is the best of the soldiers. His successor could only be worse.'

The average man grumbles; and when Dada tells Mrs Golda Meir to pack her knickers, or accuses Sir Alec Douglas-Home of being scared to visit the General in Kampala, he chuckles. But his real concern is to keep out of trouble. 'My children must eat,' he constantly reminds himself. 'I have only one life. I must stay alive.'

AMIN'S WIVES

We now see that not even Amin's close relatives are safe. On 26 March 1974 he divorced three of his wives. On 11 April a pretext was found to arrest one of them on a smuggling charge. She was held in gaol till 22 April. On 13 August we were told that the dismembered body of his third wife Kay had been found in a doctor's car. The report said that Kay was 3–4 months pregnant; the foetus had been dragged out by instruments; the doctor responsible had given poison to his wife and 7 children, then killed himself. No one believed this story. It was known that Amin was harrying Kay and her relatives. Her cousin Ondoga, former Foreign Minister, had been thrown to the fishes (10 March). Her brother Wilson, caught with a pistol, had narrowly escaped with his life (8 April). Colonel Toko, of the same family, had been dismissed from his post as Air Force Commander (June 1973) and sent to Nairobi. Kay had shortly before been accused by Amin of having a firearm. Clearly her time was up. Kay had been my student, a jolly, bright girl, her father a clergyman in Arua. I know Africans who wept when they heard what happened to her. At her wedding it had rained heavily, and Obote in his speech had told the couple they were marrying 'at an appropriate time, as rain was a blessing for Uganda'. Another close friend of Amin, fellow Kakwa Brig. Arube, died on 24 March of bullet wounds ('self-inflicted').

Amin's latest Foreign Minister, Miss Bagaya, shamefully accused by the General (29 Nov.) of 'making love to an unknown European in a Paris airport lavatory', was arrested, and a picture of her nude put in the press.

THE HOMESTEAD

The Homestead

The huts with their twisted old posts are losing their thatch. Bits of stick and rags, chewed sorghum cane and ground-nut shells litter the grey dust of the compound. An overturned calabash, a bow and a spear are all that is left from last night's drinking party.

I can see Mr Okello sitting under a butternut tree whose big crumpled leaves rattle in gusts of hot air. He is getting old, calls for *pombe* at breakfast, and has pains in his back and shoulders. Most of the time he stays in the shade, shifting his stool with the wheeling of the sun, a black and white dot on a patch of baked earth.

Mrs Okello is not at home. Despite her swollen arm she has gone early to the plot to pull up ground-nuts. The half-dozen grandchildren are playing in the dust. Pot-bellied and spidery, with snotty noses, they will grow up tall and straight, with wide shoulders and long iron legs.

Three daughters still share the homestead – the eldest, whose husband has gone off as driver with a diamond prospecting outfit, and two younger girls, one of whom has a stiff hip ('A pity,' says her mother, 'for she will have to marry some old or ugly man').

The three girls are magnificent. Without them Mr Okello and his extended family would collapse. They fetch water and firewood, milk the three cows, grind millet, prepare beer, cook millet dumplings with ground-nut sauce and sweet potatoes, watch, feed and bathe the children, sweep the compound and work in the fields.

Just now, after hungry June and July, which are the months of empty food bins, it is harvesting time: ground-nuts, maize, cassava. Cotton, which is picked at the end of the year, is Mr Okello's only cash crop. With the few hundred shillings it fetches Mr Okello, like other small Acholi farmers, must pay school fees, buy clothes, paraffin, sugar, salt, soap and matches. The two or three *dukas* are over a mile away. People complain that they are often closed and constantly changing hands; for the owners or their wives waste the takings instead of buying fresh goods.

From time to time there is a hubbub in the compound as two thin dogs that roam ceaselessly for food with their muzzles to the ground like mongooses are chased and thrashed by the children (whose excrement, immediately it is voided, the dogs eat). Winged termites are spiralling from holes in a great mound; as quickly as they emerge, the waiting kites eat them. A woodpecker is laughing among the *olim* trees.

White clouds that bear no rain rumple the bed of the sky. The heat dazes me. Mr Okello and his neighbours have adapted themselves to the dry, merciless radiation of the sun but they have not conquered it. Indeed it has defeated them. As they grow older the men give up, send their wives into the sun's glare to do their work. They have many visitors, who come quietly out of the bush along the twisting paths. Several have walked over to greet me: a shopkeeper on a Japanese motor cycle; schoolboys who want to practise their English; old men with bows and spears and ragged khaki shorts too wide for their thin legs; women with breasts pulled into the shape of tubers or dried to tiny dugs.

At night, sitting on logs with a calabash of beer, Mr Okello and his friends talk at first in low droning voices that grow louder as the beer warms them and women, their chores over, come up softly. A young man strums his *okemi*; the tinkling notes of his nailed board sound like water running over stones, like cow bells, or the music of tree frogs. Some of the women move their hips to the rhythm and giggle. They have put on dresses that cover their breasts. Their heads are shaved, they are clean, and very black. When they laugh the gaps show in their strong white teeth. Their hands, when I shake them, feel like lizards.

Last night someone spoke of a woman who had foretold that a certain girl wearing a certain dress would attend prayers in a certain church and then die. The neighbours, hearing this had driven her and her husband from the village. 'If you come back,' they told the couple, 'we will burn you. You will see what the monkey saw in the bean field.'

Mr Okello says that spitting chewed sorghum cane on the ground offends the spirits, who then bring down hail to destroy crops.

The neighbourhood is free from soldiers, the dirt roads discourage traffic, no one seems interested in the instant politics and posturings of Kampala. True, many of the Acholi tribe who were serving with Obote's security forces have been killed or have run away. That was to be expected. If a leader is thrown down by a stronger man, his followers must suffer too. 'Our son is dead,' said one man. 'His brother has dug the grave and married the widow.'

From a high rock where hydraxes hide in holes I look down on the homesteads of neighbours. With the sun on them the burnished roof tops with their circular bands of yellow thatch shine like inverted brass trays. A young boy who follows me up the rock tells me that when he broke his thigh the Italian fathers at Kalongo mended it free of charge.

At the nearby dam I watched a darter bird with its wings spread out to dry on a tree stump as though crucified. What I thought at first was a bright blue flower in a shrub was the woodland kingfisher. As I was walking back slowly through the dark, a Land-Rover caught me up. It stopped, and a white man whom I took to be an Italian priest asked me with a look of concern if I was lost, or wanted help. 'Don't worry,' I said, 'I live here.'

I appreciated his kindness, and the kindness of Mr Okello who gave me, when I left, a cock to boil in Kampala. At Patongo I called on a shopkeeper I had not seen for over two years. He was no longer wearing his white vest with a Black Hand printed on it. 'I have shut my mouth since then,' he said.

Near the leper hospital I gave a lift to an old man. 'Amin's soldiers have strange ways,' he said, 'like Nubians or Arabs, they cut off heads.'

'After the shooting in the barracks,' he went on, 'Acholi women who had called there to ask after their husbands were told "We do not deal here with the living." Some were shown, with laughter, headless corpses.'

Evil Made Flesh

On the bridge over the Nile at Karuma Falls a five-ton army lorry had smashed into the rails and was blocking the carriage way. During the killings of 1971, the bridge had been a favourite place for tossing bodies into the water.

What was it Wole Soyinka, the Nigerian playwright and poet, wrote in his prison cell during the war with Biafra, about hirelings who commit torture on the captured and the helpless?

'These men are not merely evil. . . . They are the mindlessness of evil made flesh. One should not ever stumble into their hands but seek the power to destroy them. They are pus, bile, original putrescence of Death in living shapes. They surely infect all with whom they come in touch and even from this insulation here I smell a foulness of the mind in the mere tone of their words. They breed themselves, their types, their mutations. To seek the power to destroy them is to fulfil a moral task.' (*The Man Died*, 1972.)

I have in this book drawn attention in several places to the peccadilloes of shopkeepers and those who handle money – the petty cheating, the corruption and selfishness that have followed Amin's transfer of the wealth and property of the evicted Indians into the hands of, in many cases, the wrong people. Their small villainies are venial. They pale to nothing compared with the cold-blooded killings done by Amin's soldiers and security agents. It is these deeds that are, for me, the ultimate crime by which their commander, though he may plead ignorance or loss of control, should be judged. I think of my old student Karuhanga, tied to a tree in a field and publicly executed (for 'harbouring guerillas') by firing squad.

Yet I ought perhaps to qualify even this assertion. For it is arguable that, though Africans know all about cruelty, there is still in the violence of Uganda a sort of innocence. Portal

(1893) noticed the terrible mutilations – cutting out eyes and lips – practised among the Baganda. A drunken herdsman, we now read in our local newspaper, is not only robbed of three shillings; a stick is thrust up his anus;[1] or an army corporal is accused of 'cannibalism',[2] while another soldier burns a villager alive.[3] But in Uganda people still kill each other with rudimentary equipment, with bullets or a panga, with their hands, by strangulation or beating. Soldiers may burn 'rebel' huts, but they have no high explosive to drop on crowded markets. No one (as the Irish do) has left a plastic bomb in the tea room of the YWCA; no one as yet (repeat, *as yet*, for the Palestine Liberation Organisation has established itself in Kampala) has blown up a passenger aeroplane in the sky. The calculated sophistication of Western methods of killing people has not quite reached Uganda.

[1] The *Voice of Uganda* (12 November 1973) reported that Augustino Kato, a herdsman of Namugongo, had been murdered by men who pushed a stick up his anus and stole from him three shillings. The dying man named his assailants, but the judge ruled that as the herdsman was a 'habitual drunkard', and in spite of the 'extraordinary injuries he had suffered after being roughed through the anus he was still drunk next morning when he named the murderers', his evidence must be rejected.

[2] 'Army Corporal Rashid Bahemuka' (reported the *Voice of Uganda*, 29 January and 12 February 1974) 'liked law and order to prevail while he served as a Jago chief in Padyere county, West Nile. And to demonstrate his toughness he cut off two ears from two of his subjects who were suspected of practising witchcraft and made them eat the ears. "Cutting off a man's ear is in itself a shocking act, but then forcing him to eat part of his own body goes beyond the imagination of modern times", said the chief magistrate on sending him to prison.' In his appeal against the sentence Corporal Bahemuka said, 'The villagers accused these people of practising witchcraft. I was trying to help the villagers. They told me that according to the regulations of the administration any witchdoctor arrested should be punished either by *putting a stick through his anus or hammering a stick into his chest or his navel*.' The corporal's appeal failed, and he was gaoled for six years.

[3] When Private Kitakwenda was acting as gombolola chief in Magoro sub-county, Teso district, he arrested a man called Andrea for being in possession of stolen penicillin and capsules. 'He forced Andrea, by beating him, to eat the medicine, then pulled him to the nearest ditch where he burnt him to death using grass. He then turned to the man's wife and beat the life out of her. . . . He ordered the relatives of the deceased not to mourn.' In his plea to the military tribunal for mercy, Private Kitakwenda said 'in a low voice, "since I knew no administration, whatever I did I thought I was helping the people".' (*Voice of Uganda*, 21 November 1973.) His plea failed. He was executed on 14 March 1974.

THE KINGFISHER

Kingfisher

The garden township of Entebbe, on Lake Victoria, looks
scruffy. There are holes in the hedges and ragged washing
lines. The cricket field is overgrown, its sightscreen broken.
The stretch of silvery beach where I used to like reading has
been partly churned up by excavators. Disturbed by the
machines, there seem to be fewer birds about. But fish eagles
still call out of the sky, black-legged egrets stand with their
yellow feet in the small swishing breakers, and a pied kingfisher
flutters its wings like spinning wheels before it stabs the water's
glassy face.

Entebbe used to be thronged with picnicking Indian families.
There are no more brown bodies splashing among the bilharzia
worms, no girls with waist-length hair walking with young men
carrying transistor sets tuned in to the love music of India.
A children's play garden, whose completion coincided with their
eviction, is their memorial. When I last visited the beach a
soldier stopped to watch me; I saw only two fishermen coiling
a rope, and a boy shitting in a hollow.

Bats

The greatest single change that has come over Kampala is
likewise the absence of the Indians whose evening *corso* made
them so conspicuous. From the residential suburbs the English
memsahib, too, her *ayah* and pram, have virtually disappeared.
The new '*Mzungu*' is a dumpy Russian woman, a Korean lady,
or an Egyptian housewife carrying a brown-paper parcel.
Kampala looks, and rightly so, authentically African at last –
even in its growing shabbiness. Yet not completely African.
There is too much of Anglo-Indian in its architecture, its
bungalows, dukas and gardens for that.

Unchanged and unchanging are the native shanty districts:
after dark, places of scuffling sounds and rotting smells; with
the returning dawn, whose great flamingo flush is quickly
swallowed into the dazzle of an equatorial morning, vivid with
grass and red earth compounds where sheets are spread to dry
and women scour pots.

Every evening at dusk the fruit bats still lurch across the sky, silent, blind, in untold numbers, harried by crows and kites. The rain and the drought alternate, termites are ceaselessly at work, one can still catch the stare of a night owl on a telegraph pole. The painters have failed to dislodge the swifts that nest under my roof. They twitter when I lock up, and geckos like transparent fingers run down the wall.

November 1974, Kampala

"Let a Man Lie in Prison"

1 *April* 1975. *Arrest*

Two security officers with an escort of two armed policemen woke me in my flat at 2 a.m. and said, 'You are writing a book, where is it?' I showed them part of the manuscript of the book I was in fact engaged on – an account of war-time experiences. They were not deceived. 'The book about the Kabaka (King),' they insisted.

I had usually kept my manuscript copy of *The White Pumpkin* under sacks in my garage. But that night I had brought it into my flat to confirm some references for my publisher. The publisher's correspondence was on the table. The manuscript sheets I had put in a box. It was the night of Easter Monday. I had gone to bed.

The officers scanned the correspondence and said, 'You are not co-operating.' I spent the rest of the night in a cell at the Central Police Station.

The security officers who drove me back to my flat in the morning quickly found the main part of *The White Pumpkin* manuscript; with it was an earlier draft of the epilogue. Other pages which I feared were even more compromising to me I was able during the search to bury among a pile of harmless papers. The mass of irrelevant material I now pressed zealously on the officers would be enough, I hoped, to keep the police busy sifting through for weeks.

All this the officers carried off together with letters, photographs, and books – one of them Solzhenitsyn's *Gulag Archipelago* which I had annotated (the senior officer was a literate man, and he recognised the title), another a trashy French novel

L'Espionage whose discovery was to cause me embarrassment.

So the police had got my epilogue. But at this stage I hoped I might be able to persuade a reasonable interrogator that the remarks it contained were 'fair comment'. It was the hidden sheets with the reference to Amin's treatment of his wives[1] and the Brecht quotation at the end of the preface that, if discovered, would be lethal.

As we were leaving, a full-page *Times* picture of Amin caught one officer's eye. The folded sheet made a crease that bisected Amin's face. 'This is bad,' he said, and took it with him.

3 *April* – 29 *May. Luzira Prison*

On 3 April, in the British Consul's presence, I was given a detention order and transferred to the maximum security block in Luzira Civil Prison. Everyone in Uganda knows about the detention block. It was here that Obote used to keep his political opponents. It was known then as the 'University'. Obote's detainees were educated men, and an excellent prison library had been provided for them. I could now settle down in my cell to read John Bunyan, seventeenth-century English plays, Jane Austen, and – a bizarre find in an equatorial gaol – Fothergill's exquisitely malicious *An Innkeeper's Diary* (the book stirred memories of my Oxford days, for I had once played cricket at Thame, where Fothergill kept 'The Spreadeagle', and taken eight rustic wickets).

My first companions in gaol were a lawyer (soon released), two managers of an aviation company accused of corruption, and five alleged car smugglers; the most important detainee of all, Nyanzi, Director of the Uganda Development Corporation, was being kept in isolation in another part of the prison. We met at the toilet and sometimes during exercise in the prison yard. The smugglers had Bibles and held prayer meetings. Every evening they sang, very beautifully, 'Abide with me'. On the other side of our exercise yard, ninety-four condemned prisoners were locked in their cells.

We had one bad moment, when the Defence Council – about twenty officers in splendid military uniforms – erupted into the

---

[1] Amin's present wife Medina is the latest casualty. Not long ago she was brought into hospital with a broken jaw.

yard and we were hurried from our cells to be paraded before
them. While the Director of Prisons identified us, an assistant
in a baseball cap set up the wooden frame to which prisoners are
strapped for beating. We looked at it in alarm. Was there to be
an exhibition? I tried not to catch Major Malyamungu's eye.

Towards the end of April several new prisoners joined us:
four Uganda Development Corporation managers, and three
Transintra (a state transport company) executives – all accused
of corruption. All the nine persons now detained for corruption
complained that they had been arrested by order of one man: a
man whose shadow has suddenly appeared behind Amin's
shoulder to darken the lives of many wretched people. 'He came
into our offices with police,' they told me, 'and whisked us away.'

Through a hole in the gate we watched another part of the
gaol fill up with small traders and businessmen charged with
hoarding and other trading offences. They were on remand, and
they were awaiting, under Amin's most recent decrees, trial by
military tribunal. During exercise they sat quietly on the grass,
like men with little hope.

We detainees – we wore a distinctive uniform of blue shirt
and white shorts – were the most privileged people in the gaol.
We had our grumbles: grubs in the beans, sodden cabbage leaves,
stale, coarse *posho*. The O.C., a correct and kindly man,
regretted he could not feed us better. 'We haven't the resources,'
he told us.

When Smolen (a European charged with hoarding tins of
cooking oil) was brought in, I lent him my copy of *Oliver Twist*.
It was thought that Smolen and I might be plotting an escape,
and we were kept apart. 'The British built this prison,' said the
warders, 'so you must know its secrets.' It had indeed occurred
to me that the prison was not secure against a sophisticated
rescue attempt. The football field round which the cells are
built would be a good landing place for a helicopter or light
aircraft. The approach over the lake (half a mile away) is easy;
warders are not armed.

Mengo District Court
A fortnight had passed before Mr Burton, the British Consul,
and my wife Ingrid were first allowed to visit me. We spoke

through a glass panel. I now made several rapid visits to Mengo District Court. During these jack-in-the-box appearances before four different magistrates (one African, three Asians), I was formally charged with sedition (the 'village tyrant' reference), refused bail, given a date for my trial (25 June, later brought forward to 5-6 May), and told I could engage defence counsel. As no African lawyer dared handle my defence, and the last British lawyer in Uganda to try to protect a British expatriate, Mr Gordon, against seizure of his property and instant deportation had himself been expelled together with his client, I asked for Mr Wilkinson of Nairobi.

I naturally looked forward to discussing my affairs with Mr Wilkinson before I appeared in the witness box. This was not permitted. I saw him for the first time in court on 5 May, when the public prosecutor surprised us all by requesting an adjournment until the 9th. On that day Mr Wilkinson stood up to argue that the sedition charge against me was timebarred and ought to be dropped. The Asian magistrate agreed and awarded him costs. The public prosecutor was not interested in these quibbles. The sedition charge, he said, was in any case being withdrawn. I was to be charged with treason and would appear before a military tribunal.

Sedition carries a penalty of five years' imprisonment or a fine of 10,000 shillings; and I could have appealed, if found guilty, to the Supreme Court of East Africa. That would have been bearable. Treason was punishable by death. I now felt that the Government was determined to get me.

Meanwhile in Luzira the arrival of an army surgeon detained for 'desertion' had given us sufficient numbers to form a Detainees Football XI. We played barefoot on the big football pitch. I was full-back.

On 29 May I was reading Joyce's *The Dubliners* when I was suddenly told to dress. My friends cheered and waved me goodbye. 'You're going home,' said the office clerks. I did not believe them.

Outside the prison gate a squad of military policemen was waiting for me in an open Jeep and Mercedes Benz. I counted two officers and ten armed men. I was handcuffed and put in the Benz. The Jeep went ahead, waving down traffic. I tried to hide my hands. I was wearing my suit – Ingrid had brought it to the gaol for me to wear in court – and I might, I hoped, look like a distinguished foreign person with special protective escort.

29 *May. Transfer to Bombo*

Where was I going? Naguru? Makindye military police head-quarters? An army barracks? Naguru execution block was the place I feared. We passed it by. Nor was it to be Makindye. When we turned along the Hoima road I guessed I was bound for the Malire regiment at Bombo, thirty miles away. For I remembered Amin's threat to David Martin after he had pub-lished his book about him: 'If I get Martin, I will put him in Malire custody.'

We found Colonel Sule, C.O. of Malire Special Mechanised Reconnaissance Battalion, on the football field. He had no shirt on and looked embarrassed. 'Welcome to Malire,' he said.

The officer who escorted me to the guardroom said, 'You are a very dangerous man.' Soldiers took me to a cell at the end of a passage. They threw me on the floor, stripped me, and tried to force a second pair of handcuffs over my wrists. Six automatic rifles were aiming at me. I pointed to my abdominal scar, hoping the soldiers would not beat me. I was glad when they locked me in and I was left alone. Through the grille I could see the top of a mango tree, and there were weaver birds perched on it. Former prisoners had scratched calendars on the wall. Someone had written 'I shall not again see this world'.

I lay down on the cement floor to think over my new situation. In Luzira prison the warders had been obliged to obey the rules; but soldiers would make their own. Whatever I did, I must not upset the guard. I could hear them laughing outside in the passage. I noticed a long nail sticking in the door, and I remem-bered I had a safety-pin which I had been using in place of fly buttons. If things became unbearable, I could at least choose my own exit. The two blankets I had been given would help soak up the blood. I pondered this thought for a minute or two, then dismissed it for ever from my mind.

Colonel Sule visited me in the morning. He removed my handcuffs, returned my belongings, and sent for breakfast. I sensed immediately that there was humanity in him. Now I could relax. I had five books with me, and started to reread Evelyn Waugh's *Brideshead Revisited*.

I also had Waugh's *A Little Learning*; but the malice that, for me, flaws his writings did not suit my mood. I wanted robuster characters than Waugh's debauched aesthetes and his Captain Grimes. His pages were without courage.

I studied the guard. It was changed each morning. They were young men – Sudanese, and Lugbara from the West Nile: keen, and very black. Six of them pointed their rifles at me when I went to the toilet. A gun mounted on a tripod, with a soldier behind it, faced me at the end of the passage. I had a bucket to wash in. To avoid exciting the soldiers, I tried not to look into their eyes.

I was given the amended charge sheet and a week to prepare (without pen or paper) my defence. The prosecution would have a dictionary and I could not hope to gloss over the phrase 'village tyrant'. My reference to 'the black Nero', if the prosecution had spotted it, or indeed dared to mention this insult even in closed court, was worse. Then there was the preface; had it been discovered? I thought a little about these things, then put them out of mind.

9-11 *June. Military Tribunal*

The first I knew of the trial was on the morning of 9 June when the guard gave me ten minutes to wash and dress, and I was hurried to Battalion H.Q. My arrival at the court room, with an elegantly kilted officer and surrounded by automatic rifles, struck me as theatrical. Soldiers' wives and children stared at me.

Chairman of the tribunal was Major Juma Ali. Four junior officers were sitting with him. I had looked forward to being tried by men of sufficient seniority to have opinions of their own. The four junior officers – one of them so young that his tunic was too big for him – were obvious passengers, while the major – he wore paratroop wings but no medal ribbons – would be the Defence Council's mouthpiece. He had a thin, malevolent face. We disliked each other immediately.[1] The officers had stacked their ceremonial swords against a wall. There was a civilian

[1] Ali was notoriously involved in killing two Americans in Mbarara barracks (1971).

lawyer present to advise on procedure, a few press men and photographers, a female stenographer. The sight of my 40-year-old typewriter among the police exhibits saddened me more than anything: a spool was broken, the case was missing. The prosecuting officer was a captain. I recognised the worn typescript of my epilogue on his table, and my correspondence with the publisher, but I could see no other parts of my book in his file. For the benefit of the tribunal, the proceedings were to be in Swahili as well as English. The young half-caste interpreter looked sympathetic.

My first request was for defence counsel. 'Not allowed,' said Major Juma. I pleaded that it was a 'human right' to have counsel. 'Am I not human too?' replied the major.

Then the door opened and Mr Wilkinson trundled in. I was overjoyed to see him. He stood to attention before the Chairman and asked his permission to represent me. 'Not granted,' said the major. Mr Wilkinson – I had barely time to nod my thanks to him – trundled out. Never mind, I felt no longer totally alone.

The first day was taken up with police evidence. This was very lengthy and was, I thought, a waste of time; for I had no intention of denying that the manuscript before the court was written by me. A handwriting expert (Makerere degree) who gave evidence next morning with blow-ups of my handwriting and typescript, gave us a lecture of such pedantry that we all began to smile.

The last prosecution witness to be called was my wife Ingrid. The prosecution had already, on the first day, referred to her as my 'former wife' (*bibi zamani*), and I had protested. It was now for Ingrid herself to tell the tribunal that under Uganda law a wife could not be constrained to give evidence against her husband. The chairman listened, and said one word to her: '*Kwenda* (go away)'.

It was during these proceedings that the telephone rang, and Major Juma leant out of the window with his back to the court room to answer it. It was Amin himself who was speaking. No wonder the major answered 'Yes, sir – Yes, sir – Yes, sir.'

'I think the President wants us to hurry up,' I whispered to one of the police witnesses. He pretended not to hear.

The trial went more quickly now. The prosecuting officer

stated his case against me. I had called the president a 'tyrant ruling by fear', and this was treason.

In my defence I tried to gloss over the context of the phrase. I told the tribunal that Amin, by assuming the role of Kabaka (King), was in effect returning to a form of government (Kabaka and chiefs) that was traditional to African society. Tradition, I said, was something all Africans valued. Tradition indeed was an honourable thing, and village tyrants . . . As for the element of 'fear', I pointed out that my Uganda students, for that very reason, had long ceased to run their debating and current affairs societies.

It was no good. The tribunal was not interested in my evasions.

When I accepted to be cross-examined I knew I was taking a risk; for the prosecuting officer could not only use the statements I had made to the police in evidence against me; he could now, if he wished, quote from the whole of my book. I could see, however, that he still had only the epilogue pages, and my correspondence with the publishers, in his file. I took the risk.

The phrase now quoted from the epilogue was my reference to 'the black Nero'. The chairman asked what it meant. 'The cruellest of all the Roman emperors,' explained the captain.

This was a bad moment. The court room was silent. I looked through the window.

In my defence I tried to shift the responsibility for this insult on to *Punch*. The phrase was not mine. Had I not written it in quotation marks? The argument was too sophisticated for the tribunal. The insult had been written, and that was enough.

My reference to the removal of King George V's statue was next quoted against me. It meant, said the prosecuting officer, that I was an Imperialist, and that I regretted the end of colonial rule in Uganda. Then there was my sneer at men in 'round Moslem caps'.

The reference to 'round Moslem caps' was more difficult for me to explain away than an Englishman's natural anger at seeing the head of his king 'being hammered to pieces by laughing workmen'. Nevertheless, I argued that the 'Arabs' who had been supplanting British experts were indeed less competent;

and that many of them – Somalis, for instance – had already been expelled for cheating and smuggling.

Now for my passage on 'spies'. ('Amin calls us spies, and there is truth in it. For we expatriates, whether we like it or not, are the eyes and ears of the outside world.') The passage was clumsily phrased, and the prosecution insisted strongly that it was a literal admission of widespread espionage activities by the British community in Uganda.

In my defence I pointed out that many of my own friends had been robbed or injured during the events of 1972-73. The press did not report the incidents. We expatriates were aware of them; we talked about them, and the news spread. Was that espionage?

'If these things were happening,' commented the chairman, 'you should have told the President. It was bad to write them in a book.'

Finally, there was the reference, in my correspondence with the publishers, to 'corpses'. Why did I wish to damage Uganda's good name by showing pictures of corpses in my book?

The corpses, I pointed out, had been lying in a public place for days. The police had not removed them. If there was no secrecy about their existence, then there could be no objection to photographing them.

I think that at this point both the captain and I had grown tired of bandying words that were clearly only lines in a pantomime. Major Juma too had had enough. 'Words,' he had exclaimed a little earlier, 'words, many, many words.'

The prosecuting officer now summed up. I had, he said, abused the hospitality shown me by Uganda to spy for the British Government and write bad things. My book was intended to harm the Uganda Government. It was therefore treasonable, and I was a spy.

In my own address, I denied treasonable intent. 'I am a teacher,' I said, 'and teachers believe in discussing ideas and opinions.'

I was not, I pointed out, a well-known writer and I did not expect my book to have large sales. It would in any case be banned in Uganda. My book, in fact, was a 'mere mosquito bite' (the female stenographer gave a squeak when I said this). Why make so much fuss about it?

'Above all,' I concluded – it sounds priggish now, but I was moved, 'I wish to stand here in this room as a man of integrity. I have not denied that I wrote the book. I have not contradicted the police evidence. Though I am willing to express my regrets for the expressions I have used, I have written what I thought was true.'

My appearance before the tribunal next morning was brief. Major Juma had little to say. I was bad, he said, and (he rose from his chair and projected two fingers in front of his eyes) I had bad eyes, a bad look in my eyes.

I was taken out of the court room, then brought back to hear the verdict. The tribunal had found me guilty. 'I accept your decision,' I said, 'and I thank the tribunal for listening to my defence.'

I was taken away again, and brought back for sentence.

'You will be shot by firing squad,' hissed (he really did hiss) Major Juma, speaking in English for the first time, and immediately went out. The junior officers sheathed their swords and followed. I was left among the scattered papers.

A kilted sergeant-major took me back to my cell. I pointed to the smouldering green hillside below the barracks and told him how much I liked Uganda. He did not answer; but he shuffled to get into step with me, and he gave me his cigarettes.

11-21 *June. Waiting*

I heard nothing of my request to appeal. Colonel Sule no longer visited me. I turned again to the *Memoirs* of Cellini (1500-1571). What times, and what a man! I read and reread the poem he wrote while lying with a broken leg in the dungeon of St Angelo:

> Whate'er ill fame he's gotten in the world
> Let a man lie in prison . . .
> He'll come out holy, wise.

Cellini had another line:

> Then chirped a solitary sparrow loud
> Upon the keep; and I took heart.

It was the glossy starling whose grating voice came to me

through the grille, and the caw of hooded crows. I could hear them pecking among soldiers' rubbish.

I was also given a Bible. I found little comfort in the Old Testament: too much wrath and punishment. I felt that Amin himself belonged in the ranks of those vengeful captains with their slaves, their concubines, their threats and cruel prophecies. In the New Testament there was compassion.

About this time, twice a day, I began to focus my eyes on the cell wall before me, on the finger stains and splashed blood of mosquitoes and the scratched dates, and as I stared the marks seemed to gather into a pattern and then form shapes: one of them was God – in the figure of Michelangelo's Moses: severe and bearded, seated on a throne, with one arm lifted in judgment. The other shape was Jesus – the Jesus of Italian village church paintings: handsome, gentle. Here, personified for me on the greasy wall, were Justice – and Compassion: two things the world wants most. Compassion I felt I deserved. But justice? The balance of one's life shows many debts: perhaps I was here to pay the bill.

I tried to calculate my chances by watching the guards. A smile gave me hope, a gloomy stare depressed me. 'Don't joke about your life,' a corporal told me, after some banter. 'It is in God's hands. Pray.'

One young soldier from Arua told me to read Psalm 6, where David complains of aching bones. It was a good psalm. It held out hope of deliverance. 'All mine enemies shall be confounded,' says David. 'They shall be turned back, and put to shame suddenly.' Another soldier told me to read Psalm 88. This was a bad psalm. 'I am shut up, and I cannot come forth.' I did not look at it again.

About 18 June Colonel Sule let me exercise for the first time in the compound for an hour a day. I walked round and round a tree within a circle of ten armed guards. When I had covered about a mile I sat down on the grass and ground down my toe and finger nails on a stone. Children were climbing trees for mangoes. They came and looked at me over the wire. They did not wave.

But there was another hopeful sign; the guard were now sharing their rations with me. When I asked for bread and potatoes, the Super Garden bar near by sent me a plate with twenty potatoes on it, half a loaf of bread, and a cup of brown sugar to eat it with. And once I think I saw an officer's lady smile at me through a window.

21 *June. Meeting with Amin*

On the afternoon of 21 June a lieutenant hurried me to the officers' mess. 'British government men are coming to see you,' he told me. 'Perhaps the President too.' I took it as a good omen that he gave me a pot of tea and a bottle of beer. The mess occupies what used to be the British C.O.'s living room. Its walls were bare except for a newspaper picture of General Amin stuck crooked on the whitewash.

Just as I had been given a second bottle of beer, we heard a helicopter land. The bottle was snatched from me, the mess waiter in his excitement dropped the Japanese-made ordnance issue teapot on the floor, and I was put in an anteroom. Everyone scurried. The President himself had arrived.

When I was led back into the mess, President Amin was waiting for me. He introduced me to Lt.-Gen. Blair, who was in uniform, and Major Grahame. 'This is a most extraordinary situation,' General Blair said to me. 'I have brought with me a letter from the Queen. Kampala is full of pressmen.'

President Amin stood up and addressed himself to me. Speaking slowly and quietly, he gave me a stern dressing-down. 'I have seen your book,' he said. 'It is a bad book. You have been mixing with the wrong people. The book is not good for Uganda's relations with Britain.'

'People you thought were your friends have double-dealt – they have betrayed you.'

'The execution order has been signed,' he went on, 'for tomorrow morning. But the Queen has written a letter to me, and the order will be reconsidered because the Queen is my friend.'

President Amin's quiet reprimand had impressed me. But an execution order that had been signed for tomorrow morning – that was too much! It was breaking the rules; for I would not have had time either to say goodbye to my family or to see a chaplain.

The President now spoke about his economic difficulties, and he again stressed his feelings of friendship for Britain. I was looking at the massive bulge in his pullover that showed his footballing days are over. There were lines in the soft flesh of his face. Then he paused, and General Blair interrupted with an unexpected remark. 'President Amin,' he said, turning to me, 'is a very great sportsman.'

The interruption served its purpose, for General Blair now asked the President's permission to speak with me alone, and we walked away. Our conversation had to be brief. It was agreed that I should straightaway write a letter formally expressing my regrets for the 'objectionable remarks' I had made in my book. Major Grahame also suggested I might ask for deportation.

General Blair asked me about the situation in Uganda. 'Better,' I said; 'bodies aren't being thrown into the Nile.' Amin meanwhile had quietly left the room, and the helicopter began to clatter in the dark.

'We are going to a place called Cape Town something,' General Blair remarked as he turned to go, 'do you know it?' 'One of the finest houses in Kampala,' I told him, 'recently seized from Mr Gordon and renamed Cape Town View.'

'I suppose you will retire now on the royalties from your book,' he said, '– if it is not suppressed.'

At 10 o'clock that night two officers – one had been a tribunal member – came into my cell with pen and paper, and told me to write a letter immediately to the President, 'explaining everything'.

'A long letter?'

'Tell what you feel, tell everything.'

It was not an easy letter for me to compose, with one officer standing over me and the other boisterously pulling at my blanket, both of them urging and advising and telling me to hurry. The right phrases would not come.

'Don't alter what you have written,' they told me when I tried to rewrite a sentence. In ten minutes I had scribbled the draft, and they took it away to be typed.

Left alone, I turned the letter over in my mind. Had I given in? Or had I not gone far enough? I was worried.

In my opening paragraph I had expressed 'my regrets for the objectionable remarks' I had written 'about the Uganda Government' following the events of 1972-73. In my second and third paragraphs I denied treasonable intent in writing the book, and regretted any embarrassment I may have caused to relations between Uganda and Britain. In my fourth paragraph I thanked the President for visiting me, and asked for 'magnanimity' (a word the two officers were unfamiliar with). An orderly room clerk typed the letter next morning. I signed it, and heard no more of it.

But I continued to worry about the ethics of my letter. I had regretted my objectionable remarks. Did that mean that I was in honour bound to delete them, if ever I regained my freedom and the book was published?[1]

21 June-10 July. Waiting

From the excitement and fantasies aroused in me by this Royal message dropped from the skies on to Bombo hill, I returned to the routine, the boredom and the suspense of my life in a cell. I was still closely guarded, the soldiers were still forbidden to speak with me, and I knew nothing of events in the world outside. In July I was allowed to spend more time in the compound. I sat under a tree watching rats and starlings raid the posho scraps left by soldiers. A woodpecker with a red spot on its neck was hammering at a huge gall on an acacia swarming with insects. I saw how the regimental police punished soldiers for misdemeanours: they were made to hop in circles, on one leg, till they fell down. The battalion had a kilted detachment with pipers who practised parade drill every morning. They wore the glengarry with Malire regimental cap badge (not antlers) that has become Amin's favourite headgear.

On 4 July Colonel Sule asked me to write another letter. He said there was to be a 'big government conference in Kampala' on press and publicity relations between Uganda and Britain. The President wanted my views.

I spent several hours putting together a document of 1,500

[1] I did not, as Amin (I have since learned) is reported to have said, mention espionage in my letter, or make any 'confession' concerning alleged British involvement in espionage in Uganda.

words. My reprieve had not yet been confirmed, and in phrasing it I had to steer a course between presumptuousness, candour and diplomacy. I suggested that the Uganda Government should disregard the 'sensational' type of outside reporting of Uganda affairs, and invite foreign journalists to travel freely among the ordinary people of the country. Journalists would be more impressed by what they saw of the latter's achievements than by visits to night clubs and game parks. The Uganda Government ought also to remove its ban on British newspapers and journals.

'I do not think,' I wrote, 'that references to British imperialism and British colonialism please the British people and their news media, though the British Government itself would be less sensitive.' I suggested that a new generation of British teachers, doctors, and other educational and social workers, 'not mercenary in motives', be recruited to serve in Uganda – on condition they were guaranteed 'basic facilities and personal security, e.g. against car theft and when travelling on safari'.[1]

10 *July*. *Release*

It was about now that the guard was suddenly relaxed. The soldiers put away their rifles, my cell door was left open, they invited me to dip my mess tin into their dixies of soup and beans, and I began to feel like a distinguished visitor. Colonel Sule sent soldiers to climb trees to get mangoes for me. I deduced that the visit by Blair and Grahame had been a turning-point. I felt the worst that could happen to me now was imprisonment in Luzira.

Then on 9 July Colonel Sule told me to get ready to go to Kampala with him. On 10 July he drove me in his Mercedes Benz to a 'safe house' in Kololo where I sat waiting with his

---

[1] Since my release I have read, with mixed feelings, the monitored copy of my letter as read out on Kampala radio on 11 July. Ordinary Ugandans have been isolated long enough from their old friends, the British, and I am protesting against this. The exclusively 'buffoon' or 'murderer' image of Amin that is projected by some outside journalists is not positive enough. Amin is not Uganda. Yet Uganda's achievements, even under Amin – the creation, for instance, of a new and numerous middle class of business people and technicians – deserve to be recognised. Town workers now wear shoes. And the army has reached standards of training and discipline it did not have two years ago.

intelligence officer for the next step. (I had never liked this house, for I once saw a soldier kill a man with his bayonet in the yard.) My hair was long. I had lost some teeth. I had not looked into a mirror for many weeks. I had no fly buttons. I felt shabby.

It has been reported that a dazed-looking man stumbled into Amin's Command Post. It is true that I was startled to recognise the Foreign Secretary standing there in the sunshine, though when I exclaimed 'Mr Callaghan!' I forgot to add 'I presume'. When General Amin lifted up his son Mwanga, and said quietly to me, 'My son admires you', I took it to be his gesture of reconciliation; and I was too happy to feel resentment.

What moved me greatly was the crowd of Africans who waved (and I think cheered) as I walked up the gangway into Mr Callaghan's RAF aeroplane. They were not saluting me. They were saluting all *Wazungu*, and the end of an outrage done to their feelings by their own leader.